Welcome Aboard!
with appreceation
Full Sail

To Dick

Beverly Choebel
9/1/09

Full Sail

A 21st Century Spiritual Cruise
On Board The *Mayflower*

BEVERLY PIERCE STROEBEL

Mayflower Passenger Descendant
Cruise Host & Logbook Scribe

VMI Publishers
Sisters, Oregon

Full Sail

A 21st Century Spiritual Cruise On Board the *Mayflower*
Copyright © 2009 by Beverly Pierce Stroebel

Original cover artistry by Karah Baker.

The Jefferson (*The Jefferson*) font supposedly resembles
Thomas Jefferson's signature on the Declaration of Independence and preceding drafts.

Published by VMI Publishers
Partnering with Christian Authors, Publishing Christian and Inspirational Books
Sisters, Oregon
www.vmipublishers.com

ISBN 13: 978-1-933204-94-9
ISBN 10: 1-933204-94-X
Library of Congress Control Number: 2009933741

Printed in the United States of America

Full Sail Cruise Promotion

Full Sail Endorsements

"In *Full Sail*, Beverly Stroebel, a direct descendant from four *Mayflower* passengers, helps adults and children alike to recover the long-neglected truths about the Pilgrim foundations of American civilization."
—Rev. Peter Marshall, coauthor of *The Light and the Glory*

"Thank you, Beverly, for lovingly incorporating the Jewish strand into your rich tapestry of American life and values since the landing of the *Mayflower*. Thank you as well for discerning some of the spiritual significance of this strand, and even of the thread of Messianic Judaism. May your book stir up much prayer for the divine completion of the story of America!"
—Rabbi Russell Resnik, Executive Director, Union of
   Messianic Jewish Congregations

"Keep up your noble work for such a great cause. You have a gift for making things so interesting."
—David Beale, Professor of Church History,
   author of *The Mayflower Pilgrims*

"Beverly is a true reconciler as she is walking in God's true Love that brings new life and blesses all who embrace it. My wife is a *Mayflower* descendant, so *Full Sail* has special meaning for our family."
—Ed La Rose, Host Nation Native, author of *Our Trail of Tears*

"Because of her genealogy, her passion, and her dedication to Christian and American values, Beverly Stroebel is uniquely positioned to write *Full Sail*. It is both an educational and engaging read."
—Jack Osborne, Silicon Valley engineer/businessman,
   author of *Makers of Mischief: A Boomer's Adventures in Childhood*

"As a Messianic Jew and dual citizen of America and Israel, I can especially identify with the spirit of the *Mayflower* as Beverly brings it forth in her anointed writing and shows me that the spirit of the *Mayflower* is very much at the heart of my deep love for both the land of my birth and the Land of my inheritance. *Full Sail* is a must-read for all Americans and all Israelis."

—DR. RAYMOND "BOB" FISCHER, author of
The Ways of the Way, OlimPublications.com

"The *Full Sail* logbook comprises both factual and symbolic descriptions. Factual, because it presents and examines historical facts. Symbolically, it applies spiritual truths to experiences and historical facts. Passengers are *Full Sail* readers. As readers of this book, we automatically become a civil or a spiritual passenger, or both. Along with our Cruise Host and other passengers, we will see the world through timeless eyes, thus enjoying being present at any given moment and place in history—sort of omnipresent, that is. There is nothing mystical about this since it is typically the privilege enjoyed when we read a history book, or a novel, or the Bible."

—PHILEMON ZACHARIOU, author of
The Proselytizer: The Diaries of Panos T. Zachariou,
Pioneer Minister of the Gospel in Greece

Invitations to Join this Pilgrimage

"Using her genealogical calendar, Beverly Pierce Stroebel found proof to document the credibility and fulfillment of the Mayflower Compact goals to advance the Christian faith and glorify God from the seventeenth to the twenty-first centuries. I found that joining ancestors on board the *Mayflower*, in a spiritual way, is rewarding and meaningful. Once again, steadfast and courageous 'pilgrims' have the opportunity to follow a scriptural course. The difference between our first Pilgrims and now is that twenty-first-century passengers can bathe America and other nations in prayer and participate in activities to preserve, protect, and strengthen our liberties. As a concerned citizen, a father, a retired military man, a leader in the *Mayflower* descendant community, and a man of faith, I say that the need is great. Therefore, I invite all liberty lovers and spiritual and physical *Mayflower* descendants to join me on board the *Mayflower* in the twenty-first century. Working together to fill sails, we can continue to fulfill the Mayflower Compact goals. As you prepare to board *Full Sail*, welcome aboard, and my best wishes and prayers are with you.
—EDWARD DELANO SULLIVAN,
   Mayflower Society Governor General 2005–2008

"We the daughters of *Full Sail* Logbook Scribe and Cruise Host, Beverly Pierce Stroebel, invite you to come on board. She didn't threaten to disinherit us if we didn't write this invitation. We wrote it because we are supportive of her writing and believe in her. The *Mayflower* was filled with families, so we think it fitting that our family extend an invitation to yours. Enjoy the journey!"
—SUSAN S. TAMAOKA, *Mayflower* Descendant,
   Former Campus Crusade for Christ Staff, Special Education Teacher

—CAROLINE S. GRIP, *Mayflower* Descendant, Sunday School Teacher,
   Executive Director of Rebuilding Together, Sacramento

—JANE S. GREGG, *Mayflower* Descendant,
   Volunteer Parent at Daughter's Christian School,
   Management Development Consultant,
   Instructional Designer/Technical Writer

"*Full Sail* is something big, and it could have important educational impact on a generation that has little opportunity to explore the faith foundation upon which our free nation was built. I proudly invite you aboard *Full Sail* for a truly American journey, sailing in the wake of my ancestors whose unique faith-filled leadership helped shape this one nation, under God! The onboard music and drama will not only entertain, but continue to point you toward the author of all art. I know that God has this wonderful project in his hands, and I look forward to seeing what becomes of it."

—DARIN ADAMS, John Adams and John Alden Descendant,
    Composer, Playwright, Performer, Broadway Voice Teacher,
    and Church Worship Leader

Logbook Opening Prayer and Course-Setting for Pilgrims Through the Centuries

Lord God Almighty, our help in ages past and hope for years to come—You whose Word at the beginning of time charted courses for centuries and pilgrims—

Bring on board your people dispersed and living from sea to shining sea. Then hear us pray as we open this logbook. Shout aloud to awaken scribes from the past to fulfill what was left unfinished.

Breathe your life and love into us, the twenty-first-century Passengers, as we set sails to fulfill our duty to the world and future generations.

Open floodgates and fountains to satisfy our thirst and desire for deeper depth.

Grant faith to see light in the darkness and discern truth for each day. Instill passion to preserve and protect liberty.

Sharpen spiritual senses for penetrating historical haze and the biblical mystery maze.

Authorize angelic harvesters and warriors to fulfill your Word and protect pilgrims.

Hurl regretted and confessed personal, family, and national sins into the sea.

Lift curses and heal individuals, families, congregations, communities, and nations.

Release prisoners held in physical, emotional, and spiritual bondages.

Redeem and unite Abraham's seed to bless the nations.

Send Elijah before that great and dreadful day of the Lord comes.

Demolish strongholds and avenge arguments and disobedience against you.

Speak as we meditate on your works and words and tell of your mighty acts. "That we may know thy way upon earth, and thy saving health among all nations.

Let the people be glad and rejoice; for thou shalt judge the people righteously, and govern the nations upon the earth.

"Let the people praise thee, O God: let all the people praise thee.
Then shall the earth bring forth her increase, and God, even our God
shall be merciful and bless us and the ends of the earth shall fear him."

We praise you, O God, for sharing your Son's life and love
and the fullness of his grace so we can abide the day of his coming
when our Redeemer will stand upon the earth.

May all fullness dwell in him as you reconcile all things to him on
earth and in heaven.

Open your book and record names who ask for spiritual power
and zeal to embark on a great work—an offering to purify and
dedicate all that is within us and on earth to your glory and honor for
ever and ever.

Hallelujah! Our righteous God reigns! Amen.

Last and not least, they cherished a great hope and inward zeal of laying
good foundations, or at least of making some way towards it, for the propaga-
tion and advance of the gospel of the kingdom of Christ in the remote parts
of the world, even though they should be but stepping stones to others in the
performance of so great a work. (Plymouth Governor William Bradford, *Of
Plymouth Plantation*, 1909 Edition edited by Harold Paget)

Prayer Scriptures: Genesis 12; Job 19:25; Psalm 65, 67; Isaiah 40, 41, 55;
Micah 5, 7; Malachi 3, 4; Matthew 13; John 1, 7, 8, 15–17; Romans 9–15; 2
Corinthians 10:4–6; Galatians 3:26–29; Colossians 1, 2; Revelation 20, 21.

Bevery Pierce Stroebel Lineage

Great is the Lord and most worthy of praise; his greatness no one can fathom. One generation will commend your works to another; they will tell of your mighty acts.
Psalm 145:3–4

Beverly Pierce Stroebel

Francis Cooke *Mayflower* Line

1. Francis Cooke
   Hester Mathieu

2. Jane Cooke
   Experience Mitchell

3. Elizabeth Mitchell
   John Washburn, Jr.

4. Joseph Washburn ← ←
   Hannah Latham

5. Ebenezer Washburn
   Patience Miles

6. Rebecca Washburn
   Timothy Carver

7. Mehitable Carver
   Daniel Pierce I

8. Timothy Pierce
   Katie MacDonald

9. Daniel Pierce II
   Mary Reynolds

James Chilton *Mayflower* Line

1. James Chilton
   Mrs. Chilton

2. Mary Chilton
   John Winslow

3. Susanna Winslow
   Robert Latham

→ → 4. Hannah Latham
   Joseph Washburn

10. Marcus Pierce
    Adelaide Cramer

11. Lewis Grant Pierce
    Bertha Moore

12. Ray H. Pierce
    Lillian Weaver

13. Beverly Pierce
    William Stroebel

> We envisage our history in the proper light, therefore, if we say that each generation—indeed each individual—exists for the glory of God; but one of the most dangerous things in life is to subordinate human personality to production, to the state, even to civilization itself, to anything but the glory of God." (L.H. Butterfield, *Christianity and History*)

On Board

An Introduction to the *Full Sail* Cruise Logbook

My physical and spiritual ancestors sailed on board the seventeenth-century *Mayflower*. After reviewing and relating to their civil and Christian covenant—the Mayflower Compact—I rechartered the vessel in a spiritual sense.

Alone as the first onboard twenty-first-century Passenger, I began playing four roles: a descendant of the seventeenth-century *Mayflower* and Plymouth Pilgrims, the logbook writer transcribing—not authoring or rewriting—history, the Cruise Host connecting faith-and-fact history from the seventeenth century to twenty-first century, and a sinner regretting and asking God to forgive personal, family, and national sins.

For transcribing history, I carefully chose and invited other voices on board to help tell the American faith-and-fact story, and some to lead prayers. As the Host, realizing that even those from the distant past deserved an audience, I asked God to bring you and other Passengers on board.

My ability to see and confess sins results from years in Bible study, prayer, and a personal relationship with Jesus Christ, who died to save humankind from punishment for sins—though confession is not always easy. For example, ignoring the recorded sins of my possible ancestors and definite namesakes, the Pierces, would have been easy; instead, and specifically because this sin still affects so many and hangs over our nation like a cloud, I chose to confess and regret that a Pierce was the first New England slave trader. Perhaps you will relate to or consider forgiving that sin and others confessed on board, as these are powerful sail-setting and caring actions to take.

Potential Passenger, if you agree with me that America and other nations need us—citizens of America and those from other nations who appreciate an incredibly blessed, rich, and spiritually founded, grounded, caring, and motivated nation—please set your priorities according to God's guidance, take responsibility for personal, family, and national matters of conscience, and schedule times to cruise alone or with a group.

As you join me on board and we sail, the Pilgrims' seventeenth-century Plymouth covenant—as recorded in the Mayflower Compact and signed by forty-one male Passengers—will advance to the twenty-first-century Passenger dedications of our national, Judeo-Christian, and personal lives and liberty to God's glory and honor.

By embarking with that daily destination and motivation in mind, and with responsibilities undertaken, We the Passengers will help preserve, protect, and purify America's civil and spiritual legacies—and at the same time, fulfill our duties to the world and to God.

Yes, those goals can be accomplished just by reading a book, most notably and essentially if We the Passengers will use Scripture as the greatest wave-breaking pilgrimage, precedent, language, and challenging course ever charted for humankind.

This logbook was written and formatted and is now introduced as a spiritual cruise with you the twenty-first-century Passenger—the reader—in my mind, heart, and prayers. Because God answered those prayers, your importance is indicated by the capitalization of "Passenger" throughout the cruise.

I needed to learn unfamiliar language for writing a spiritual cruise logbook. Speaking from experience, I guarantee that you will quickly become comfortable with the navigational terms and words—used allegorically and spiritually—such as "on board," "charter," "baggage," "Passenger," "Scripture Course," "headings," "embarkation," "Daily Destination Dedications," "coming about," "tacking, trimming, setting, and filling sails," and "disembarkation." With that, I hope you are prepared to get underway.

New World Charters

The seventeenth-century *Mayflower* sailed in the "wake" of other chartered ships. Columbus and crew on the *Santa Maria*, *Niña*, and *Pinta* come to mind. English Protestants, whose intent was to advance Christianity in the New World, wrote, signed, and paid for the Jamestown and Plymouth New World charters. Consequently, our twenty-first-century spiritual pilgrimage sails in wakes as well—the tracks of waves left by other chartered ships moving through the water.

Charter for the Jamestown Ships and Settlement

Chartering a ship means signing a contract for leasing part or all of a vessel for a voyage or a stated time. The Virginia Company of London was formed to charter sailing ships for voyages to America; in 1607, the *Susan Constant*, *Godspeed*, and *Discovery* were chartered and commissioned to convey 104 male colonists to build a New World settlement on the James River.

The Jamestown, Virginia, settlement was a profit-making and political venture with a spiritual charter:

> There are two great providential landmarks to the dawn of American liberty. The first is Jamestown and the second Plymouth. Both were birthed out of evangelical zeal to see the spread of Christianity. Both involved intrepid men who risked much in the hope of blessing generations yet to be born.
>
> Jamestown's founding in 1607 resulted in North America's introduction to the ancient Christian common law with its origins in the Law of Moses and the Magna Carta. This common law would later be incorporated by direct reference into the United States Constitution. To Jamestown we owe America's first great experiment, a model that would later be adopted by the Founding Fathers as the basic construct of civil government in a free society. Jamestown gave the American people their first Protestant Christian worship services, church buildings, and baptisms.[1]

---

1. Douglas W. Phillips, President and Founder of the Vision Forum, Inc., "We Must Rejoice in Providence If We Are to Persevere as a People," Providence & Perseverance Vision Forum Family Catalog 2007. San Antonio, TX: Vision Forum, 2007. www.visionforum.com. Used by permission.

Chartering and Rechartering the *Mayflower*

In 1609, Christopher Jones was the *Mayflower* master. By 1612, four Eng-lishmen including Jones owned the *Mayflower*, and they contracted space and time to transport material goods from one European port to another.

Eleven years later, the *Mayflower* was chartered by Englishmen called Mer-chant Adventurers to cross the Atlantic Ocean and dock in Virginia. The cargo was men, women, and children with their personal belongings, Bibles and other books, and supplies needed first for the voyage and later to establish and defend a free-style settlement in the New World.

At ease with stating spiritual intent, vision, and resolve, in his journal Plymouth governor William Bradford unknowingly rechartered the *Mayflower* for future Passengers:

> What, then, could now sustain them but the spirit of God, and His grace? Ought not the children of their fathers rightly to say: Our fathers were Englishmen who came over the great ocean, and were ready to perish in this wilderness; but they cried unto the Lord, and He heard their voice, and looked on their adversity . . . Let them therefore praise the Lord, because He is good, and His mercies endure forever ... Let them confess before the Lord His loving kindness, and His wonderful works before the sons of men![2]

Edward Delano Sullivan, a twenty-first-century Mayflower Society Gover-nor General, looks back to explain our forefathers' motivations:

> The Pilgrim leaders were passionate, Bible-reading, praying Christians who were unafraid to voice their great faith in God. These separatists set the stage for religious free-dom on the North American continent. Their goal was to worship God as they thought right, following God's Word and not the dictates of the established Church of England. ... Before landing, the *Mayflower* passengers developed the first written declaration of self-government. That document, the Mayflower Compact, was a precursor of the Constitu-tion of the United States.[3]

---

2. Bradford, *Of Plymouth Plantation*, ed. Paget, 66.
3. General Society of Mayflower Descendants online welcome, 2005–2008, while Edward D. Sullivan was Governor General. www.themayflowersociety.com

Full Sail Logbook

In his seventeenth-century farewell letter to his parishioners—men, women, and children who became America's Pilgrims—the Reverend John Robinson wrote, "There are divers motives provoking you above others to great care and conscience."[4] So it has been with transcribing this logbook. The chapters and topics, and the motives underlying them, are diverse, each one following the sail-setting precedent laid down by the Pilgrims.

Those first colonists, and many American citizens since, set sails with motives of caring and conscience that have led to free-style Judeo-Christian and American life—life in "full sail." *Full Sail* chapter contents address various topics—listed as Cruise Day Headings on our navigational logbook cruise—that move chronologically through America's development as colonies and then as a nation of free and united states. Thus, on Cruise Day One, Passengers will remember that by planting corn with Native help, the Pilgrims established an agricultural system and economy. Family and friend occupations and interests also determined topic choices for this literary voyage.

Seventeenth-century Pilgrims sailed into the unknown with little preparation compared to ours. We have been introduced to sailing language, rechartered the *Mayflower*, and reviewed New World history made by our spiritual and physical ancestors. As we head toward the dock to sense the power of the wind and waves God created for the American national adventure to last from the seventeenth to the twenty-first centuries, let's use this time to become acquainted with the daily headings and programs.

---

4. Bradford, *Of Plymouth Plantation* 1620-1647, ed. Morison, 369. From Rev. John Robinson's farewell letter to the Pilgrims, written in Leiden in the Netherlands, 1620.

Daily Headings and Programs

Daily Headings and Programs

Final Boarding Preparation: Setting Sails to Catch the Wind

*He who forms the mountains, creates the wind, and reveals his
thoughts to man, he who turns dawn to darkness, and treads
the high places of the earth—the Lord God Almighty is his name.*
Amos 4:13

Before embarking on this twenty-first-century Full Sail free-style cruise alone or with a group, please ensure that your boarding passes are in good order:

★ If you are boarding to review civil and/or church history, and you wish to read more than the snippets in these chapters or to augment facts in *Full Sail*, acquire library cards and borrow or budget to purchase books listed in the Cruise Library Catalog. Also learn how to research on the Internet. Some books can be downloaded for free (or for a fee) on the Internet or Kindle.

★ If you are boarding as a person of faith, if you are seeking faith, or if you are just curious about a relationship with Christ, please take your Bible off the shelf or purchase a version or versions quoted in Full Sail.

★ Optional for individual Passengers: acquire a hymnal and biblical commentary. Groups will benefit by possessing at least one of each.

★ Open your heart to receive and love Jesus Christ—and your enemies, your neighbors, and one another—as commanded by him.[5]

★ Ask to be filled with the Holy Spirit, who will give you free-style understanding.[6]

★ Prepare to sing, study, serve, prosper spiritually, and receive God's gracious and holy peace.

★ Practice addressing prayers to the Almighty Master of our cruise ship.

★ Invite others to come on board to strengthen and protect free-style life and liberty.

★ Prayerfully commit your time, mind, and heart as an offering to God.

★ Prepare now to review and advance sail-setting history before setting twenty-first-century sails.

---

5. Matthew 5:43, 19:19; Luke 10:25.
6. Joel 2; Acts 2.

Setting Sails in the Seventeenth Century

In the year 1620, 102 English men, women, and children boarded the *Mayflower* at Plymouth, England. They sailed across the Atlantic for over sixty perilous days. The ship they sailed on disappeared long ago, but the passengers' names are recorded history.

In those days, masters managed merchant ships, and captains managed naval ships. Master Christopher Jones charted and mastered the *Mayflower's* course, with the crew setting and trimming sails to catch the wind.

Due to wintry weather and seemingly off-course winds, the *Mayflower* crew and passengers sighted land far north of their Virginia destination and disembarked at Plymouth in New England. Fishermen and explorers had already named Plymouth and partially mapped the coastline area.

Before disembarking, forty-one male *Mayflower* passengers, including my ancestors James Chilton and Francis Cooke, signed a solemn agreement known as the Mayflower Compact. The Compact was a covenant, an agreement with each other and with God to govern the conduct of the settlers and establish guiding principles for Plymouth Colony. To this day, it is believed that the Compact initiated American "government of the people, by the people, for the people."[7]

The Seventeenth-Century Mayflower Compact

IN THE NAME OF GOD, AMEN:

We whose names are underwritten, the loyal subjects of our dread Sovereign Lord, King James, by the Grace of God, of Great Britain, France, and Ireland, King, Defender of the Faith, &c.

Having undertaken, for the Glory of God, and advancement of the Christian Faith and the Honor of our King and Country, a voyage to plant the first colony in the northern parts of Virginia, do by these presents solemnly and mutually in the presence of God, and one of another, covenant and combine ourselves together into a civil body politic, for our better ordering and preservation, and furtherance of the ends aforesaid; and by virtue hereof to enact, constitute, and frame, such just and equal laws, ordinances, acts, constitutions, and offices, from time to time, as shall be thought most

---

7. The Declaration of Independence, as quoted in Catherine Millard's *Rewriting of America's History*, 19.

meet and convenient for the general good of the Colony, unto which we promise all due submission and obedience.

In witness whereof we have hereunto subscribed our names at Cape Cod, the eleventh of November, in the year of the reign of our sovereign lord, King James, of England, France and Ireland, the eighteenth, and of Scotland the fifty-fourth. Anno Domini, 1620.[8]

Meeting Seventeenth-Century Passengers

The *Mayflower* was chartered by passengers wanting to live and prosper in a civil society based on biblical guidelines and religious freedom. Not all passengers sailed for free-style reasons; among those on board were orphan children rescued from London streets and paying passengers called "strangers" by the Pilgrims.

The crew and a cooper (the barrel-maker and caretaker aboard historic vessels) were hired to care for the ship, steerage, and passengers. John Alden was the cooper, and Miles Standish was the military adviser paid to protect the settlers. According to Governor William Bradford, the seventeenth-century passengers were:

★ Mr. Samuel Fuller and a servant called William Button. His wife was behind, and a child which came afterwards.
★ John Crackston and his son John Crackston.
★ Captain Myles Standish and Rose his wife.
★ Mr. Christopher Martin and his wife and two servants, Solomon Prower and John Langmore.
★ Mr. William Mullins and his wife and two children, Joseph and Priscilla; and a servant, Robert Carter.
★ Mr. William White and Susanna his wife and one son called Resolved, and one born a-shipboard called Peregrine, and two servants named William Holbeck and Edward Thompson.
★ Mr. Stephen Hopkins and Elizabeth his wife, and two children called Giles and Constanta, a daughter, both by a former wife. And two more by this wife called Damaris and Oceanus; the last was born at sea. And two servants called Edward Doty and Edward Lester.
★ Mr. Richard Warren, but his wife and children were left behind and came afterwards.

8. Bradford and Paget, *Of Plymouth Plantation*, 75–76.

★ John Billington and Ellen his wife, and two sons, John and Francis.

★ Edward Tilley and Ann his wife, and two children that were their cousins, Henry Sampson and Humility Cooper.

★ John Tilley and his wife, and Elizabeth their daughter.

★ Francis Cooke [twenty-first-century Cruise Host ancestor] and his son John; but his wife and other children came afterwards.

★ Thomas Rogers and Joseph his son; his other children came afterwards.

★ Thomas Tinker and his wife and a son.

★ John Rigsdale and Alice his wife.

★ James Chilton and his wife, and Mary [twenty-first-century Cruise Host ancestors] their daughter; they had another daughter that was married, came afterward.

★ Edward Fuller and his wife, and Samuel their son.

★ John Turner and two sons; he had a daughter came some years after to Salem, where she is now living.

★ Francis Eaton and Sarah his wife, and Samuel their son, a young child.

★ Moses Fletcher, John Goodman, Thomas Williams, Digory Priest, Edmund Margesson, Peter Browne, Richard Britteridge, Richard Clarke, Richard Gardiner, Gilbert Winslow.

★ John Alden was hired for a Cooper at Southampton where the ship victualed, and being a hopeful young man was much desired but left to his own liking to go or stay when he came here; but he stayed and married here.

★ John Allerton and Thomas English were both hired, the latter to go master of a shallop here, and the other was reputed as one of the company but was to go back (being a seaman) for the help of others behind. But they both died here before the ship returned.

★ There were also other two seamen hired to stay a year here in the country, William Trevor, and one Ely. But when their time was out they both returned. These being about a hundred souls, came over in this first ship and began this work, which God of His goodness hath hitherto blessed. Let His holy name have the praise. (Governor William Bradford, *Of Plymouth Plantation*, 1650)[9]

---

9. www.pilgrimhall.org

Power for Setting Sails in the Twenty-First Century

As we prepare for our own journey, we cannot just jump on board to set sail. For playing twenty-first-century roles that fulfill America's conscience, causes, and callings, we need the power generated by certain history-making citizens who advanced and connected the "civil body politic" and spirituality. Hear the sail-setting wind in their words.

William Bradford (1590-1657)

Many of the things feared might never befall; others by provident care and the use of good means might in a great measure be prevented; and all of them, through the help of God, by fortitude and patience, might either be borne or overcome.[10]

John Winthrop (1638-1707)

When God gives a special commission, He looks to have it strictly observed in every article. Thus stands the cause between God and us. We are entered into Covenant with Him for this work . . . We must delight in each other, mourn together, labor and suffer together, always having before our eyes our Commission and Community in the work. So shall we keep the unity of the Spirit in the bond of peace.[11]

Jonathan Edwards (1703-1758)

Fathers and mothers, husbands, wives, children or the company of earthly friends, are but shadows; but the enjoyment of God is the substance. These are but scattered means; but God is the sum. These are but streams; but God is the fountain. These are but the drops; God is the ocean.[12]

Benjamin Franklin (1706-1790)

Here is my creed: I believe in one God, the Creator of the universe. That he governs it by his providence. That he ought to be worshipped. That the most acceptable service we render to him is in doing good to his other children. That the soul of man is immortal, and and will be treated with justice in another life respecting its conduct in this.[13]

Samuel Adams (1722-1803)

During his farewell address as governor of Massachusetts on Jan. 27, 1797, Samuel Adams made a plea for moral education, expressing hope that "our

---

10. Bradford and Paget, *Of Plymouth Plantation*, 23.
11. Dunn and Yeandle, eds., *The Journal of John Winthrop*, 9–10. From Winthrop's "Model of Christian Charity" sermon, written on board the *Arrabella* on the Atlantic Ocean, 1630.
12. Quoted in Turnbull, *Jonathan Edwards The Preacher*, 46.
13. Quoted in Smyth, *Writings of Benjamin Franklin*, 10:84.

children and youth, while they are engaged in the pursuit of useful science, may have their minds impressed with a strong sense of the duties they owe to their God, their instructors, and each other."[14]

Abigail Adams (1744-1818)

A patriot without religion in my estimation is as great a paradox as an honest Man without the fear of God. Is it possible that he whom no moral obligations bind, can have any real Good Will towards Men? Can he be a patriot who, by an openly vicious conduct, is undermining the very bonds of Society? . . . The Scriptures tell us "righteousness exalteth a Nation."[15]

John Jay (1745-1829)

It has often given me pleasure to observe that independent America was not composed of detached and distant territories, but that one connected, fertile, widespreading country was the portion of our western sons of liberty. Providence has in a particular manner blessed it with a variety of soils and productions, and watered it with innumerable streams, for the delight and accommodation of its inhabitants. A succession of navigable waters forms a kind of chain round its borders, as if to bind it together; while the most noble rivers in the world, running at convenient distances, present them with highways for the easy communication of friendly aids, and the mutual transportation and exchange of their various commodities.[16]

The Writers and Signers of America's Declaration of Independence: Excerpts from the Declaration of Independence

We hold these truths to be self-evident, that all men are created equal, that they are endowed by their Creator with certain unalienable Rights, that among these are Life, Liberty and the pursuit of Happiness. That to secure these rights, Governments are instituted among Men, deriving their just powers from the consent of the governed.

. . . WE THEREFORE, the Representatives of the UNITED STATES OF AMERICA, in General Congress, Assembled, appealing to the Supreme Judge of the world for the rectitude of our intentions, do, in the Name and by the Authority of the Good People of these Colonies, solemnly publish and declare, That these United Colonies are, and of Right ought to be FREE AND INDEPENDENT STATES . . . And for the support of this Declaration, with a firm reliance on the protection of Divine Providence, we mutually pledge to each other our Lives, our Fortunes and our sacred Honor.

14. Stoll, *Samuel Adams*, 248.
15. Quoted in Federer, *America's God and Country*, 3. Abigail Adams to her friend, Mercy Warren.
16. Federalist Paper #2.

The United States Constitution

We the People of the United states, in Order to form a more perfect Union, establish Justice, insure domestic Tranquility, provide for the common defence, promote the general Welfare, and secure the Blessings of Liberty to ourselves and our Posterity, do ordain and establish this CONSTITUTION for the United States of America . . . Done in Convention by the Unanimous Consent of the States present the Seventeenth Day of September in the Year of our Lord one thousand seven hundred and Eighty seven, and of the Independence of the United States of America the Twelfth. In Witness whereof We have hereunto subscribed our Names.

Daniel Webster (1782-1852)

If we and our posterity reject religious institutions and authority, violate the rules of eternal justice, trifle with the injunctions of morality, and recklessly destroy the political constitution which holds us together, no man can tell how sudden a catastrophe may overwhelm us that shall bury all our glory in profound obscurity. Should that catastrophe happen, let it have no history! Let the horrible narrative never be written![17]

Abraham Lincoln (1809-1865): Second Inaugural Address, March 4, 1865

With malice toward none, with charity for all, with firmness in the right as God gives us to see the right, let us strive on to finish the work we are in, to bind up the nation's wounds, to care for him who shall have borne the battle and for his widow and orphans, to do all which may achieve and cherish a just and a lasting peace among ourselves and with all nations.

Frederick Douglass (1818-1895)

Douglass began publishing the North Star on December 3, 1847, with this motto on the masthead: "Right is of no sex—Truth is of no color—God is the Father of us all, and we are all Brethren."

Chief Joseph (1840-1904)

Chief Joseph, chief of the Nez Percé, said to several congressmen and government officials, "All men were made by the same Great Spirit Chief. They are all brothers."[18]

---

17. From "The Dignity and Importance of History," an address to the New York Historical Society, February 23, 1852. www.dartmouth.edu/~dwebster/speeches/dignity-history.html
18. Baron, *Soul of America*, 43–44.

Booker T. Washington (1856-1915)

This experience of a whole race beginning to go to school for the first time [after Emancipation], presents one of the most interesting studies that has ever occurred in connection with the development of any race . . . The great ambition of the older people was to try to learn to read the Bible before they died. With this end in view, men and women who were fifty or seventy-five years old would often be found in the night-school.[19]

Theodore Roosevelt (1858-1919)

Liberty and justice simply cannot be had apart from the gracious influences of a righteous people. A righteous people simply cannot exist apart from the aspiration to liberty and justice. The Christian religion and its incumbent morality is tied to the cause of freedom with a Gordian knot; loose one from the other and both are sent asunder.[20]

Franklin Delano Roosevelt (1882-1945)

This nation has placed its destiny in the hands and heads and hearts of its millions of free men and women; and its faith in freedom under the guidance of God.[21]

Ronald Reagan (1911-2004)

General Secretary Gorbachev, if you seek peace, if you seek prosperity for the Soviet Union and eastern Europe, if you seek liberalization, come here to this gate. Mr. Gorbachev, open this gate. Mr. Gorbachev, tear down this wall! . . . As I looked out a moment ago from the Reichstag, that embodiment of German unity, I noticed words crudely spray-painted upon the wall, perhaps by a young Berliner, "This wall will fall. Beliefs become reality." Yes, across Europe, this wall will fall. For it cannot withstand faith; it cannot withstand truth. The wall cannot withstand freedom.[22]

Billy Graham (1918–)

The early Americans were angry, disturbed, articulate people. They were angry at tyranny, prejudice, intolerance and injustice, and angry enough to talk about it and do something about it. It was not the fearful and the soft who made this country, but the articulate and the courageous men who changed this wilderness into the mighty nation that it is today.[23]

19. Washington, *Story of My Life and Work*, 29–30.
20. Quoted in Grant, *Courage and Character of Theodore Roosevelt*, 188.
21. Quoted in Baron, *Soul of America*, 108. From FDR's "Four Freedoms Speech" on January 6, 1941.
22. Remarks on East-West Relations at the Brandenburg Gate in West Berlin, June 12, 1987. http://www.reagan.utexas.edu/archives/speeches/1987/061287d.htm. President Reagan's June 12, 1987 speech is important Cold War history. The Berlin Wall stood from 1961 to 1987; Germany was reunified on October 3, 1990.
23. Quoted in Flint, *The Quotable Billy Graham*, 21.

We the People in the Twenty-First Century

We are passionate or complacent or somewhere in between concerning our nation's past, present, and future, and toward fulfilling our duty to the world and to God.

We are indifferent toward, disagree with, or consider it important that America's founders, pastors, and presidents believed that a nation prospered when government and faith worked along with Providence. We may have been careless toward the past, or we may have freely chosen to preserve and protect historical treasures such as speeches and signatures. We are Americans with or without the power generated by confession, passion, importance, preserving, and protecting.

If you are without this power or merely indifferent toward the past, I suggest that praying together will help everyone board and set sails.

Setting Free-Style Sails in the Twenty-First Century

Prayer for Sail Setting

Almighty Providential Master and Forgiving Judge,
we are deeply indebted to you for our freedoms in Christ and your
agenda for America. Please hear as we confess unwisely taking
our liberties for granted, that power has been lost because we failed
to respect, protect, and preserve. Trusting that through confession in
Christ's name and sacrifice we are forgiven, we ask for time, faithfulness,
wisdom, love, conscience, risk-taking courage, enthusiasm, and
caregiving power to praise you and purify nations. As on board the
seventeenth-century *Mayflower*, bless us with the same provision,
protection, presence, and sail-filling power for our twenty-first-century
pilgrimage as has been articulated by those who preceded us.
Hear our prayers for unseeing eyes to be opened and Satan's walls
of oppression to crumble wherever they stand in opposition
to your will, agenda, and truth. —*Amen.*

The Twenty-First-Century Mayflower Compact

We the Twenty-First-Century Passengers covenant with one another in the name and presence of God Almighty, Supreme and Sovereign Ruler of all Nations, the Alpha and Omega of time and events and authority over wind and waves. *We the Passengers* believe in the power of this declaration, and with a firm reliance on Divine Protection and Providence, we pledge alliance and allegiance to this covenant in the style and spirit of the Mayflower Compact. We will connect our past with our future to perform our duty to the world and to advance Judeo-Christian faith. We will bathe America and other nations in prayer and confess sins to purify glory and honor.

In WITNESS whereof to prophetic fulfillment and faithful duty, we agree to dedicate the United States of America and all nations to God's glory and honor—and to promote the furtherance of the ends aforesaid to bless God and all nations. —*Anno Domini 2009*

Meeting Twenty-First-Century Passengers

Several of the Passengers on board in the twenty-first century relate to dedication headings. For example, Native American Ed LaRose and Rabbi Richard Rubinstein are Passengers on Cruise Day One, when we will dedicate races, tribes, and agricultural systems to God's glory.

Other modern-day Passengers are imaginary, though based on historical figures—like Chap and Coop in the conversation you're about to take part in. If you are cruising as a group, here is your first opportunity to role-play, ad-lib, and relate to other Passengers in conversation.

"Chap," short for Chaplain, represents spiritual leadership on board the American pilgrimage from the seventeenth to the twenty-first centuries. "Coop," short for Cooper, represents citizens whose lives are touched by spiritual leadership but who are burdened with sins in our lives, families, nations, and world.

The seventeenth-century *Mayflower* passengers probably packed their belongings, and certainly their supplies, in barrels watched over by Cooper John Alden. Barrels are no longer extensively used, but this is a spiritual, not a material cruise. Please picture in your mind our twenty-first-century cooper caring for heavy baggage—representing our attitudes, regrets, successes, and sins, as well as the positive potential that We the Passengers have brought on board.

Let's listen as Chap and Coop talk and answer questions you may have on your minds as we prepare for our spiritual cruise through time.

A "Chap and Coop" Conversation

COOP.   Chap, the *Full Sail* boarding and sail-setting information says that Almighty God is Master of this ship and that he uses his Word to chart courses. Who is the helmsman of the ship?

CHAP.   Your question demands an answer based on hindsight and visionary faith. Securely moored to the dock or at sea, the *Mayflower* vessel and voyages then and now are forever tied to the premises that our Almighty Providential God and Master uses his Word to chart free-style courses, that his Spirit fills sails, and that he stations his Son Jesus Christ at the helm.

COOP.   Chap, what is the dock, and how will we head out to sea to sail free-style if we are so securely moored to it?

CHAP.   The dock is our personal, family, and national history, as well as our free lifestyles, cultural traditions, and systems. Think of America's mooring security as a very strong, three-stranded, woven rope that connects our economic, civil, and spiritual flagship to the dock on shore. The economic strand pays for the rope. The civic strand protects and governs the use of the rope—its tie to the dock. The spiritual strand is when citizens trust God—that his Providential sovereignty over the affairs of humankind will preserve, strengthen, lengthen, and manage the rope—no matter if and especially when our will conflicts with Providential will. The rope is to last until the old earth and the history, lifestyles, cultural traditions, and systems we are attached to pass away and the sea is no more.

COOP.   Is *no more* a scriptural prophecy and compass point for this voyage?

CHAP.   Yes; the warning is in Revelation 21:1: "Then I saw a new heaven and a new earth, for the first heaven and the first earth had passed away, and there was no longer any sea."

COOP.   Any flexibility?

CHAP.   The Bible and history cannot be rewritten, so no, there is no flexibility—the Bible is always relevant.

COOP.   Okay, I understand the woven-rope metaphor and accept the warning. Now tell me more about staying moored to the dock.

CHAP.   The rope length represents free-style time from the seventeenth to the twenty-first centuries. Those who tried to cut it short by attacking American and Judeo-Christian life and liberty have failed. When chafed, the rope has healed and grown more durable. In fact, because every strand now stretches as one rope from sea to shining sea, the rope is more than three times stronger and more sturdy and dependable than each individual strand.

COOP.   So as we head out to sea, the ship will stay moored to the dock representing history, lifestyle, cultural traditions, and systems, and the rope will lengthen and strengthen as each day goes by.

CHAP.   By faith and figuratively speaking, yes, and our sturdy rope and secure mooring to the dock will hold the ship steady and stable even as passengers participate and baggage shifts—when God hurls sins into the sea—and as we set daily sails to catch the wind and ride the waves.

HOST.   Please pardon my interruption in the Chap and Coop conversation. As we meet twenty-first-century Passengers, several of you may share concerns in group discussions. In this next segment of the conversation, offered for role-playing, the tension between Chap and Coop and Host and Passengers brings to modern-day attention the tension between the chartering passengers and the secular, paying passengers—also known as Saints and Strangers—onboard the seventeenth-century *Mayflower*, as well as the tension which exists in our daily lives and conversations in the twenty-first century. Please don't fear doing this; it will help you get acquainted if you are boarding as a group, and you are as free to role-play as I am: the conversation obviously portrays my experiences, observations, and personal reflections.

      Now that we've overcome the fear obstacle on our way to getting acquainted with one another and with our cruising goals, let's picture ourselves standing next to or sitting on baggage stacked on the *Mayflower* deck.

COOP.   Chap, because we're on a spiritual and not a literal cruise, there is no holding space. What do I do with the baggage?

CHAP.   Holding space isn't needed because God has promised to hurl our sins—our baggage—into the sea. Have you inspected any baggage?

COOP.   Isn't a personal baggage inspection intruding on privacy?

CHAP.   Not in this security-minded day and age.

COOP.   I certainly agree with that! Now, whose baggage should I inspect? Ha, here's someone with a suspicious amount of baggage. Sir, may I ask, what you have brought on board?

PASSENGER 1.   I packed poor choices, errors in judgment, and avoidable mistakes. How do I get rid of all that baggage?

CHAP.   Those are burdensome excuses. I advise that you don't hide behind your carry-on contents, because 1 John 1:8–10 clearly says, "If we claim to be without sin, we deceive ourselves and the truth is not in us. If we confess our sins, he is faithful and just and will forgive us our sins and purify us from all unrighteousness. If we claim we have not sinned, we make him out to be a liar and his word has no place in our lives."

PASSENGER 1.   This is beginning to sound like a judgmental guilt trip.

PASSENGER 2.   Sure, if you want to see it that way. I thought that way too, until I opened my Bible and read Luke 1:50: "His mercy extends to those who fear him, from generation to generation."

PASSENGER 3.   Let's hear what other Passengers are saying.

PASSENGER 4.   I think it's presumptuous for Americans to purify and dedicate other nations.

PASSENGER 5.   I disagree, because we send missionaries to many nations, and we're *from* many nations. If you don't believe me, listen to the accents and observe our diversity on the deck.

PASSENGER 6.   I'm Caucasian, Polish, and American. God seemed to be someplace else the first year I lived in America. After I saw my Polish forefathers' sins in me and confessed, God spoke and worked in my life again. So I'm on board to pray for and dedicate my homeland to his glory and honor.

HOST.   You've brought up an interesting point. Scripture says that the sins of the fathers are carried down even to the third generation. We who are alive today are able to confess those sins that are family traits, habits, regrets, and character flaws that hurt others, ourselves, and our communities and nations. Let me repeat in a personal way: I cannot confess my forefathers' sins to save their souls or baptize them into faith. But I can express regrets and confess their sins, which were passed on and are now in me and our nation. For example, my temper was inherited. When I began studying the Bible as an adult, God opened my spiritual eyes to see and my mouth to confess the trait. God forgave me. Now I seldom lose my temper because I am more accountable to him, and when the sleeping trait that hurts others occasionally awakens, I can recognize it and again confess, repent, and ask for mercy.

PASSENGER 7. Sounds like my old temptation: an addiction I will deal with all my life. My father and grandfather lived and died as addicts. God, have mercy on me and my children and all their descendants.

PASSENGER 8. I spend more than my income. Lord, have mercy on me.

CHAP. Listen! Other passengers, too many to count, are asking for mercy:

PASSENGERS,
one at a time. "My ancestors brought disbelief to America. God, have mercy on me and my children."

"I'm stuck-up and arrogant, just like my parents and grandparents. God, have mercy on me and my children."

"My ancestors brought criminal tendencies. My son is in prison, and a grandkid is heading that way. I'm willing to do anything to help him. God, have mercy on our family and community."

"Mine brought addictive eating habits that are still mine and my family's. God, have mercy on us."

"My family has a rudeness habit; our tongues and actions hurt each other and others. God, have mercy on us and those we encounter and offend."

"I'm Native American. I'm on board to forgive Europeans for moving and murdering my ancestors so they could use the land—and to ask God and Passengers to forgive Native atrocities. Lord, have mercy."

"I'm African-American. I boarded to hear if anyone cares about prejudice."

"Me too. I'm Jewish."

"I'm sensing responsibility to forgive and reconcile. Lord, have mercy."

CHAP.   Spirit, fill sails so America can go back out to sea on the *Mayflower*, where you will hurl our sins into the sea as promised in Micah 7:18–20.

COOP.   Chap, I've heard other Passengers ask this question. Do you and the Cruise Host love America more than God?

CHAP.   Absolutely not! God prioritized that order through Paul: "Everyone must submit himself to the governing authorities, for there is no authority except that which God has established."[24]

HOST.   My answer is this: God established the nations—"When the Most High gave the nations their inheritance, he set up boundaries according to the numbers of the sons of Israel."[25] Therefore, he is the sovereign authority over all nations and leaders. I love him with all my heart and ask him daily to use me for his glory and honor where I live and serve. He led me to search out my family history, as well as American, Judeo-Christian, and world history, to find a way to do that. My *Full Sail* boarding process—the researching and Providential role-playing—was slow but sure, not unlike the boarding process you are experiencing.

PASSENGER 9.   Will this voyage be dangerous?

CHAP.   We will trust Christ to calm the sea and storms, as in Luke 8:22–25.

PASSENGER 10.   Any famous people on board?

HOST.   Yes. Some are well-known American heroes and patriots; others are not.

---

24. Romans 13:1.
25. "Song of Moses" in Deuteronomy 32:8.

PASSENGER 11. Is this cruise partisan?

PASSENGER 12. And denominational?

HOST.   No, this cruise is nonpartisan and nondenominational. I invite people from every political or theological persuasion to participate and pray, along with citizens from other nations, to protect, preserve, and dedicate purified life and liberty and our individual nations to God's glory and honor. Please join me in prayer.

Personal and Group Prayer
Almighty Master of this historical flagship—
I wish to participate. I salute, and I will try with all my heart and
mind to trust and honor your course for this pilgrimage.
Please add my name to the twenty-first-century *Mayflower* Passenger list.
We the Passengers humble ourselves to turn from wicked ways,
and we ask for your help to reconcile and bring order
and hope into the twenty-first-century chaos that challenges personal,
family, national, and international lives and liberties. —*Amen.*

Life Preservers

Passengers on modern-day cruise ships gather on decks for life-preserving drills. *Full Sail* life preservers are the allegiances, creeds, documents, pledges, and songs—many written in response to dramatic historical episodes—that became national treasures to help keep free-style American and Judeo-Christian life and liberty strong and steady through the passage of time.

We will begin with a pledge of alliance to the American flag—the Stars and Stripes. The word "allegiance" immediately brings to mind a flag or banner. A Cruise Library book, the *Dictionary of Biblical Imagery*, gives reasons to raise a national flag:

> Banners are identifying flags or streamers attached to the end of a standard. Throughout history they have served three main purposes: to identify a group, to claim possession of a space or territory and to lend festivity to a celebration. Banners are rallying points, physically and/or emotionally . . . In the Psalms too it is God who sets up a banner for his people (Ps 60:4) . . . Jeremiah's prediction of Babylon's destruction is prefaced by the statement, "Declare among the nations

and proclaim, set up a banner and proclaim, conceal it not"
(Jer 50:2 RSV), along the lines of a warrior boldly planting a
banner as a sign of taking possession.[26]

The two British flags flying on the original *Mayflower* masts were important to passengers. The Cross of Saint George had symbolized England at least
as far back as the Crusades in 1277. The British Union Flag, designed by King
James when he succeeded Elizabeth I of England in 1603, combines the red
cross symbolic of England's Patron Saint George with the white cross of Saint
David of Wales and the white, X-shaped cross of Saint Andrew, Patron Saint
of Scotland. The Saint George flag was flown on the foremast of English merchant ships, with the Union flag on the mainmast. Hence, these flags flew over
all the English New World colonies. The symbol of Northern Ireland's Saint
Patrick has been added to the modern Union Jack.[27]

As we raise the American flag over our own voyage, this seems like a good
time to affirm our allegiance to the American Constitution's intent and to clarify
confusion about what is a nation—and specifically what is a "Christian nation."
Russell Kirk, a twentieth-century lecturer and man of faith respected by adherents
to differing perspectives, fills sails with a historical and modern-day explanation:

> The United States of America is not a Christian state,
> for the country's Constitution forbids the establishment of
> a national church by Congress, and stands tolerant of all
> religions. But the words state and nation signify different
> concepts. "State" means the governmental organization of
> a country, political society with sovereign power; while "na-
> tion" means the people of the land, with their culture—and
> not merely the people who are living just now, but also their
> ancestors and those who will descend from them: that is, a
> nation is extended in time and shares a culture: those par-
> ticipants in a common culture who are living today, and the
> participants in that culture who have preceded them in time,
> and those participants in the common culture who are yet to
> be born. One might call a nation a community of souls. In
> that proper understanding of what a nation amounts to, the
> American nation is Christian.[28]

---

26. Ryken, Wilhoit, and Longman, *Dictionary of Biblical Imagery*, 70–71.
27. http://www.americanrevolution.org/flags.html
28. Kirk, "Renewing a Shaken Culture," lecture at the Heritage Foundation on December 11, 1992.
    Archived at www.heritagefoundation.org

This "Tribute to the American Flag" by Charles Evans Hughes (eleventh Chief Justice of the United States), delivered in June 1916 to a Washington DC graduating class, explains how Americans feel about our flag.

What the Flag Means

This flag means more than association and reward. It is the symbol of our national unity, our national endeavor, our national aspiration.

It tells you of the struggle for independence, of union preserved, of liberty and union one and inseparable, of the sacrifices of brave men and women to whom the ideals and honor of this nation have been dearer than life.

It means America first; it means an undivided allegiance.

It means America united, strong and efficient, equal to her tasks.

It means that you cannot be saved by the valor and devotion of your ancestors; that to each generation comes its patriotic duty; and that upon your willingness to sacrifice and endure as those before you have sacrificed and endured rests the national hope.

It speaks of equal rights; the inspiration of free institutions exemplified and vindicated, of liberty under law intelligently conceived and impartially administered.

There is not a thread in it but scorns self-indulgence, weakness, and rapacity. It is eloquent of our community interests, outweighing all divergences of opinion, and of our common destiny.

Given as a prize to those of the highest standing, it happily enforces the lesson that intelligence and zeal must go together, that discipline must accompany emotions, and that we must ultimately rely upon enlightened opinion.[29]

We can pledge and sing without fear, with hearts filled with thanksgiving, because many sacrificed their hopes and dreams, even their lives, to sustain the power of our allegiance and anthem.

Pledge of Allegiance

I pledge allegiance to the Flag of the United States of America,
and to the Republic for which it stands, one Nation under God,
indivisible, with liberty and justice for all.

American National Anthem: The Star-Spangled Banner

Oh say! Can you see, by the dawn's early light,
What so proudly we hailed at the twilight's last gleaming?
Whose broad stripes and bright stars, thro' the perilous fight,
O'er the ramparts we watch'd, were so gallantly streaming?
And the rockets' red glare, the bombs bursting in air,

---

29. Quoted in Molotsky, *The Flag, The Poet & The Song*, 217–8.

Gave proof thro' the night that our flag was still there.
Oh, say, does that Star-spangled Banner yet wave
O'er the land of the free and the home of the brave?

Oh, thus be it ever when free men shall stand
Between their lov'd homes and the war's desolation!
Blest with vict'ry and peace, may the heav'n-rescued-land
Praise the Pow'r that hath made and preserved us a nation!
Then conquer we must, when our cause it is just,
And this be our motto: "In God is our trust!"
And the Star-spangled Banner in triumph shall wave
O'er the land of the free and the home of the brave![30]

"God does not show favoritism but accepts men from every nation" (Acts 10:34–35). Citizens of all nations, please pledge your allegiances to your nations and causes as we sing:

In Christ There Is No East or West

In Christ there is no East or West, In Him no South or North;
But one great fellowship of love Throughout the whole wide earth.

In Him shall true hearts ev'rywhere Their high communion find;
His service is the golden cord Close binding all mankind.

Join hands then, brothers of the faith, Whate'er your race may be;
Who serves my Father as a son Is surely kin to me.

In Christ now meet both East and West; In Him meet South and North.
All Christly souls are one in Him Throughout the whole wide earth.[31]

The Twenty-First-Century Mayflower Passenger Pledge

Fellow Passengers, I hope you are ready as I am to embark on this journey! However, to honor the Mayflower Society and descendants who preserved Plymouth and Pilgrim history without our help for centuries, let's pause to recite the Society's meeting pledge. As we recite, picture Passengers from all tribes and races gathered on the *Mayflower* deck with the Stars and Stripes flying overhead—and feel the wind gathering to fill our sails.

---

30. Lyrics (1814) by Francis Scott Key. Melody (1780) probably by John Stafford Smith.
31. Lyrics (1908) by John Oxenham/William A. Dunkerley; music (1836) by Alexander R. Reinagle.

In the name of Almighty God, Amen:

I pledge myself to hold aloft, the lamps of civil and religious liberty lighted by the Pilgrims at Plymouth Rock. To recall and cherish the sacrifices and struggles made by them for the common good; to study their lives, deeds, faith, courage and character, and to draw inspiration therefrom—to emulate their spirit, to be loyal to the flag and institutions of the Country whose founding was so greatly aided by their work and wisdom; to do everything within my power to deserve and preserve the heritage, at all times and in all ways to profit by their Pilgrim example. (Centennial History, General Society of Mayflower Descendants 1879–1997)

Daily agendas are in your logbook. Sails are set.

Spirit of Almighty God, fill our sails! Amen.

Bon Voyage!

Beverly Pierce Stroebel

Cruise Day One Program
First Things First

~~~~~~~~~~~~~~~~~~~~~~~~

Scripture Course

Wake-Up Calls!

First-Generation Introductions
Francis and John Cooke
James, Mrs. Chilton, and Mary Chilton

First Briefing: Connecting Historical and Spiritual Potential and Power

Free Time Options

Last Briefing: Releasing the Power of Reconciliation and Hope

Cruise Library Visit

Cruise Bonus
Bookends: Judeo-Christian History and a Twenty-First-Century
Jewish and Gentile Conversation

Covenant and Dedications
Judeo-Christian Faith and America's Races, Tribes,
and Agricultural Systems

Night Watch
Scripture Course and Focus Points

~~~~~~~~~~~~~~~~~~~~~~~~

Scripture Course

> *O Lord Almighty, my King and my God. Blessed are those who*
> *dwell in your house; they are ever praising you. Blessed are those*
> *whose strength is in you, who have set their hearts on pilgrimage.*
> Psalm 84:3–5

Scripture: Genesis 12:1–3; Leviticus 11:36; Deuteronomy 28; 2 Chronicles 7:13–14; Psalm 122:1–9; Isaiah 10–11, 42:7; Ezekiel 36:22–23, 37:24–25, 28; Hosea 10:12; Habakkuk 2:2–3, 14; Luke 4:18; Acts 13:48; Romans 1:8, 1:16, 2:9–11; 9–15; Philippians 3:5–8; Colossians 1:15–17; Revelation 5:5, 14:6–7, 22:16.

Wake-Up Calls!

*Write down the revelation and make it plain on tablets so that a
herald may run with it. For the revelation awaits an appointed time;
it speaks of the end and will not prove false. Though it linger, wait for it;
it will certainly come and will not delay . . . The earth will be filled with
the knowledge of the glory of the Lord, as the waters cover the sea.*
Habakkuk 2:2–3, 14

*The hour has come for you to wake up from your slumber, because
our salvation is nearer now than when we first believed. The night is
nearly over; the day is almost here. So let us put aside the deeds
of darkness and put on the armor of light.*
Romans 13:11–12

Powerful voices—biblical, historical, and modern-day—jolted me awake from deep slumber while writing this logbook. They became the "great multitude, like the roar of rushing waters" of Revelation 19:6, shouting to be heard. By *awake*, I mean that my ears, eyes, heart, and mind were opened to see and understand Providence throughout history and to mingle old and new information with sea sounds, sights, and meaning. I was especially stirred as I read the words of Habbakuk and the book *The Ways of the Way* by Dr. Raymond Robert Fischer. Suddenly, a restless, roaring wave, demanding revelation and glory, released wake-up calls for our days on board the *Mayflower*. We sail across the ocean, hanging on tight to Providence and prophecy, to seek purification and dedication to God. Hold on, Pilgrims! We're heading out to sea.

The historical roots of the *mikvah* [a Hebrew word that includes oceans] reach all the way back to the Garden of Eden. By eating the fruit, Adam and Eve brought death into the world. Most of the Jewish traditions that relate to impurity are connected to some form of death. Those who come into contact with one of the forms of death must therefore immerse themselves in water, which is described in Genesis as flowing out of the Garden of Eden (the source of life), in order to be cleansed of this contact with death, and by extension, cleansed from sin.

The Hebrew word *mikvah* in English means "a pool or gathering of water." A *mikvah* may use either stationary rainwater or flowing well water or spring water. Oceans, lakes, ponds, and springs are all natural catch basins of rain water and thus can be used for this ritual purpose (Lev. 11:36).[32]

O God, we are humbled at this opportunity to come into your presence. We stand in awe of your power and sustaining grace. We are eternally thankful that our Pilgrim forebearers had you as the center of their pilgrimage as they established a new society while they endured trials that would have destroyed a lesser people. We thank you for your spirit and providence that has brought us together today. We ask your blessing on our gathering. We pray, O God, that as you have invested in us we will be faithful witnesses to your infinite goodness, love, and justice. To God be the glory! —*Amen* (Manning Longley Balcom, New York, *Mayflower* descendant, twentieth century)[33]

They then chose, or rather confirmed, Mr. John Carver, a godly man and highly approved among them, as their governor for that year. After they had provided a place for their goods and common stores, which they were long in unlading owing to want of boats, the severity of the winter weather, and sickness, had begun some small cottages for dwellings,—as time would admit they met and consulted of law and order, both for civil and military government, as seemed suited to their conditions, adding to them from time to time as urgent need demanded. (Governor William Bradford)[34]

My ancestral and spiritual roots are English Separatist and Jewish. It gives me great joy to know that the Pilgrims and Puritans loved the Jewish people for their part in the history of redemption, the salvation that was so precious to them. Moses Wall, in his appendix to Menassah's "Hope of Israel," makes clear the debt the Puritan felt to the Jew. Their desire for the Jewish people was to see them experience the fullness of joy that the Puritans experienced in knowing the Jewish Messiah. I can in my mind's eye see my Puritan ancestors praying for my salvation. They would have been blessed to see our day when God's Spirit is moving with such power among the Jewish people. (Messianic Jewish Rabbi Richard Rubinstein, William Bradford descendant)

---

32. Fischer, *Ways of the Way*, 76. Quoting Rabbi Aryeh Kaplan, *Waters of Eden: The Mystery of the Mikvah*, OU / NCSY,1993.
33. Teal and Folger, *Pilgrims at Prayer*, 23.
34. Bradford and Paget, *Of Plymouth Plantation*, 76.

First-Generation Introductions

Francis Cooke	b. ca. 1583	d. 1663
James Chilton	b. bef. 1556	d. 18 Dec. 1620
	m. bef. 1584	
Mrs. Chilton name and	b. unknown	d. after Jan. 11 1620/1
Mary Chilton	b. 31 May 1607 (Baptism)	d. bef. 1 May 1679

First Briefing: Connecting Historical and Spiritual Potential and Power

Welcome to the first briefing on our first Cruise Day! My first-generation Pilgrim relatives are *Mayflower* passengers James Chilton, his wife and their daughter Mary, and Francis and John Cooke. John's sister Jane, my second-generation direct Cooke ancestor, sailed to America on another ship.

Sea Captain William Pierce, a family namesake, is also on board. Native American author Ed LaRose and Rabbi Richard Rubinstein have boarded from the twenty-first century so our communities can reconcile.

With the Pilgrims still on board, the *Mayflower* master and crew first let down the ship's anchor in Cape Cod Harbor. Exploration for a settling site was unsuccessful. After finally anchoring in Plymouth Harbor and choosing a location, the passengers lived on board the seventeenth-century vessel for a month. James Chilton, at sixty-four years the oldest passenger on board, died having never stepped off the ship. His daughter Mary, according to family and American tradition, was the first female to disembark and set foot on Plymouth Rock.

> In 1744, Ann Taylor, a granddaughter of Mary Chilton and John Winslow [her husband], wrote that Mary had been the first woman who stepped onto the rock of landing at Plymouth Harbor, an event now memorialized in Francis Bacon's famous painting, "The Landing of the Pilgrims." Although neither Bradford nor Edward Winslow make any mention of the event, no other family claims that distinction.[35]

Before we step ahead with Mary and the other Pilgrims, a full-scale replica now docked in Plymouth Harbor provides a picture of their sailing ship:

> The *Mayflower* had three masts and six sails. Five sails are big and square—fore and main courses, fore and main topsails, and a spritsail on the bowsprit. There is a smaller

---

35. Robert Luce (Chilton-Winslow descendant), "John and Mary (Chilton) Winslow," *Chilton's Chat*, Volume #2, Issue #4, 2006.

triangular mizzen (aft) sail. The 181-ton ship is steered with a whip staff attached to the tiller. From the back rail to the end of the bowsprit beak, length is a little over a hundred feet; keel is about sixty-four feet and board width is about twenty-five feet.[36]

From the first days at Plymouth, the Pilgrims caught glimpses of Natives. Eventually, Samoset and Squanto appeared, spoke with the Pilgrims, and helped them. Hobomok was another helpful Host Native. These first Natives whom the colonists conversed with in person were friendly and could speak English learned during previous encounters with Englishmen.

They were not "Indians," a name determined by other sailors, adventurers, and explorers sailing through uncharted seas and looking for riches in the Indies and India. They were North American tribal hosts whom the Pilgrims and other colonists met upon arrival, and they were the First Nations facilitators of the peace that lasted for decades between Natives and immigrants.

> Squanto, or Tisquantum, was a citizen of Patuxet, a shoreline settlement halfway between what is now Boston and the beginning of Camp Cod. Patuxet was one of the dozen or so settlements in what is now eastern Massachusetts and Rhode Island that comprised the Wampanoag confederation. In turn, the Wampanoag were part of a tripartite alliance with two other confederations: the Nauset, which comprised some thirty groups on Cape Cod; and the Massachusett, several dozen villages clustered around Massachusetts Bay. All of these people spoke variants of Massachusett, a member of the Algonquian language family, the biggest in eastern North America at the time.[37]

Regrettably, the decades-long peace ended when the Natives and colonists started killing one another, and now, figuratively speaking, this land which we the people—descended from many tribes and nations—love and call ours is covered with blood.

Many Americans regret the continuing plight of Native Americans and assume a responsibility to do something about it. The responsibility I assumed was to invite a Native on board to represent North American First Nations Hosts.

Please welcome Mr. Ed LaRose, an evangelist, prophet, and author, to release our spiritual potential and power for reconciliation and hope.

---

36. Beale, *The Mayflower Pilgrims*, 99.
37. Mann, 1491, 36–37. Used by permission.

BEV: Ed, please share a few words from your book, *Our Trail of Tears*, about the European take-over of native land and peoples.

ED: Certainly: "European settlers raped and plundered the land, destroying everything in their path, including the First Nations people."

BEV: Immigrants took over other nations. It was called colonization. The theoretical "right" through superiority to take over land was called "Manifest Destiny." That mindset is obsolete, we hope and pray.

ED: I agree, and now God is calling us all to be reconcilers and restorers. In my book, I challenge Native peoples to forgive sins committed by the Europeans.

BEV: Unforgiveness is one of many dark clouds hovering over North America. Forgiveness cuts through darkness and is part of our purification process before We the Passengers move on to Dedications. So I ask you to represent your Native ancestors and forgive discrimination, along with thoughts and actions of superiority by my European ancestors, and to forgive the same offenses by my great-grandparents who took over Host Nation lands in Minnesota.

ED: I forgive, and pray that others will forgive, and I also ask forgiveness for atrocities committed by Natives against immigrants.

BEV: I forgive, and I pray that others will forgive. Now, please share more from your book before leading us in a forgiveness prayer.

ED: "The Church has seen us Native people as a 'mission field' for over five hundred years. What the Church has got to realize is that as Jesus followers we are all *together* as partners in this work of the Great Commission. I also believe that the Natives will be known as a Mission Force as the Church begins to see God raising up indigenous people to go worldwide to take whole nations for the glory of God . . . Who else is poised with favor from both God and man to reach their Nation? It is the Indigenous Man of this hour; we must all rise to our calling in the body of Christ."[38] Let's pray as one body:

"Almighty Master:
We ask you to forgive us and to heal, cleanse, and purify our land and all nations. Help every tribe forgive and love one another and make peace with you. We can do that by praying: Lord, I realize that I am a sinner, and I need

---

38. LaRose, *Our Trail of Tears*, 79–80.

you to forgive me. I cannot make it on my own; I need your blood to wash away all my sins. Please, Jesus, come into my heart and make me new. Fill me with your powerful Spirit. Give me your concern about the injustices still experienced by Natives. I pray this in Jesus' name. —*Amen.*"[39]

Prayer Song

We finish our first briefing with a life-preserving drill. Singing or praying national songs and hymns silently or aloud will strengthen our resolve to preserve and empower our free-style life and liberty.

America (My Country, 'Tis of Thee)

My country, 'tis of thee, Sweet land of liberty, Of thee I sing.
Land where my fathers died! Land of the Pilgrim's pride!
From ev'ry mountain side, Let freedom ring!

My native country, thee, Land of the noble free, Thy name I love.
I love thy rocks and rills, Thy woods and templed hills;
My heart with rapture thrills Like that above.

Let music swell the breeze, And ring from all the trees
Sweet freedom's song. Let mortal tongues awake,
Let all that breathe partake;
Let rocks their silence break, The sound prolong.

Our fathers' God to Thee, Author of liberty,
To Thee we sing. Long may our land be bright
With freedom's holy light;
Protect us by Thy might, Great God, our King! Amen.[40]

Free Time Options
All free time breaks are for reflecting and meditating on what has been said during briefings. Go to deeper depth by further reading about daily topics and journaling thoughts and questions for yourself or to share and discuss if you are a pilgrimage group.[41]

---

39. Ibid., 101.
40. Lyrics set to the tune of "God Save the King" in 1832 by Rev. Samuel F. Smith, a Baptist minister. The hymn was first sung at a July 4th celebration in Park Street Church, Boston, Massachusetts.
41. For example, check Bradford's *Of Plymouth Plantation* out of a library or purchase recommended books.

Last Briefing: Releasing the Power of Reconciliation and Hope

This briefing continues our pilgrimage toward dedicating Judeo-Christian faith, races, tribes, and agriculture to God. Agriculture is a familiar aspect of American life for me, because in my first life stage, I was a farmer's daughter—and most of my generational grandfathers were farmers.

Agriculture

Agriculture was a first occupation in Plymouth. Some North American Natives were nomadic hunters, others farmed the land, and "in 1623 the colonists divided the land 'according to the year that each family had arrived on three ships—the *Mayflower* (1620), the *Fortune* (1621), and the *Anne* (1623).'"[42]

The *Anne's* master was a namesake of mine, William Pierce. He crossed the Atlantic more than any other sea captain at the time, bringing relatives of the first passengers, Rev. Cotton, and Rev. Roger Williams, among other settlers. Supplies brought to Plymouth on the *Anne* helped to end the Pilgrim's time of starvation.[43] To document the starving time, Bradford wrote,

> All their food supplies were consumed, and they had to rely upon God's providence, often at night not knowing where to get a bit of anything next day; and so, as one well observed, they had need above all people in the world, to pray to God that He would give them their daily bread. Yet they bore their want with great patience and cheerfulness of spirit, and that for upwards of two years . . .[44]

Governor Bradford also included in his journal a letter from Captain Pierce to the Pilgrims after his cargo ship, carrying Plymouth Colony goods (not slaves) for sale in England, was wrecked on Virginia's coast.

> Dear Friends,
> The news of this fatal stroke that the Lord has brought upon me and you will probably come to your ears before this comes to your hands . . . Thus with my continual remembrance of you in my poor desires to the Throne of Grace, beseeching God to renew His love and favour towards you all, in and through the Lord Jesus Christ, both in spiritual

---

42. Beale, *The Mayflower Pilgrims*, 99.
43. "The 'starving time' lasted from May 1622 to the good harvest in the fall of 1623 and the arrival of the ships *Anne* and *Little James*, bringing sixty new settlers and loaded with provisions." Duane A. Cline, "The Pilgrims and Plymouth Colony: 1620," www.rootsweb.com.
44. Bradford and Paget, *Of Plymouth Plantation*, 116–117.

and temporal good things, as may be most to the glory and praise of His name and your everlasting good, so I rest,
Your afflicted brother in Christ,
William Pierce, Virginia, Dec. 25th, 1632.[45]

As far as I can know, 377 years later in 2009, Captain Pierce never regretted owning and trading slaves, or that he was the first New England slave trader.

The beginnings of New England Negro slavery would fall somewhere between 1624 and 1630 . . . other authorities, however, who claim that Negro slaves were first brought to New England in 1638 base their contention on a statement in John Winthrop's Journal, recording on December 12, 1638 the return to Boston of Captain William Pierce in the Salem ship, *Desire.* Pierce had gone to Providence and Tortugas in the West Indies with a cargo including some captive Pequod Indians, whom he sold into slavery there . . . In exchange for his goods and chattels Pierce brought back, "salt, cotton, tobacco and Negroes" . . .

The opinion has been general, however, that colonial Massachusetts was hostile to slavery. Says William Sumner, "slavery was repugnant to the Puritans and was regarded by them with abhorrence."[46]

Another author observed, "Slavery is a story about America, all of America. The nation's wealth, from the very beginning, depended upon the exploitation of black people on three continents. Together, over the lives of millions of enslaved men and women, Northerners and Southerners shook hands and made a country."[47]

Acknowledge Our Responsibilities

Our responsibility, potential, and hope to advance Judeo-Christianity, liberty, justice, and equality in the twenty-first century are linked during this cruise to the Plymouth and Puritan immigrants' actions, values, and morals. Sadly, though, some early Americans including Pierce namesakes obviously believed that slavery was acceptable and biblical. Others did not approve of the

---

45. Ibid., 245.
46. Greene, *The Negro in Colonial New England,* 16, 17, 66. Reprinted with permission of the publisher. Green quoted John Winthrop, History of New England, Vol. 1 (Boston: Little, Brown and Co., 1853), 260. Reprinted by permission of the publisher.
47. Farrow, Land, and Frank, *Complicity,* 12, 27, 29. Used by permission of the publisher

traffic. As is well-known from history's archives, the framers of our Constitution disagreed about slavery, so equality for all did not include everyone.

Despite his earlier reservations and the continuing dialogue about his heart and mindset changes, we must credit President Abraham Lincoln for changing America's history of hurt and hate to hope. After signing the Emancipation Proclamation on January 1, 1863, he said, "I never, in my life, felt more certain that I was doing right, than I do in signing this paper. If my name ever goes into history it will be for this act, and my whole soul is in it."

He designated our responsibility in his Second Inaugural Address:

> Fondly do we hope—fervently do we pray—that this mighty scourge of war may speedily pass away. Yet, if God wills that it continue, until all the wealth piled by the bond-man's two hundred and fifty years of unrequited toil shall be sunk, and until every drop of blood drawn with the lash, shall be paid by another drawn with the sword, as was said three thousand years ago, so still it must be said the "judgments of the Lord, are true and righteous altogether."
>
> With malice toward none; with charity for all; with firmness in the right, as God gives us to see the right, let us strive on to finish the work we are in; to bind up the nation's wounds; to care for him who shall have borne the battle, and for his widow, and his orphan—to do all which may achieve and cherish a just and lasting peace, among ourselves, and with all nations.

Song

African-American spirituals are also a historical treasure for use as prayers. In the twentieth century, Martin Luther King quoted from a spiritual, "Free at Last," to end his "I Have a Dream" speech.[48] Like this logbook, his dream and vision for freedom and the advancement of Christian faith is addressed to all God's children—Jews and Gentiles—and to all people in bondage. Dr. King's speeches and the words of many spirituals are available on Web sites. For today, I chose a childhood favorite.

Swing Low, Sweet Chariot

Chorus
Swing low sweet chariot, Comin' fo' to carry me home,
Swing low sweet chariot, Comin' fo' to carry me home.

---

48. Delivered by Rev. Dr. Martin Luther King on August 28, 1963, on the steps of the Lincoln Memorial in Washington, DC.

I looked over Jordan and what did I see, Comin' fo' to carry me home,
A band of angels comin' after me, Comin' fo' to carry me home.
Chorus

If you get there before I do, Comin' fo' to carry me home,
Tell all my friends I'm comin' too, Comin' fo' to carry me home.
Chorus

The brightest day that ever I saw, Comin' fo' to carry me home,
When Jesus wash'd my sins away, Comin' fo' to carry me home,
Chorus

I'm sometimes up and sometimes down, Comin' fo' to carry me home
But still my soul feels heav'nly bound, Comin' fo' to carry me home
Chorus

Free at last! Tragically, another Web search reveals that slavery and human trafficking still exist on every continent, in several nations, even in the United States. Nearly one hundred and fifty years after the Thirteenth Amendment, the U.S. is not yet free from slavery. See proof at www.anti-slavery.org.

Prayer
Almighty Master:
Freed and using the power of light uncapped by Christ's prophetic revelation and resurrection, we ask you to release prisoners from physical and spiritual bondage. Freed, We the Passengers assume responsibility to share your ageless and amazing grace with Jews and Gentiles. Freed, we ask you to nurture us with spiritual seeds to sow and grow to enrich and provide strength to reap a harvest of forgiveness, restoration, reconciliation, righteousness, and freedom around the world. Freed, we tap into repentance and reconciliation power to fill today's sails. — *Amen*

Cruise Library Visit

Today I recommend *Our Trail of Tears: The Journey of Reconciliation* by Ed LaRose, along with other books by his publisher, Healing The Land Publishing.

Today's first Wake-Up Call introduced *The Ways of the Way* by Bob Fischer, a Jewish believer in Jesus. Check out books by other Jewish believers, a new category for libraries to list in card catalogs and for citizens to place between bookends.

Cruise Bonus

Bookends: Judeo-Christian History and a Twenty-First-Century Jewish and Gentile Conversation
by Rabbi Richard Rubinstein and Beverly Stroebel

A first in North American history: a small group of Portuguese Jewish families landed on Manhattan Island in 1654 after escaping the Spanish and Portuguese Inquisition in Brazil.

Interestingly, just as the Pilgrims first sought freedom to worship in Holland, that country had also afforded the Jews a measure of freedom from persecution, and they prospered in the Dutch colony in Brazil. In Manhattan, however, the twenty-three refugees were not welcomed until a group of Jewish merchants living in Holland, investors in the Dutch settlement, admonished the Gentile colonists.[49]

Evidently, seventeenth-century Dutch colonists failed to see the 1654 arrival as a signpost pointing to God's intent to bless and use North America for his glory. Could it be that the curse of prejudice toward the Jews—cast by Constantine like a dark shroud over Europe—had followed the colonists across the Atlantic? Is it still affecting us today?

I am not your judge; each pilgrim must personally answer this question. I confess that as a European descendant still living under the dark discrimination curse, I nearly missed the 1654 sign. Only by studying and believing truth—and at the same time experiencing God's keeping of promises—did I see the next sign pointing to the ingathering of the Jewish remnant as a blessing that has power to shred the shroud. To understand, see Scriptures such as Isaiah 10 and 11, Romans 9–15, and Ephesians 2 and 3.

See it another way. Curses covering continents allow blinding and deceptive forces to roam at will. Fanatical, political *Sharia* law is an example, a force that destroys rather than works for good. I plead with fellow liberty lovers to educate yourselves and others to recognize and fight against this approaching oppressive force.

Pilgrims, our prayers can also be a mighty force for lifting curses, and today specifically for overcoming the devil's hatred and fear of the Jewish people. According to history and to the Apostle Paul in Romans 11, the Jews were blinded by God so Gentiles could see and accept their Messiah. In our day, God is removing scales from eyes, and the word "Messianic" indicates Jewish belief in Jesus. The power of Jewish belief will help fill sails during this Cruise Bonus.

Before Messianic Rabbi Rubinstein joins us, please pray with me.

Prayer

Almighty Providential Master, Messiah's Father,

We repent and ask that you will hurl Gentile arrogance and shrouds of superiority, prejudice, deception, and discrimination into the sea. Release your mercy as power to end the sacrifice and suffering of the Jewish people.

Open Gentile and Jewish eyes and ears to see and accept truth as reality, and as beneficial to them, as you combine our gifts and enrich our

---

49. Gross, *Israel in the Mind of America*, 3–4.

pilgrimage by making us "one new man" in Messiah. Redeem Jewish men, women, and children to bless the nations as promised.[50] —*Amen*

BEV: Rabbi Rubinstein, please talk to us from your perspectives—as a history teacher, Jewish believer, and *Mayflower* descendant—about the Puritans and the Pilgrims.

RABBI: The Puritans and Pilgrims were a people who loved the Jews. They named their children Hebrew names. They wrote the first Hebrew grammars in the English language. The blind poet Milton had the Hebrew Scriptures read to him as part of his morning devotions.

Cromwell allowed Jews to return to England, and the Puritans desired to see Jews come to faith. The Puritan revival was a great move by God. Preachers were out in fields preaching to tens of thousands. All society was changed. And the heart of the Puritan and Pilgrim preachers was to see just one Jew come to faith in his Messiah. I see them expressing the same values that I pray all believers will have about the Jews. Amazingly, you and I share that *Mayflower* heritage and vision!

BEV: Where in the Bible does God say he'll keep his promises to the Jewish people?

RABBI: David Stern's translation, *The Complete Jewish Bible*, answers that question in Romans 11:1–5:

> In that case, I say, isn't it that God has repudiated his people? Heaven forbid! For I myself am a son of Isra'el, from the seed of Avraham, of the tribe of Binyamin. God has not repudiated his people, whom he chose in advance. Or don't you know what the *Tanakh* says about Eliyahu? He pleads with God against Isra'el, "ADONAI, they have killed your prophets and torn down your altars, and I'm the only one left, and now they want to kill me too!" But what is God's answer to him? "I have kept for myself seven thousand men who have not knelt down to Ba'al." It's the same way in the present age: there is a remnant, chosen by grace.

BEV: Your friend Rabbi Russell Resnik, executive director of the Union of Messianic Congregations, asks us to pray for "the new, under-forty genera-

---

50. Genesis 12:1–3; Ephesians 2:15 ("One new man": the united body of believers; the Jewish and Gentile church).

tion in the Messianic Jewish community to be larger than the current over-forty generation."[51] How does that exciting request—which we have to believe comes from God's heart—fit into Messianic Jewish history and fulfillment?

RABBI: We often view the history of the Jewish people as a universal rejection of Messiah. But if we look at history carefully, a Jewish remnant have been faithful to God and to the revelation of Yeshua[52] through the centuries. Acts 21 tells us that when Paul and Luke were reporting to James in Jerusalem, there were tens of thousands of Jewish believers who were zealous for Torah.[53] The modern revival began in the 1800s with the first modern Messianic synagogue in Kishinev, Moldova. Paul was an example of the remnant, and I am also, as are the thousands of Jewish believers in the world today. The generational "remnant" is growing as creation moves to completion.

BEV: Has God assigned a task to the growing remnant?

RABBI: Yes. The believing remnant sanctifies the whole. The remnant concept includes the idea that a holy portion makes the whole holy:

> Now if the *hallah* offered as firstfruits is holy, so is the whole loaf . . . For, brothers, I want you to understand this truth which God formerly concealed but has now revealed, so that you won't imagine you know more than you actually do. It is that stoniness, to a degree, has come upon Isra'el, until the Gentile world enters in its fullness; and that it is in this way that all Isra'el will be saved. (Romans 11:16, 25–26, *Complete Jewish Bible*)

BEV: Rabbi, what can Gentiles do to fulfill Scripture and reconcile with you and other Jews?

RABBI: As you do, Bev, respecting Torah, God's Word, means a great deal to Jews. Respect the Jewishness of *Yeshua*. Understand and honor the Jewishness of the Scriptures. Care about the Jewish roots of Christianity. Give thanks that you are "grafted in among the others and now share in the nourishing sap from the olive root, [so] do not boast over those branches. If you do, consider this: You do not support the root, but the root supports you," as Paul says in Romans 11:17–18. And finally, enjoy the blessings given through Abraham's children.

---

51. Rabbi Russell Resnik, Executive Director, Union of Messianic Jewish Congregations, May 10, 2009, e-mail to UMJC friends.
52. Hebrew for "Jesus."
53. "Torah" refers to the first five books of the First Testament, but in a broad sense can refer to the whole revelation of Scripture.

BEV: The blessings through Abraham are these: One God, his Son Messiah as Redeemer and Bridegroom, Spirit, Truth, Law and Commandments, Commissions, Feasts, Fellowship, Marriage Between a Man and a Woman, Freedom from Bondages, Worship, Healing, Miracles, Justice, Spiritual Gifts, Storytelling, Writing Techniques—such as Poetry, Parables, Allegory, Hyperbole, Imagery, and Dialogues like ours—Discipline because he loves us, Prophecy, Signs and Wonders, Angels, Hope of Heaven, Worship Dancing, Music, Instruments, Prayer, Personal Relationship with God and his Family, Mercy, Joy, Peace, Forgiveness, Grace—I could go on and on, capitalizing to stress importance, and still overlook blessings received through the Jewish people that we can and should honor.

Ancestors of modern-day Jewish people were blinded so that Gentiles could be saved.[54] Gentiles on board, let's clap loud enough for heaven and earth, sky and sea to hear that we are thankful to God and honor the Jewish people.

RABBI: I'll add another blessing: the habit of the Jewish people to say thanks because God said to praise him. America's spiritual ancestors, the Pilgrims, and also New Amsterdam colonists, brought the Christian Thanksgiving tradition to North America, but it was based on Scripture and Jewish tradition.

To honor and reconcile our Judeo-Christian traditions, I say thank you and ask other Jews to clap and praise God for using the Gentile people to bless us and preserve and honor God's Word, as in Acts 13:48.

BEV: Thank you. Please end our conversation with your personal story, then lead us in prayer.

RABBI: My faith in Messiah has been a grand adventure. Walking with God is full of surprises. When I first discovered God's love, I was astonished. He revealed himself to me in his Holy Word and broke strong bondages in my life. He spoke, saying that he had not converted me from being a Jew, he had only converted my heart. He changed my heart, not my inheritance—Jewish faith. He said that I would be a better Jew, a stronger light to the nations. Please pray with me:

Abba Father:
You know the hearts of your Jewish children. You have called us to
be different from others. You have called us to bring redemption and
blessings to the world. By your mercy and by the power of the *Ruach
HaKodesh*,[55] bring truth into the lives of your chosen nation, Isra'el.
Cause all of us to fall in love with our Jewish Messiah. Create in our

---

54. Romans 11:8–12.
55. Hebrew for "Holy Spirit."

community a people who will welcome Messiah back. Sanctify and use us to bring about *Tikkun Olam*,[56] the healing and restoration of your world as you bring all things to completion. Cause Jews and Gentiles to walk in unity. Bring healing and reconciliation to Jewish hearts.

May Gentiles know the Jewish Messiah and honor their mothers and fathers in the faith. May Gentile believers honor the Jewish root that nourishes faith and blesses their pilgrimages. Cause words of life and truth to flow in the body of Messiah between Jews and Gentiles. Help us to invite and welcome unbelievers into our Judeo-Christian walk with you. Messiah, come quickly. —*Amen*

Covenant and Dedications

We covenant to fight for equality, prosperity, and justice for all. We dedicate Judeo-Christian Faith, along with Races, Tribes, and Agricultural Systems in America and all Nations to God's Glory and Honor.

Night Watch

Ships docked or at sea are watched twenty-four hours, seven days a week by crew members. America's spiritual and national flagship and population need 24/7 watchmen. The nations need 24/7 watchmen. Your Night Watch could be spent finding Bible references to match your personal watchman assignments. The following verses and focus points recap today's cruise. Please feel free to match and share other related references.

Scripture Course and Focus Points

Scriptures: Genesis 12:1–3; Psalm 33:11–12; Isaiah 37:30–35, 58:6; Jeremiah 17:5–8; Micah 5:7–15; Luke 4:18–19; John 4:34–38; Romans 6:19–23, 11, 12:1–2; 2 Corinthians 12:9; Galatians 6:7-9; 2 Timothy 1:7.

Focus Points: Blessings, curses, inheritance, nation, injustice, oppressed, roots, slavery, freedom, remnant, fear, favoritism, power, grace, transform, impurity, holiness, harvest.

Spirit, fill our sails as we rest assured in God's Word and love until tomorrow. —*Amen*

End of Cruise Day One

---

56. Hebrew words describing the concept of partnering with God to restore and repair the world

Cruise Day Two Program
Two Systems Begin and Prosper

Scripture Course

Wake-Up Calls!

Second-Generation Introductions
Jane Cooke and Experience Mitchell
Mary Chilton and John Winslow

First Briefing: Education System

Free Time Options

Last Briefing: Entertainment System

Cruise Library Visit

Cruise Bonus
Reliable Genealogical Research and Documentation

Covenant and Dedications
Education and Entertainment Systems in
America and All Nations

Night Watch
Scripture Course and Focus Points

Scripture Course
> *Since my youth, O God, you have taught me, and to this day*
> *I declare your marvelous deeds. Even when I am old and gray,*
> *do not forsake me, O God, till I declare your power to the*
> *next generation, your might to all who are to come.*
> Psalm 71:17–18

Scripture: Deuteronomy 4:9; Psalms 100:5, 119:111–112; Proverbs 22:6; Isaiah 52:13–53:12, 54:13, 59:21; Luke 2:39–52; Romans 15:20–21; 1 and 2 Timothy; Hebrews 12; 1 John 4; Revelation 3:19–20.

Wake-Up Calls!

With Christ's precepts ruling supreme, the Pilgrims recognized all human life as sacred, to be redeemed by the blood of the Savior, and to be protected by the government as representative of God's law. Along with this divinely prescribed function of government, the Separatists had a clear understanding of an additional purpose of the ruling structure as the guardian of God-given liberties (foremost being religious freedom), and finally as the protector of property.[57]

Their ardent zeal and heavenly temper prompted them to labor in the perilous field of liberty, and their spirits, sustained by a holy trust, must have traced through the eye of faith the glorious destiny of future generations . . .

Here the first parochial school was set up, and the system originated for communicating to every child in the community the knowledge of reading, writing, and arithmetic.[58]

An outstanding event in the history of the United States was the coming from England to America of the *Mayflower* with its small band of Pilgrims. Their fame has extended to every land. Their descendants may justly be proud of being descended from this most remarkable group. All Americans have cause to be proud of the Pilgrims; every American owes them a debt of gratitude.[59]

Second-Generation Introductions

Jane Cooke	b. 1613	d. 1650
	m. Unknown	
Experience Mitchell	b. ca 1609	d. between 1685–1689
(Experience came to New England and Plymouth on the *Anne* in 1623.)		
Mary Chilton	b. 1607	d. 1679
	m. Before 1627	

---

57. Richard Wheeler, Preface to Bradford and Paget, *Of Plymouth Plantation*.
58. Thacher, *History of the Town of Plymouth*, 166.
59. Stoddard, *Truth About the Pilgrims*, 1.

John Winslow   b. 1597   d. ca 1674
(John arrived on the *Fortune* in 1621.)

First Briefing: Education System

Several children left England with their Separatist parents four hundred years ago to live in the Netherlands nearly twelve years. When the parents grew worried that their children were becoming "Dutch" in lifestyle, they initiated the 1620 pilgrimage to North America. Yes, other documented reasons—freedom to worship and interpret Scripture as they preferred and the need for more income—were on their minds in the seventeenth century. Children, however, were as much a mindful reason as the others.

My *Mayflower* ancestor Mary Chilton, who was between twelve and fourteen during the voyage and early settlement of Plymouth, was orphaned when both parents died during the First Sickness at Plymouth. She married John Winslow, who arrived on the *Fortune* in 1621, before 1627, and they had ten children.[60] Eventually, they moved from Plymouth to Boston, where the family became wealthy merchants and ship owners. Jane Cooke and Experience Mitchell were not on board the seventeenth-century *Mayflower*.

Uncapping and tapping into children's minds as a sail-filling power source is a great way to found and sustain a free and functional society. However, the educational system in Plymouth, for Mary, Jane, and other children—and thus for America—got off to a slow start.

> The first allusion to education was on January 25, 1623, when some of their adversaries residing in London said of them, "Children not catechized nor taught to read." Governor Bradford answered as follows: "Neither is true; for diverse take pain with their owne as they can; indeede, we have no commone schoole for want of a fitt person, or hitherto means to maintaine one, though we desire now to begine."[61]
>
> The first Free School was ordained by law in [Plymouth] New England in 1672. However, a prior law was ordained in the neighboring colony of Massachusetts, in 1647, for a similar purpose. But that law did not really ordain Free Schools, but a reasonable tax on the scholars was left to the direction of the towns.[62]

---

60. GSMD, *Five Generations*, 5–7.
61. Stoddard, *Truth About the Pilgrims*, 34.
62. Thacher, *History of the Town of Plymouth*, 302–307.

Now, please welcome on board three more authors to tell the Plymouth and early-American education story: George F. Willison, Rodney Stark, and Daniel Webster.

> The Pilgrims had announced their intention of providing a common school as early as 1624, excusing their delay by saying that they had been prevented by "want of a fitt person or hitherto means to maintaine one." Whatever their intentions, nothing was done about the matter for almost a half century. What little instruction youngsters received was obtained at home from their parents, many of whom were illiterate. For the wealthier and more ambitious, a few persons conducted what were virtually small private schools . . . Education of girls was a vain and idle thing, the Pilgrim Fathers agree . . . Girls were not admitted to the Massachusetts public schools on an equal footing with boys until 1828.[63]

Willison also describes efforts, mostly by missionaries and pastors such as Roger Williams, to educate the Indians, with the "aim to bring them into the fold." Some tribes responded; others refused.

Rodney Stark, a modern-day author, writes:

> When the Pilgrims arrived in 1620, one of the very first things they did was to concern themselves with educating their children. They believed that everyone must consult scripture for themselves. In 1647 the Massachusetts Colony enacted a law asserting that all children must attend school. Any community that failed to provide educational services was to be fined "till they shall perform this order." Other states soon followed suit, and free public schools became a fixture of American life.[64]

Daniel Webster, considered the greatest orator of the early nineteenth century, spoke about the regard the founding fathers had for the Bible, and that of the first Puritans who came to New England. His powerful voice from our past advances faith and fills today's sails:

> The Bible came with them. And it is not to be doubted, that to the free and universal reading of the Bible, is to be as-

---

63. Willison, *Saints and Strangers*, 384–5, 478.
64. Stark, *Victory of Reason*, 226–7. Used by permission of the publisher.

cribed in that age, ascribed in every age, that men were much indebted for right views of civil liberty. The Bible is a book of faith, and a book of doctrine; but it is also a book, which teaches man his own individual responsibility, his own dignity, and his equality with his fellow man.[65]

Reading

Educating children to read made history and also advanced Mayflower Compact goals when the first 106 of the 108 colleges in America were established and administered by Christians. A few examples:

★ Congregational Church: Harvard (1936)
★ Anglican Church: William and Mary (1693)
★ Congregational Church: Yale (1701)
★ Presbyterian Church: College of New Jersey, later Princeton (1746)
★ Anglican Church: King's, later Columbia (1754)
★ Baptist Church: Brown (1764)
★ Dutch Reformed Church: Queens, later Rutgers (1766)
★ New Light Congregational Church: Dartmouth (1769)
★ Presbyterian Church: Hampden-Sydney (1775)

In the next century, on December 22, 1820, Daniel Webster could say,

> The country has risen from a state of colonial subjection; it has established an independent government, and is now in the undisturbed enjoyment of peace and political security. The elements of knowledge are universally diffused, and the reading portion of the community is large. Let us hope that the present may be an auspicious era of literature. If, almost on the day of their landing, our ancestors founded schools and endowed colleges, what obligations do not rest upon us, living under circumstances so much more favorable both for providing and for using the means of education?[66]

Returning to our Pilgrims as we cruise through the minds and experiences of *Mayflower*, Plymouth, and other early-American children, we experience hunger, harsh weather, illness, death—more than half the *Mayflower* passengers

---

65. Address delivered at the completion of the Bunker Hill Monument, June 17, 1843. Speech in the Digital Library of the University of Missouri Library Systems, http://digital.library.umsystem.edu.
66. "First Settlement of New England" speech at the foundation of the Pilgrim Society.

died the first winter—and fear of Natives and wild animals. We hear, read, recite, and study, using Bibles and books from William Bradford's and William Brewster's libraries that were brought on the *Mayflower* and other vessels sailing to North America.

John Alden also brought Bibles on board. During the Cruise Bonus drama on Cruise Day Four, John reads the Bible to James and Mary Chilton. Mary was probably illiterate—her will, dated 31 July 1676 in Boston, was signed with an "M."

The original Geneva Bible is difficult for twenty-first-century pilgrims to decipher, but a new modern-day translation of the 1599 Geneva by Dr. Marshall and Gary D. DeMar is now available and used during our cruise.

Also sailing into the twenty-first century with us is my friend, retired teacher Marty Martin. This authentic and sincere pilgrim believes that even if only one capable American child receives a "D" or "F" in reading, then our system and tools and techniques are failing, not our children. Further, she maintains that it is past time—but not too late—for teachers, parents, grandparents, friends, and Passengers cruising today to humbly bathe our children in prayer, then act on their behalf and on our nation's.

Prayer

Almighty Master on board with us today and everyday:
Sensing your concern about the state of education today, we ask you to protect our liberties and release America's educational system and children's minds as power sources. We confess and repent that we have failed to educate and live to exemplify and please you. And now we ask, in keeping with your promise in Micah 7:18–20, that you would hurl into the sea our sin of disbelief in your Word's power to teach, correct, discipline, and instill hope, courage, and confidence. Guide officials at every level to provide equal education and facilities for all races and communities. Remove disrespect and confusion's power from classrooms and from the hearts and minds of students, parents, teachers, and officials. Fill the purified rooms and lives with the power of your Word and Spirit. —*Amen*

Writing

Noah Webster (1758–1843), a William Bradford descendant who is often considered the father of American education, fills sails for dedicating purified educational systems to God:

Noah Webster's 1828 American Dictionary of the English Language was produced during the years when the American home, church and school were established upon a Biblical and patriotic basis. Webster, descended on his mother's side from Pilgrim Governor, William Bradford of Plymouth Plantation, made important contributions to an American educational system which kept the nation on a Christian Constitutional course for many years. The famous "blue-backed Speller," his "Grammars," and "Reader," all contained Biblical and patriotic themes and Webster spear-headed the flood of educational volumes emphasizing Christian Constitutional values for more than a century.

It is not surprising, therefore, that the 1828 American Dictionary should contain the greatest number of Biblical definitions given in any reference volume. Webster considered "education useless without the Bible" and while he cautioned against too extensive use of the Bible in schools as "tending to irreverence," he reiterated, "In my view, the Christian religion is the most important and one of the first things in which all children, under a free government, ought to be instructed . . . No truth is more evident to my mind than that the Christian religion must be the basis of any government intended to se-cure the rights and privileges of a free people . . . "

Today when the Biblical basis of education is under sys-tematic attack we need to capitalize upon the availability of our first American Dictionary—the only dictionary in the world to "draw water out of the wells of salvation"—to uti-lize God's written word as a key to the meaning of words. Historically, it documents the degree to which the Bible was America's basic text book in all fields.[67]

Arithmetic

The Geneva Bible was the first English translation numbered according to chapters and verses. So perhaps in the home, and later in public and parochial schools, Plymouth and early American children practiced counting while look-ing for Bible chapters and verses.

By reading Numbers, a First Covenant book, early American children learned

★ the exact number of days the Israelites wandered in the desert,

★ the number of spies Joshua, son of Nun, sent into the Promised Land, and

---

67. Chesapeake, VA: Foundation for American Christian Education, www.face.net. See Appendix One, the Two Dictionaries word Chart, revealing the erosion of vocabulary that elevates man's sovereignty and rights above natural law and God.

★ the Israelite tribes by name and number.

From the Second Covenant, they learned how many

★ generations from Abraham to David,
★ generations from David to Christ,
★ angels appeared to Joseph and Mary, and
★ wise men followed how many stars hovering over how many baby saviors.

If a test question asked for Messiah's first- and second-coming references, they could list books, chapters, and verse numbers in the First and Second Covenants.

If asked who is accountable to God, they could recite Hebrews 4:13: "Nothing in all creation is hidden from God's sight. Everything is uncovered and laid bare before the eyes of him to whom we must give account."

They learned that Psalm 51 was usable as a plea for mercy in English courts.

They knew that God promised, in Psalm 139, to write the "number of their days" in his book.

By reading Psalms 139 and 56 and Revelation 21:26–27, they learned that God records the names of people he will allow in when the purified "glory and honor of the nations are brought into the Holy City of God, the new Jerusalem."

Could we pass seventeenth-century reading, writing, and arithmetic tests?

Free Time Options

Use this free time to search your minds for school memories.

Praise God for good memories and actions!

Use bad memories to motivate you to investigate behavior in your community's classrooms. Ask God to alert you to hear children if they tease or bully, or are treated that way, because such treatment could explain, and also affect, future behavior.

If needed, take immediate action: Children who are rejected and abused repeat what they have experienced, and some join gangs whose goals are to kill, burn, and steal, among other ways to seek revenge. Some commit suicide. Please—so they will learn early on to live at peace with themselves and others, knowing that God will avenge—read Romans 12:18–20 and pray with children and grandchildren.

For more on this topic, see the Memoirs and Letters category in the Cruise Library.

Last Briefing: Entertainment System

In their time, *Mayflower* and Plymouth children and parents most likely sang psalms. Today's music accentuates and empowers movie, stage, and television entertainment. Figuratively speaking, though, the notes played and songs sung during musical productions in worship and on secular stages are less than one melody or lyric line when compared to the great American musical drama. Military marches, regional and war ballads, Native drumming and dancing, Broadway show tunes, dance music, children's songs, religious hymns—each has inspired American generations to sing, dance, tap, honor, pray, and praise.

If the distance between heaven and earth is less than the shortest vibration of one bell ringing for freedom because the Divine Inspiration for psalms, the Author of life and liberty, is listening, then we entertain heavenly thoughts— even heaven itself—when we count our blessings and uncap a sail-filling source for dedicating education and entertainment to God's glory.

Song
Count Your Blessings

When upon life's billows you are tempest-tossed,
When you are discouraged, thinking all is lost,
Count your many blessings, name them one by one,
And it will surprise you what the Lord hath done. *Chorus.*

Are you ever burdened with a load of care?
Does the cross seem heavy you are called to bear?
Count your many blessings, every doubt will fly,
And you will be singing as the days go by. *Chorus.*

When you look at others with their lands and gold,
Think that Christ has promised you wealth untold;
Count your many blessings, money cannot buy
Your reward in heaven, nor your home on high. *Chorus.*

So, amid the conflict, whether great or small,
Do not be discouraged, God is over all;
Count your many blessings, angels will attend,
Help and comfort give you to your journey's end. *Chorus.*

Chorus:
Count your blessings, Name them one by one;
Count your blessings, See what God hath done;
Count your blessings, Name them one by one;
Count your many blessings, See what God hath done.[68]

---

68. Johnson Oatman, Jr., 1856–1926, and Edwin O. Excell, 1851–1921.

Cruise Library Visit

Today, for children I recommend *Sarah Morton's Day: A Day in the Life of a Pilgrim Girl* by Kate Waters, photographs by Russ Kendall. For very young children, I suggest *The Very First Thanksgiving Day* by Rhonda Gowler Greene, artistry by Susan Gaber. They confirmed my title by portraying and writing about the *Mayflower* in *full sail.*

For young girls, I highly recommend Wendy Lawton's book, *Almost Home*, a fictional story about my ancestor Mary Chilton and other *Mayflower* children.

For young teenagers, check out Rev. Peter Marshall's Crimson Cross Adventure Series for young teenagers.

I also recommend books by Lynne Cheney, including *America: A Patriotic Primer*, *A is for Abigail: An Almanac of Amazing American Women*, and *Our 50 States: A Family Adventure Across America.* The books are beautifully illustrated, with artistry for children of all ages to appreciate by Robin Preiss Glasser.

Several *Mayflower* books are listed in the Cruise Library Catalog for supplemental reading.

Read *Bridge to Terabithia* and see the movie to remember what childhood teasing looks and feels like.

Cruise Bonus
Reliable Genealogical Research and Documentation

Organizations, families, and individuals by the thousands are now spending time on genealogical searches. This can be a fulfilling pastime, but first, consider this sail-filling warning. Before choosing to head into or continuing in that direction, consider biblical genealogy guidelines.

Psalms 71:14–18 and 100:5 challenge us to "declare God's marvelous deeds and faithfulness to the next generation." First Timothy 1:3–7 warns that "endless genealogies promote controversies rather than God's work—which is by faith."

Millions of Mayflower *Descendants*

You may be surprised to hear that millions of *Mayflower* physical descendants are alive today. Yet only twenty-six male and two female passengers have descendants.

Eight U.S. presidents are documented descendants, and a number of other famous people, including astronauts, poets, politicians, actors, directors, and inventors are descendants as well.

The Society of Mayflower Descendants in the Commonwealth of Pennsylvania Web site provides this short "celebrity" list in alphabetical order:

★ John Adams (second U.S. president)—John Alden and William Mullins
★ John Quincy Adams (sixth U.S. president)—John Alden and William Mullins

* Maude Adams (stage actress)—John Howland
* Humphrey Bogart (film actor)—John Howland
* Marie Corinne ("Lindy") Morrison Claiborne Boggs (U.S. ambassador to the Vatican, congresswoman)—William Brewster
* Phillips Brooks (wrote "O Little Town of Bethlehem")—John Howland
* William Cullen Bryant (poet)—John Alden and William Mullins
* George Herbert Walker Bush (forty-first U.S. president)—John Howland, Francis Cooke, and John Tilley
* Barbara Bush (U.S. First Lady)—John Howland and Henry Samson
* George W. Bush (Texas governor, 1994–2000; forty-third U.S. president, 2001–2009)—John Howland, Francis Cooke, Henry Samson, and John Tilley
* John Ellis "Jeb" Bush (Florida governor, 1999–2007)—John Howland, Francis Cooke, John Tilley, and Henry Samson
* Bing Crosby (film star and singer)—William Brewster
* Bob Crosby (Big Band leader, Bing's brother)—William Brewster
* Ralph Waldo Emerson (poet)—John Howland and John Tilley
* James A. Garfield (twentieth U.S. president)—John Billington
* Nathaniel Gorham (Continental Congress president)—John Howland
* Ulysses Grant (U.S. general and eighteenth president)—Richard Warren
* Hugh Hefner (founder of *Playboy* Magazine)—William Bradford
* Esther Allen Howland (produced the first American Valentines)—John Howland
* Josiah Granville Leach (originator of Flag Day)—Francis Cooke
* Henry Cabot Lodge, Jr. (U.S. senator)—John Howland
* Henry Wadsworth Longfellow (poet)—John Howland
* Marilyn Monroe (actress)—John Alden and William Mullins
* Anna Mary Robertson "Grandma" Moses (twentieth-century American primitive painter)—Francis Cooke
* Sarah Heath Palin (Governor of Alaska, 2006-2009 Republican vice-presidential nominee in 2008) John Tilley, John Howland, Stephen Hopkins, William Brewster, and Richard Warren
* Dan Quayle (U.S. senator and vice president)—Myles Standish, John Alden, and William Mullins
* Cokie Roberts (political analyst for ABC and NPR)—Elder William Brewster
* Franklin Delano Roosevelt (thirty-second U.S. president)—Isaac Allerton, Francis Cooke, John Howland, Digory Priest, John Tilley, and Richard Warren
* Lillian Russell (stage and film actress)—John Howland

★ Deborah Samson (took part in Revolutionary War battles disguised as a man)
—William Bradford, Myles Standish, John Alden, and William Mullins

★ Alan B. Shepard, Jr. (first American in space and fifth man to walk on the moon)—Richard Warren

★ Joseph Smith (founder, The Church of Jesus Christ of Latter-day Saints)—John Howland

★ Zachary Taylor (twelfth U.S. president)—William Brewster and Isaac Allerton

★ John Trumbull (painter of Revolutionary War scenes, soldier, and aide to General Washington)—John Alden

★ James Mitchell Varnum (Brigadier General, Continental Army) —Francis Cooke

★ Noah Webster (author of the first American dictionary)—William Bradford

★ Orson Welles (stage and film actor, director, and producer) —John Alden, Francis Cooke, and Richard Warren

★ Leonard Wood (U.S. general, colonial administrator, and surgeon; commander of the Rough Riders)—Francis Cooke, Stephen Hopkins, and Richard Warren

Genealogy Questions and Answers

I am not a genealogist compared to those who make a living researching for others or spend hours and a lifetime researching. So I can only answer basic questions:

Q: Our family believes that we are original *Mayflower* passenger descendants. How do we research this, then join the Mayflower Society?

BEV: Begin by reading the Mayflower Society Web site. Download the Society application form. Then list your ancestors and grandparents to see what you know and/or can document. Talk to older relatives, because they may have documents and information. Because the Mayflower Society has documented the first five generations, begin with the sixth generation. Or, as I did, work backwards from yourself and your generation.

When you've done this, make sure that each generation is descended from the previous generation. "Possible" is not acceptable; I've been told that "probable" is seriously considered by the Mayflower Society. Positive proof is a primary source: the single-event record made when something happened, for example, birth, marriage, and death certificates.

Q: Where can I find help for proving *Mayflower* ancestry?

BEV: My answers are about doing it yourself, but remember that professionals are available and very capable. State and county genealogical and historical libraries and archives, especially in New England, contain vital records.

Each state's Mayflower Society contacts are listed on the Web (see Duane Cline's Web site, www.rootsweb.com, or the Mayflower Society Web site). Contact the Society in your state to ask questions, such as, do they have members with your lineage? I found a very distant relative and proof of parentage by going through files at the Connecticut Historical Society Library in Hartford. When you find documentation for each generation, ask a state historian for a preliminary application and cost information.

County and state archives and records are an important source. I found forms to order Pierce family birth, marriage, and death certificates on a Minnesota county Web site. The Public Library Web site for Plymouth, Massachusetts, contains local history and lists of genealogy research Web sites.

You can also submit your lineage online to the Mayflower Society. If you are approved for further consideration, the Society will give directions for proceeding.

Q: Does the Mayflower Society honor genealogy provided by the Mormon Church genealogy Web site and services?

BEV: No. You must supply your own documentation. But I do suggest that the Mormon Web site www.ancestry.com and Mormon libraries are useful, and some are free for initiating or confirming other research.

Just type "genealogy" into your search engine for many ways to begin and more information than you need. The Cruise Library contains a few research book titles and Web sites.

Q: Is the U.S. Census Bureau Web site reliable, useful, and accepted?

BEV: Yes, but the site says that it is limited in the answers to questions and information it provides. Another government source is www.vitalrec.com.

Q: What about DNA?

BEV: I asked Myrle L. Savage, the Mayflower DNA Committee Chair, to answer:

> In 1997 the ISPGG (International Society of Genetic Genealogists) published two proposed versions of the *Guidelines for the use of DNA in Genealogy*; it is currently being revised again. In May 2007, a Mayflower YDNA Website

was begun in Family Tree DNA. Later a MTDNA Component was added. Several requests to join the Project have been made, but most did not have the "straight line" descent required to join (Father to son to son, etc. and Mother to daughter to daughter, etc.). It has the potential of being a recruitment source.[69]

I found important information on the "northern" Pierce DNA Project Web site: http://www.piercednanorth.com/index.html. (Change "north" to "south" if you are descended from southern Pierces.)

A male Pierce cousin's DNA test disproved the idea that our Pierce English-American lineage began with Michael Pierce, who is famous for fighting and dying in King Philip's War in 1676. Therefore, a warning for all Pierces: the New England Historic Genealogical Society (NEHGS) does not accept Frederick Chifton Pierce's *Pierce Genealogy Being the Record of the Posterity of Capt. Michael, John and Capt. William Pierce* as reliable proof that the three were brothers. During research requested by me, they found that writers were just cross-referencing each other without citing primary documentation. The brother's birthplace in England was also not documented. If you know or suspect that you are descended from any of the three "brothers," and have a male lineage going back several generations, please contact the Pierce DNA Project.

Q: What about Ellis Island data?

BEV: Stephen Morse, who refers to himself as an amateur Jewish genealogist, makes Ellis Island data research easy at www.jewishgen.org/databases/EIDB/ellis.html. Also, see www.ellisisland.org for research help.

Q: What genealogical information is available for descendants of slaves?

BEV: Do a Web site search, including this new site established in 2008 to mark the bicentennial of the official end of the trans-Atlantic slave trade in 1808: Emory University spearheaded the two-year project, "Voyages: The Trans-Atlantic Slave Trade Database," which is free to the public at www.slavevoyages.org.

Q: Can adopted people join the Mayflower Society?

BEV: Only if their birth records include *Mayflower* lineage documentation from a birth parent. My adopted grandchildren are told that, like all Ameri-

---

69. GSMD, *The Mayflower Quarterly*, Vol. 73, 376–7.

cans, they are "spiritual descendants" of the Mayflower passengers. If desired, genealogy research is a way for adopted and foster children to reunite with their birth families.

Q: Do you know of other organizations to join if you know that you have early-American ancestors?

BEV: Yes! I joined the National Society of Sons & Daughters of the Pilgrims (NSSDP). Applicants can qualify if they can prove lineal descent from immigrants to the American colonies prior to 1700. I suggest that you investigate organizational objectives before joining to be sure that you agree with them and have good reasons and ways to promote the objectives.

Q: Have you had fun researching and writing? Is time allowed for fun during the cruise?

BEV: Absolutely yes, and I hope you have fun too—beginning with the ending to today's bonus.

Genealogy Pox!

Respected and professional genealogists, please forgive me. I end today's bonus with entertaining Mayflower-Society humor to poke fun at ourselves. Passengers, please smile and rejoice with me, because research that began as a hobby became seriously meaningful—to me and I hope to all those on board— as We the Passengers in the twenty-first century head further out to sea on the historic *Mayflower*. This was once printed in *Canadian Pilgrim Magazine*, from the General Society of Mayflower Descendants in Canada:

Warning: Very Contagious to Adults!

> Symptoms: Continual complaint of a need for names, dates, and place. The patient has a blank expression and a strange, far-away look in the eyes. Sufferers are sometimes deaf to spouse and children and tend to mumble to themselves. They have no taste for work of any kind except for feverishly looking through records at libraries and courthouses. They have a compulsion to write letters and get angry at the mailman when he doesn't leave mail. They frequent strange places such as cemeteries, ruins, and remote country areas.
> Treatment: Medication is useless. Disease is not fatal but gets progressively worse. Patients should attend genealogy

workshops, subscribe to genealogy magazines and newsletters and be given a quiet corner in the house where they may be left alone.

Remarks [prognosis]: The unusual nature of this disease is—the sicker the patients get the more they enjoy it.

Covenant and Dedications

Because God's teachings and his pilgrims have crossed borders and seas for centuries, we will dedicate most daily subjects in all nations, not in America only.

Today We the Passengers covenant:
To provide the best and right education for all children
to grow in wisdom and stature, and in favor with God and humankind.
To work without ceasing to provide an environment
that protects children. To entertain heavenly thoughts and heaven.

We dedicate Children, Educators, Textbooks, Classrooms,
Discipline, and the Educational and Entertainment Systems of the
United States of America and all Nations to God's Glory and Honor.

Night Watch

Children around the world need 24/7 watchmen. We are cruising today because the Pilgrims, and other spiritual ancestors who are now dust, prayed. I heard my grandparents pray for their family. God has blessed me with prayer partners for over forty years. Partners are praying with me for every Passenger on this cruise. Communicating with God in prayer is an unending power source available to humankind for filling our sails; and it is desperately needed for twenty-first-century children, education, and entertainment.

If you agree, pause now during our Night Watch to pray in your own words, by name, for the children in your life and in your community, America, and the nations of the world.

Scripture Course and Focus Points

I rest better assured by reading Scripture into my mind and back to the Lord as my prayers at day's end. If we do this before closing the logbook at the end of each Cruise Day, sails will stay filled and trimmed as we rest. Assured courage and confidence will chase away any confusion that has crept in during the day.

These verses and passages could also be assigned for weekly discussions, perhaps with group members taking leadership turns.

Scripture: Psalms 90:1–4, 97; Matthew 6:19–21, 7:1–2, 11:28–30; Luke 12:15, 20:37–38; Romans 15:4–5; Colossians 1–2; 2 Thessalonians 1:11–12; 1 Timothy 6:20–21.

Focus Points: Favor, watching, music, account, correcting, training, knowledge, wisdom, pleasing, wandering, measures, hope, treasures, purpose, false teaching.

We rest assured in Christ's blessings as he ends this day.

End of Cruise Day Two

Cruise Day Three Program
Records, Law Enforcement, and Correction and Court Systems

Scripture Course

Wake-Up Calls!

Third-Generation Introductions
Elizabeth Mitchell and John Washburn, Jr.
Robert Latham and Susanna Winslow

First Briefing: Records and the First Trial and Verdict

Cruise Library Visit

Free Time Options

Last Briefing: Records and the Second Trial and Verdict

Cruise Bonus
A Prison Visit

Covenant and Dedications
Records, Law Enforcement, and
Correction and Court Systems

Night Watch
Scripture Course and Focus Points

Scripture Course
The Lord is righteous, he loves justice; upright men will see his face.
Psalm 11:7

Scripture: Exodus 20:1–17; 2 Chronicles 19:6–7; Psalm 84:10; Isaiah 58:6; Zechariah 8:16–17; Matthew 6:9–13; Acts 24–25; Romans 12; Hebrews 10–13; 1 John 5.

Wake-Up Calls!

The administration of the law by the Pilgrims was remarkably mild for the standards of their day. The Pilgrims introduced much of our criminal code. When they lived, England had 149 capital crimes. The Pilgrims adopted only five which were practically the same as our laws today. They extended trial by jury so as to apply to all people. The Pilgrims established the public recording of deeds and mortgages and introduced our method of conveying land. They established the probating of wills and recording of births, marriages and deaths by towns. These were made applicable to all the people, a practice which had not previously existed. They introduced our system of administering estates. Instead of the oldest son inheriting all of his father's estate, the Pilgrims provided that the estate was to be divided equally among all children. This was a recognition of the rights of women. The Pilgrims introduced almost all of our system of equity. They introduced our system of free public education. Much of what they introduced was taken from the Dutch because no such institutions existed in England at that time.[70]

Even when every English life was precious to the settlements, the Pilgrims did not hesitate to execute three Englishmen for the murder of one Indian. In flying from civilization to the desert in pursuit of liberty, the Pilgrims did not fly so fast and far as to leave majestic law behind them.[71]

The first written records of Plymouth Colony date to 1627, when Governor William Bradford commenced the first volume of Deeds, recording the garden plots laid out in 1620, the division of lands in 1623–24, and the division of cattle in 1627. The recording of wills and inventories began in 1633, with the will of Samuel Fuller, the elder, dated 30 July. All estate administration was handled through the Court at Plymouth until 1685, when a change took place in the judicial system of the Colony, and separate county court registries were created for Barnstable, Bristol and Plymouth.[72]

---

70. Stoddard, *Truth About the Pilgrims*, 9–11.

71. The Centennial Issue, *Bulletin of the Pilgrim Record Society*, published in 1876 by David P. Holton, Appendix, from speech given by General Sargent for the Consecration of the Monument Grounds at Duxbury to honor Captain Myles Standish.

72. Patricia Scott Deetz, "The Plymouth Colony Archive Project, Index to Plymouth Colony, Wills and Inventories, 1670–1685." www.histarch.uiuc.edu/plymouth/index.html

Third Generation Introductions

Elizabeth Mitchell	b. ca 1628	d. 1684
	m. 1645	
John Washburn Jr	b. ca 1621	d. 1686
Susanna Winslow	b. ca 1627	d. 1685
	m. ca 1649	
Robert Latham	b. ca 1623	d. 1685

First Briefing: Records and the First Trial and Verdict

Today you will meet my third-generation ancestors from the seventeenth-century *Mayflower*, not to be seen as spooky ghosts, but as a meaningful relationship because their story is also America's. Susanna Winslow was Plymouth Governor Edward Winslow's niece, the daughter of John and Mary (Chilton) Winslow.

I know, because good records were kept, that my Cooke and Chilton lines merged when the Lathams' daughter Hannah married Joseph Washburn. Thus, from tomorrow forward, only one *Mayflower* lineage will cruise with us in a relational sense on my genealogical calendar.

While trimming flagship sails to find the wind and tack through time to advance Christian faith during the first two days of our cruise, our nautical headings led to dedicating American education, entertainment, education, children, races, tribes, and agriculture to God's glory and honor.

Today's course is set to uncap and tap into new energy sources to fill sails for heading toward the dedication of records, law enforcement, and correction and court systems.

The seventeenth-century colonists found no jails or prisons on the North American continent. The first offences were John Billington's 1621 contempt of lawful commands and opprobious[73] speeches and Edward Doty and Edward Leister fighting a duel with sword and dagger. Punishment was the tying of head and feet together and being made to go without food and drink for twenty-four hours.[74] In 1630, Billington's execution for murder was another Plymouth first.[75]

The first record I found for a jail was one built in 1820,[76] but certainly we can assume that even before then, the Pilgrims separated accused and convicted troublemakers and lawbreakers from those attempting to live according to godly civil laws and authority. According to the excellent account written

---

73. "opprobious": outrageously disgraceful, dishonorable, ignominious, abusive, shameful. Correct spelling: Dictionary.com.
74. Thacher, *History of Plymouth*, 37–38.
75. Ibid., 72.
76. Ibid., 309.

about courthouses, jails, and Plymouth records by Rose T. Briggs, found at the Pilgrim Hall Web site,[77] the 1820 courthouse was still in use in 1966.

According to a Plymouth newspaper and Web site article, a new courthouse was finally built and opened for use in December 2007:

> The new $70 million courthouse on Obery Street opened for business in September. In just the short time since then, First Justice of the Plymouth District Court Thomas F. Brownell said the effect of moving from the small and crumbling 1820 courthouse downtown to the large and ultramodern facility has already paid off . . .
>
> Lynda M. Connolly, Chief Justice of the District Court, stressed that the new courthouse is about more than providing comfortable digs for its employees.
>
> "The only matter that is important to people is the matter that brings them to the court, so it's important we treat them with respect," she said . . .
>
> "What gets measured gets managed," she said. "We are on top of our numbers."
>
> Those efforts appear to be paying off. In the last fiscal year, the district court had a 103 percent clearance rate, meaning more cases were disposed during that time than were filed.
>
> That's the kind of news the justices are happy to share, and part of that success is recognizing the needs of both the court administration and the people who find themselves involved in the justice system.
>
> "We have a great story to tell, and I'm delighted to tell that story whenever I can," Connolly said.[78]

Thank you, Plymouth citizens and officials, for another great story and example for other communities to follow.

Regretfully, many other communities have very crowded jails and prisons, along with old courthouses. Court docket schedules in cities and counties often run behind, sometimes by years in large cities. Newspaper article and book writers, correction officials, leaders in faith and government systems, and prisoners are calling for prison reform and facility upgrades.

What can we do, other than dedicate these systems to God?

---

77. Briggs, "The Court Houses of Plymouth," www.pilgrimhall.org.
78. David R. Smith, www.wickedlocal.com/plymouth. Plymouth, MA: Gate- House Media, Dec. 7, 2007.

Charles "Chuck" Colson answers, filling today's sails by repeating what he said to Norman Carlson, head of the Bureau of Prisons, that opened prison doors for Christ:

> More than half of those who come out of prison commit new crimes. The repeat offender rate is 80 percent in some states. Prisons simply do not rehabilitate.
>
> We are spending billions on prisons but four out of five crimes are committed by ex-convicts according to one study. It's futile and a horrid waste. We must do better, do things to turn lives around. It's the only answer.[79]

Now the Prison Fellowship Web site explains the ministry founded in 1976 by Mr. Colson after his release from prison:

> Prison Fellowship reaches out to prisoners, ex-prisoners, and their families both as an act of service to Jesus Christ and as a contribution to restoring peace to our cities and communities endangered by crime. For the best way to transform our communities is to transform the people within those communities—and truly restorative change comes only through a relationship with Jesus Christ.[80]

More Reasons to Dedicate

Many law enforcers, attorneys, judges and juries, and court and correction systems deserve the nation's respect and appreciation for their protection and for justice served. Attorneys and organizations fight and achieve justifiable victories for faith, families, and communities.

Whether all who serve and win or lose cases deserve honor in either civil or God's hallowed halls of justice is a national question and worldwide concern. Personal and civil discipline, law enforcement, and corrections, along with court systems, verdicts, and structures, may evoke memories that many of us would rather avoid and erase from our minds because the scenes experienced and words said were dark, distasteful, and oppressive.

Personally, I would rather erase or rewrite today's family and American story, a Plymouth trial recorded in many history books—but I cannot.

---

79. Colson, *Life Sentence*, 45.
80. "Inside Prison Fellowship," www.prisonfellowship.org

A Plymouth and Family Trial, and Today's First Trial and Verdict

Records reveal that Hannah Latham—my grandmother ten generations back—was one or two years old in 1654/55 when her parents, Susanna and Robert, abused teenage servant John Walker until he died. The twelve-man jury's report is in the *Records of the Colony of New Plymouth in New England,* Volume III, *1651–1661,* in the Mayflower Society Library. The following verdict review is from a Cruise Library book:

> Robert Latham was indicted for "felonious cruelty" and found guilty of manslaughter. The case is one of the rare instances in New England of a citizen claiming the ancient English custom of "benefit of clergy." In England, after a guilty verdict was returned by a jury, particularly in a trial carrying the death penalty, the prisoner was asked if he had any reason why judgment should not be given, and if he could read, he could ask for a Bible and read out Psalm 51, verse 1, "Have mercy upon me, O God, after thy great goodness, according to the multitude of thy mercies do away mine offences." This was known as the "neck verse." After this the court would proceed to judgment, but being able to read the verse would save the prisoner from being hanged for murder.[81]

Latham was burned in the hand, and as he had no lands, all his goods were confiscated. All the charges against Susanna were dropped, even though witnesses were asked to testify. No one did. The record was not erased, just crossed out—so it remains.

The explanation for Susanna's escape is probably found in her identity. Susanna was John Winslow's daughter; her mother was Mary Chilton, a Mayflower passenger. Her uncle had already served three terms of office as governor of Plymouth Colony, "and the court's willingness to give Robert Latham benefit of clergy makes sense when it becomes clear that he was John Winslow's son-in-law and married to the niece of one of Plymouth Colony's governors."[82]

Verdict?

I suspect you agree: guilty. If today's American free-style jury and court systems are used, the Lathams are convicted, and justice is finally served when both are severely punished. Sadly, twenty-first-century jurors can only hope

---

81. Deetz and Deetz, *Times of Their Lives,* 119–121.
82. Ibid., 119-121.

that other Plymouth citizens cared enough to share the Lord's love with John Walker. Today we regret, confess, and repent of abuse, murder, and any evasions of justice from the seventeenth to the twenty-first century, and we ask God to hurl those sins into the sea.

Introducing a Boston Trial, Today's Second

The Puritans, the Massachusetts Bay Colonists, only stayed in Salem about three years, moving in 1630 to establish the Boston settlement. Led by John Winthrop, a London lawyer, in 1641 the Bay Colony adopted its first code of law, the "Body of Liberties." Tolerating no religion other than their own, they evicted other religious groups and individuals from the colony—for example, Roger Williams. He will come on board on Days Four and Five, invited by my son-in-law, a documented Williams descendant.

This sending away, along with the outgrowth of the Bay Colony, led to the establishment of Connecticut in 1635, of Rhode Island in 1636 by Anne Hutchinson and Roger Williams, and of Maine in 1652. Plymouth and the Massachusetts Bay colonies combined into one colony in 1691.

The Cruise Library is today's best place to learn more about early courts and Anne Hutchinson's case.

Cruise Library Visit

The Puritan court system is explained in Eve LaPlante's excellent book, American Jezebel: The Uncommon Life of Anne Hutchinson, The Woman Who Defied the Puritans. (We will also look at this case during today's second briefing.) Hutchinson is LaPlante's grandmother eleven generations back.

I also suggest books by Charles Colson and Gerald Sittser.

Free Time Options

Support and serve with a prison ministry. Find ways to help prisoners' families. Investigate prison systems in county and state, and even work with others to demand changes so that systems become interested in helping and rehabilitating inmates. Pray for, visit, and write letters to prisoners. Contact prison chaplains about providing Full Sail and Bibles for prisoners.

Song
The Love of God

The love of God is greater far Than tongue or pen can ever tell;
It goes beyond the highest star, And reaches to the lowest hell;
The guilty pair, bowed down with care, God gave His Son to win;
His erring child He reconciled, And pardoned from his sin.

When years of time shall pass away, And earthly thrones and kingdoms fall,
When men, who here refuse to pray, On rocks and hills and mountains call,
God's love so sure, shall still endure, All measureless and strong;
Redeeming grace to Adam's race—The saints' and angels' song.

Could we with ink the ocean fill, And were the skies of parchment made,
Were every stalk on earth a quill, And every man a scribe by trade,
To write the love of God above Would drain the ocean dry.
Nor could the scroll contain the whole,
Though stretched from sky to sky.[83]

Prayer

Almighty Master:
We are pardoned and redeemed to see that injustice is an
unacceptable free-style verdict. We need your intervention.
Release power into twenty-first century courts and prisons to overcome
where injustice is accepted and administered. Uncap spiritual power
for use by faithful servants of the people administering justice in civil
and faith courts. We feel energized to ask more:
uncap spiritual power around the world and from sea to sea
to set oppressed citizens and nations free from mental, emotional,
and physical bondages. For your glory and honor we ask. —*Amen*

Last Briefing: Records and the Second Trial and Verdict

Anne Hutchinson was brought to trial in 1637 before forty male judges of
the Massachusetts General Court. She was a midwife, wife, mother, and Bible
teacher who taught, for example, that people can communicate with God without the help of ministerial biblical teaching. The Puritan theologians disagreed,
saying their Bible teaching and interpretations were the only way. Women were
not to teach and interpret the Bible.

Because there was little separation of church and state in her day, and because she strayed from Puritan orthodoxy by allowing both men and women to

---

83. Words and music by Frederick M. Lehman, written in 1917 in Pasadena, California; published in *Songs That Are Different*, Volume 2, 1919. The lyrics are based on the Jewish poem "Haddamut," written in Aramaic in 1050 by Meir Ben Isaac Nehorai, a cantor in Worms, Germany; they have been translated into at least eighteen languages.

"One day, during short intervals of inattention to our work, we picked up a scrap of paper and, seated up on an empty lemon box pushed against the wall, with a stub pencil, added the (first) two stanzas and chorus of the song . . . Since the lines (3rd stanza from the Jewish poem) had been found penciled on the wall of a patient's room in an insane asylum after he had been carried to his grave, the general opinion was that this inmate had written the epic in moments of sanity." (Frederick M. Lehman, "History of the Song, The Love of God," 1948, http://www.cyberhymnal.org/htm/l/o/loveofgo.htm)

meet together at her house, the verdict against Anne was blasphemy and lewd conduct. After leaving Massachusetts, she lived in the area that became Rhode Island, but she was living on Long Island, New York, when she and several family members were killed by Natives in 1643.

Please welcome Eve LaPlante, a Hutchinson descendant, to explain why Anne was convicted.

> The entire controversy, according to historian David Hall, was "not about matters of doctrine but about power and freedom of conscience." Moreover, according to Charles Francis Adams, author of the first major study of the Hutchinsonian controversy, published in 1892, the many documents of theological controversies "may, so far as the reader of to-day is concerned, best be described by the single word impossible." Adams concluded that the ministers' language during this controversy was "a jargon which has become unintelligible"—an overstatement that may reassure readers of the transcript of Hutchinson's church trial . . .
>
> . . . In a community devoted to evangelical preaching, people cited Bible passages at will, from memory, and discussed the resurrection of the body and the evidence of justification in the casual manner that people now chat about sports scores or new films.[84]

Today's verdict?

Cruise Bonus
A Prison Visit

We all live in various degrees of denial and stages of bondage—perhaps to eating and drinking habits, to driving too fast or carelessly, to living beyond our income, to anger or foolishness, to laziness or busyness, to having our own way, or to cultish religiosity that doesn't preach the true gospel (see Paul's warning about this in Galatians 1). These bondages may be less, as, or more serious and dangerous than physical bondage. But victory and deliverance are available.

Listen: the wind is blowing at our backs and filling our sails to hear from a former prisoner (speaking anonymously) now living on the outside:

> Hello. My name and prison number could be yours. I wore blue for 17½ years while locked up for the crimes I

---

84. LaPlante, *American Jezebel*, 172–3.

committed. I confessed the horrible crimes and expressed my regret in courts, in letters to victims, and personally to family, friends, and God.

While incarcerated in eight different prisons and a state hospital, I endured humiliating and torturous treatment. To relieve boredom and earn a few pennies, I worked at jobs ranging from chair-side assistant in a prison dental office to clerk for a correctional captain.

Now, please listen to the other side of my prison story. All my life I believed that I was "born again," and I blamed God for not protecting me against the horrible things that had happened. But on January 15th, 1997, while sitting in a county jail facing a petition that could potentially incarcerate me for the rest of my life, the Holy Spirit invaded my life and set me free from sin and death.

I found freedom in Christ even though I was still incarcerated. Even though I might spend the rest of my life behind prison walls, I knew that I had a place in God's heaven. That means I will spend all of eternity with my Lord. After being set spiritually free, I became active in the prison chapel ministry, using my knowledge of the Scriptures, as well as my vocal and musical talents, to become a leader in Christian ministry in most of the prisons.

Now physically and spiritually free, I am still learning that God is far more interested in my character than my comfort. Out of his love for me, he allowed my physical freedom to be withheld so I would learn the true meaning of freedom in Christ.

Along with forgiveness and love, God showed me that he is in control because he is sovereign and that I was to trust him completely, honor him with the remainder of my life, and comfort those in prison who have no comfort. With God's help, my focus and all my energies are forward, not backward. My hope and prayer was and is that my mistakes and experiences will help boys and girls and men and women avoid the things I have been through.

This warning is to parents: Watch for negative distress signs and talk with your children, often, about anything and everything, letting them know that you care about them. If you show that you are interested in the little things in their lives, they will share the big things with you. If you see negative changes, create an environment that is safe for them to express their thoughts.

If you are committing crimes, know that you will be caught, because the Scriptures say, "God is not mocked, whatever a man sows that will he reap." Never forfeit your physical freedom for a moment of pleasure or for a few bucks! Seek help, and seek people to be accountable to. Repent and follow hard after Jesus Christ.

If you are male or female reading this from inside prison walls, you know the agony and humiliation of having your freedom and humanity stripped away. You have no doubt felt the gut-wrenching frustration of having your life placed in the hands of attorneys, judges, and prosecutors—some who have so many cases that he or she has no time to care about you, even if they wanted to.

Does all that sound familiar? Are you bitter from the things you have experienced? Then listen to Gerald Sittser talk about the poison of bitterness before praying with me.

Regret is not the only way our past can control us. Bitterness can do the same thing. Regret usually involves choices we have made; bitterness usually results from choices other people make. It arises when we become acutely aware that we have been wronged.

Bitterness can turn the mind into a black hole of anger and revenge from which it is all but impossible to escape. The only thing a bitter person can think about is the hurt caused, the wrong done, the pain inflicted.

Bitterness can poison everything else, too. A leader of the Warsaw ghetto uprising describes in the documentary film *Shoah* how he felt about Nazi brutality: "If you could lick my heart, it would poison you." Bitterness ruins health, destroys relationships, punishes friends and enemies alike, and wreaks havoc wherever it goes.

Regret, bitterness, and revenge will only ruin us. We will become prisoners in our own dark souls, suffocated by our own brooding thoughts.[85]

---

85. Sittser, *Will of God*, 157, 159.

Prayer

Lord and Master:

I kneel at the cross of the Savior and repent of my sins in order
to find the only true freedom. Please forgive and help me and others
overcome bitterness and brooding thoughts. Use my small voice,
calling from outside to behind the walls, to give others in black-hole
bondages assurance of freedom in eternity. —*Amen*

Covenant and Dedications

Today We the Passengers covenant:

To stay on course in order to restore and administer justice,
mercy, reconciliation, comfort, and order across our
nation and around the world.

We dedicate Records, Law Enforcement, and Correction
and Court Systems in America and all Nations to
God's Glory and Honor.

Night Watch

Scripture Course and Focus Points

As we end today's journey, let us rest assured that God's Word will chase
away any confusion or anxiety that has crept in during the day. As before, the
following Scripture Course and matching Focus Points are provided for day's
end. A personal and group judgment: consider reading aloud so our Master
hears that We the Passengers believe his Word.

Scripture: Psalm 1:1–3; Proverbs 24:23–25; Isaiah 1:26, 3:13, 9:6–7, 16:5,
28:5–6, 42:6–7, 61:1–2; Ezekiel 33:6–7; Amos 5:24; Matthew 25:35–40; Luke
4:18–19; 1 Corinthians 5:12–13; 2 Peter 3:17–18.

Focus Points: Verdict, judging, injustice, righteousness, day, partiality,
bribery, court, freedom, captives, law, meditation, discipline, justice, good
news, saints, deliver, grace deceived, secure position.

Spirit, fill sails and grant peace and rest as
this day ends.—*Amen*

End of Cruise Day Three

Cruise Day Four Program
Four Scenarios and Stages in History

~~~~~~~~~~~~~~~~~~~~~~~~~

Scripture Course

Wake-Up Calls!

Fourth-Generation Introductions
Joseph Washburn and Hannah Latham
Roger Williams

First Briefing: Two Scenarios and Stages

Cruise Library Visit

Free Time Options

Last Briefing: Two More Scenarios and Stages

Cruise Bonus
How to Pass the Great American Dream Test

Covenant and Dedications
Communities, Cities, Congregations, Campuses

Night Watch
Scripture Course and Focus Points

~~~~~~~~~~~~~~~~~~~~~~~~~

Scripture Course
Praise the Lord from the heavens, praise him in the heights above.
Praise him, all his angels, praise him, all his heavenly hosts.
Praise him, sun, and moon, praise him, all you shining stars.
Praise him, you highest heavens and you waters above the skies . . .
Praise the Lord from the earth, you great sea creatures and all ocean depths.
Psalm 148:1–4, 7

Scripture: Numbers 14:17–19; Psalms 91, 139:7–12; Daniel 12:2–4, 13; Colossians 3:1–2; Hebrews 12:22, 13:1–2; 1 Peter 1:3–5; Revelation 21:26–27.

Wake-Up Calls!

Of those 100 or so of persons who came over first [on the *Mayflower*], more than half died in the first sickness. Of those that remained, some were too old to have children. Nevertheless in those thirty years there have sprung up from that stock over 160 persons now living in this year 1650; and of the old stock itself nearly thirty persons still survive. Let the Lord have the praise, Who is the High preserver of men ...

James Chilton; his wife; their daughter, Mary. Another daughter, who was married, came after. Mr. and Mrs. Chilton died in the first sickness. Mary Chilton married, and has nine children.

Francis Cook; his son, John. Mrs. Cook and other children came over afterwards. Three more children were born here. His son, John, is married. Mr. Cook is a very old man, and has seen his children's children have children.[86]

The religious diversity of the American colonies—though largely within the Puritan tradition—called for a new understanding of the church. We may call it the denominational theory of the church. The use of the word denomination to describe a religious group came into vogue about 1740 during the early years of the Evangelical Revival led by John Wesley and George Whitefield. But the theory itself was hammered out a century before by a group of radical Puritan leaders in England and America ...

In the English colonies of America, however, the denominational theory gained increasing acceptance. It seemed to be God's answer for the multiplying faiths in the New World.

Few advocates of the denominational view of the church in the seventeenth century envisioned the hundreds of Christian groups included under the umbrella today.[87]

To the spiritual heirs of Roger Williams, to those who agree with him that "Having bought truth dear, we must not sell it cheap, not the least grain of it for the whole world."[88]

---

86. Bradford and Paget, *Of Plymouth Plantation*, 342-344.
87. Shelley, *Church History in Plain Language*, 306, 308.
88. Gaustad, *Roger Williams*, dedication.

Fourth-Generation Introductions

Hannah Latham	b. ca 1653	d. 1725
	m. by 1677	
Joseph Washburn	b. 1652	d. 1733
Roger Williams	b. 1603	d. 1684

Hannah Latham and Joseph Washburn are my fourth-generation ancestors from the *Mayflower*. Hannah was Susanna and Robert Latham's daughter. Joseph's parents were Elizabeth Mitchell and John Washburn. James Chilton was Hannah's great-grandfather. Hannah was born in 1652 or 1653 in Bridgewater; Joseph probably in 1652 in Duxbury, Massachusetts. A Stroebel granddaughter and son-in-law are Roger Williams descendants.

Many fourth-generation descendants have more than one, and in fact, some have several *Mayflower* ancestors. The marriage of Hannah and Joseph by 1677 merged my family's Chilton and Cooke *Mayflower* ancestries into one lineage. Born in the mid-seventeenth century and living into the eighteenth century, perhaps this couple discussed colony and church diversification and growth.

Records were kept, so I know that this generation of *Mayflower* descendants inherited land from their parents: "On 28 Feb. 1688/9 Joseph Latham of Bridgewater sold land bought by 'my father Robert Latham late of Bridgewater decd.'"[89]

First Briefing: Two Scenarios and Stages

First Scenario and Stage

During this fourth generation's stage in Judeo-Christian and American history, citizens and immigrants were beginning to realize the great American prosperity dream. At the time, their primitive lifestyles and struggles for survival were far from meeting our standards for a comfortable prosperity dream coming true. In modern times, realizing the American dream usually means materialistic thinking. But the prosperity we enjoy today is ours because this generation in history established colonies that became thriving rural communities and urban centers that became cities, states filled with citizens, and commercial sites, school campuses filled with classmates, and churches filled with congregations.

The time setting is early pre-Revolutionary War. Most colonists are still loyal British citizens, and figuratively speaking, are still on board the *Mayflower* with British flags flying on the masts.

---

89. GSMD, *Five Generations*, 11.

For a moment, let us return to Day One on our historic platform as we set and begin filling today's sails to head toward Dedications. Because it was winter, Captain Jones and the crew postponed their return to England, and *Mayflower* passengers were allowed to remain on board the seventeenth-century vessel for a month after arriving at Plymouth Harbor. Several men went ashore to explore and choose the location for Plymouth village.

Hopes and dreams for the colony diminished when half the colonists died the first winter, but the dismay was temporary. The colony began to grow as new settlers arrived each year. By 1630, the population was 390; 1,020 in 1640; 1,566 in 1650; and 1,980 in 1660; and the colonists established other towns in the area.

> The colony was governed by a legislature of the freemen called the General Court. They elected the governor and his assistants, made laws, set up courts, appointed officials, distributed land, and levied taxes. … Plymouth Colony at first tried to function with common property, but failed, after 1623 permitting settlers to have individual plots of land . . . Farming, cattle-raising, and fur trading were the major means of subsistence. In 1643, Plymouth Colony entered the New England Confederation, a loose relationship with the colonies of Massachusetts Bay, Connecticut, and New Haven for the settlement of boundary and jurisdictional disputes and for mutual defense.[90]

The preceding scenarios came about because a small group of Separatists from the Church of England decided to sail across the sea and settle in the New World. Their voyage and settlement were funded by Englishmen called Merchant Adventurers. Two of my family namesakes, John and William Pierce, were among the fifty to seventy adventurers. You have already heard William's story. I tell John's story today to prepare twenty-first-century citizens to purify communities, cities, congregations, and campuses for God's glory and honor by asking God to hurl *greed* into the sea.

My family may never know until heaven if we are related to John and William. Despite trying twice, John failed to cross the sea to America. We are still looking for a Pierce with documentation and DNA to prove a relationship with William, who lived in Boston. But even without proof of blood relation, John Peirce/Pierce's greed is a family namesake sin and regret. It is also documented

---

90. George K. Schweitzer, *Massachusetts Genealogical Research*, 10–11. Used by permission.

national and international history, because Governor William Bradford, Frederick C. Pierce, and also the unknown author of *Mourt's Relation* wrote that John cheated the Pilgrims.

John Peirce himself tells a different story, recorded in Charles M. Andrews's Plymouth history book and footnote. His different vantage point is included during today's briefing to remind us to always look for and consider both sides of a story before passing judgment—a necessary reminder, because church and state are soon to be separated.

> In 1621 conditions in the colony were very bad and the merchants, discouraged, divided among themselves and without funds, turned to Peirce for help. Peirce says that James Sherley and four or five others sent Robert Cushman to persuade him to provide a ship and to undertake a voyage to New England, in order to help the plantation in its distress, and they promised to recompense him for his outlay. With considerable difficulty he got a ship, stocked it with passengers, provisions, and goods, part of which the merchants provided, and twice, once in October 1621, and again in January, 1622, tried to cross the ocean, but each time was forced to return. The merchants blaming him for these failures, which involved them in further loss, sued a writ out of the court of admiralty and placed him and the ship under arrest. They charged him not only with the losses of the voyage but also with "some supposed unjust dealing touching the said plantation and untruely pretended that your Orator had not fulfilled his bargain but had broken some covenants and donne great wrong unto them." At Portsmouth, where he was arrested, Peirce could not get bail, so his brother Richard gave bond for 600 *li*, which secured his release and he returned to London. From this time forward, the merchants, through his brother Richard, tried to persuade him [John] to give up the patent, promising to deal "bountifully" with him. But he refused. Then they brought pressure to bear on Richard (just what hold the merchants had on the latter does not appear), and finally, because his ship and goods were "under arrest," he yielded and under compulsion assigned the patent to Sherley, on pretence of a valuable consideration (perhaps the 500 *li*), which was never paid. After a year's delay, he struck back, first offering to submit the case to arbitration, then appealing to the king, and finally, these attempts coming to nothing, carrying the case into chancery.

What Peirce sued for was recompense for his losses in money and reputation, and payment of the full value of his patent, "according as it was then worth when it was taken from your Orator." Regarding the outcome we know nothing.[91]

We do know the outcome of robbing God. Malachi 3 reveals the repercussions of this sin, along with the promised blessings for testing and obeying God by bringing a tithe into his house.

Let's focus on another way the Lord looks at robbing: he knew that greed for material wealth would grow out of our personal, family, and national history, from our prosperity and free-style capitalist democracy. Surely, greed is a sin in our inherited subconscious and conscious natures that differs from God, who is generous in every way and in every day with his grace.

Poem Set to Music
He Giveth More Grace
by Annie Johnson Flint

> He giveth more grace as our burdens grow greater,
> He sendeth more strength as our labors increase;
> To added afflictions He addeth His mercy,
> To multiplied trials He multiplies peace.
> When we have exhausted our store of endurance,
> When our strength has failed ere the day is half done,
> When we reach the end of our hoarded resources
> Our Father's full giving is only begun.
> Fear not that thy need shall exceed His provision,
> Our God ever yearns His resources to share;
> Lean hard on the arm everlasting, availing;
> The Father both thee and thy load will upbear.
> His love has no limits, His grace has no measure,
> His power no boundary known unto men;
> For out of His infinite riches in Jesus
> He giveth, and giveth, and giveth again.

Prayer

Generous Almighty Master,

Thank you for testing your people, for your generous grace and patience with us. To lift the curse of greed and robbery, we confess and ask you to forgive and hurl our personal, family, and national greed for material goods and money into the sea. Show us how to reimburse if we or our ancestors, back to the first generations in the land, have robbed you.

---

91. J. Gardner Bartlett, "John Peirce of London and the Merchant Adventurers," *The New England Historical and Genealogical Register*, 67, 1913. Quoted in Andrews, *Colonial Period of American History*, 283.

We thank and praise you for scenarios and stages that illustrate your generous Spirit and rich grace. Give us your greed for souls and enough love to submit to your will. Purify our ungodly greed and change it to godliness, the reputation and application we covet, so that we may be ready and willing to covenant and dedicate today's headings to your glory and honor. —*Amen*

Cruise Library Visit

"*Four Early Bibles In Pilgrim Hall*"
by Rev. Dr. Charles C. Forman
Pilgrim Society Note, Series One, Number Nine, April 1959

Among the books in Pilgrim Hall Museum in Plymouth, Massachusetts are four Bibles of unusual interest. One belonged to Governor William Bradford, the Pilgrim Governor, and one to John Alden. These are among the very few objects existing today which we feel reasonably sure "came over in the Mayflower." Of the history of the two others we know little, but they are Geneva Bibles, the version most commonly used by the Pilgrims. John Alden's Bible, rather surprisingly, is the "King James" version authorized by the Church of England but he also owned a "Geneva Bible," which is now in the Dartmouth College Library.[92]

On the other side of my evolving life story and sanctification process, my greedy and growing yearning to see the prophetic scenarios and stages in God's Word fulfilled led to my writing the script, not the music, for a musical stage play called *How to Pass the Great American Dream Test*. The drama portrays and brings together important scenarios, stages, and characters from the seventeenth to the twenty-first century.

Roger Williams is the main player, both today and tomorrow, because he envisioned and ordained the separation of church and state in his independent settlement at Providence, Rhode Island.

Born in England circa 1603, Williams emigrated to Massachusetts in 1630 on board the *Lyon*. William Pierce was the ship's master. Rev. Williams died in 1683/4. Some of my seventeenth-century Pierce and *Mayflower* relatives could have personally known or heard about him. This historical innovator and protagonist was "a charming, sweet-tempered, winning man, courageous, selfless, God-intoxicated—and stubborn—the very soul of separatism."[93]

The following quote from a Williams family history book honors his influential role in American history:

---

92. The four Bibles belonging to the Pilgrim Society have been carefully examined by the Rev. Dr. Charles C. Forman, pastor of the First Parish in Plymouth. See the Pilgrim Hall Web site for his notes on the evolution of the Geneva Bible, its characteristics and historical importance. www.pilgrimhall.org
93. Morgan, *Puritan Dilemma*, 116.

Let us unite in bestowing honor upon Roger Williams for the great contribution he made to religious liberty, by insisting that the State limit its authority to civil government, leaving to the Church all matters of religion. To Roger Williams we owe the first government that recognized the complete separation of Church and State, and accorded to all men complete religious liberty.[94]

Author Edwin S. Gaustad tells how Roger Williams still advances Christian faith and enriches twenty-first-century scenarios and stage settings:

For the subsequent history of what became the United States, Roger Williams possesses one indubitable importance, that he stands at the beginning of it. Just as some great experience in the youth of a person is ever afterward a determinant of his personality, so the American character has inevitably been molded by the fact that in the first years of colonization there arose this prophet of religious liberty . . . The image of him in conflict with the righteous founders of New England could not be obliterated; all later righteous men would be tormented by it until they learned to accept his basic thesis, that virtue gives them no right to impose on others their own definitions . . . He was thinking on a deeper plane than that which simply recognizes religious liberty as a way for men to live peaceably together . . . His decision to leave denominations free to worship as they chose came as a consequence of his insight that freedom is a condition of the spirit . . . His bequest to America, then, of liberty, responsibility, and civility has enriched the American past and can help to preserve the American future.[95]

Free Time Options

Whether you are alone or cruising with a group, you may want to pause and take time to reflect upon or discuss a Providential plan in your life and family—perhaps, as I did, seeing reputations and evolving scenarios in ways you formerly ignored or just considered happenstance in your family's history.

---

94. Rev. John Sampey, title-page dedication in Anthony, *Roger Williams of Providence*.
95. Gaustad, *Roger Williams*, 124, 129.

Last Briefing: Two More Scenarios and Stages OR
Cruise Bonus: How to Pass the Great American Dream Test

How to Pass the Great American Dream Test is a two-act, several-scene musical drama written as a metaphor to portray the dramatic influence of the *Mayflower*, the Pilgrims, and Roger Williams in American history, and to cross over into the influence of the American Revolution and Constitution on modern-day life. My American dream is to see the entire drama published, then adapted and produced for the stage.

Today, we premier the drama in the first scene, as Mary Chilton says good-bye to her father James on the *Mayflower* stage, and we say "hello" to this moment's influence on us—her physical and spiritual descendants. In the second scene, a modern-day Mary, also an immigrant, is a classmate of my granddaughter Andrea, a Williams and Chilton descendant.

In today's fictitious good-bye scene, Mary and James discuss the opportunity for Mary to be the first female to step on Plymouth Rock in 1620. Because no pictures were taken, Mary did not keep a journal (or it has been lost), and the journals and diaries of William Bradford and other seventeenth-century cast members do not document her step, I can only support that historical supposition through family and American tradition, and through other authors whose words are worth our consideration.

Our first support for this historic moment repeats a previous quote:

> In 1744, Ann Taylor, a granddaughter of Mary Chilton and John Winslow, wrote that Mary had been the first woman who stepped onto the rock of landing at Plymouth Harbor, an event now memorialized in Francis Bacon's famous painting, "The Landing of the Pilgrims." Although neither Bradford nor Edward Winslow make any mention of the event, no other family claims that distinction.[96]

If we listen carefully to other recorded history, we can hear Mary's voice and even see her personality introduced by Thomas, son of John Faunce, who arrived in Plymouth in 1623 on the *Anne*.

> A well known story originated in a talk given in the 19th century at Plymouth's Old Colony Club that at age ninety-five Elder Faunce was driven to town in an open wagon from Eel River and taken to Plymouth Rock. He told the people gathered there how he had talked to John Howland and his

---

96. www.chiltonschildren.org

wife, John Alden, Giles Hopkins, George Soule, Francis Cooke and his son John, and Mrs. Cushman, born Mary Allerton, who "died but yesterday." All of these, he said, told him that upon that rock they had stepped ashore, and John Winslow's wife, Mary (Chilton), had come there on her seventy-fifth birthday and laughed as she stepped on the rock, and said she was the first woman to have stepped on it. This story, relayed to posterity verbally by one who claimed to hear it from a person who had been in Elder Faunce's audience that day, is as far back as we can go to authenticate that what we today call Plymouth Rock was in fact the first land at Plymouth touched by the *Mayflower* Passengers.[97]

Mary's first step for posterity is also considered as plausible in *Mary Chilton's Title to Celebrity* by Charles T. Libby, published by the Society of Mayflower Descendants in the State of Rhode Island in 1978. The accounts were written and verbalized by her grandchildren and great-grandchildren. To believe this requires respect for Libby's "old-lady" rationalization:

> We have one old lady telling an interesting anecdote of her own girlhood to her grandchildren, and another old lady telling a story of her grandmother to her grandson. Both old ladies were eminently proper and highly respected—none more so. We must either accept the narration as true, at least the pith of it, or believe that one of the other of these old ladies blandly lied in order to deceive their own grandchildren into making false boasts to no purpose!
>
> If Mary Chilton was not the first ashore, what occasion ever was there for saying anything about it?
>
> On this evidence alone, and in the absence of counter evidence, what antiquary can feel so insecure in his historical judgment as to shrink from the unqualified statement, as matter of history: The first woman or girl of the Mayflower passengers to get ashore at Plymouth was Mary Chilton.[98]

These vantage points are shared to avoid slanting the truth and to introduce *Dream Test* as a creative, fictional drama based on tradition and truth. John Alden is also in the scene because he owned books, including Bibles; thus we can assume that he could read—an assumption we cannot make about Mary. James's literacy is more probable because he was a businessman.

97. Stratton, *Plymouth Colony*, 291.
98. Libby, *Mary Chilton's Title to Celebrity*, 9.

In *Dream Test*, John Alden offers to step ashore with Mary, because for many generations the first-ashore claim "has been contested between the Alden and Chilton descendants."[99]

Please relax now, and watch as Mary, her father, and John prolong the contest in a drama that I dreamed up for passing time on the American stage.

Lights are dim, and a stage light shines on a seventeenth-century stage and *Mayflower* passengers. They are still and silent until a choir sings the "Amen" for the following hymn. Feel free to sing along and read the script aloud. If cruising as a group, you may create the suggested stage settings and role-play to bring the drama to life.

Song
O God, Our Help in Ages Past
Psalm 90, Isaac Watts, William Croft

> O God, our help in ages past, Our hope for years to come,
> Our shelter from the stormy blast, And our eternal home!
>
> *Under the shadow of Thy Throne Still may we dwell secure;*
> *Sufficient is Thine arm alone, And our defense is sure.*
>
> Before the hills in order stood, Or earth received her frame,
> From everlasting Thou art God, To endless years the same.
>
> *A thousand ages in Thy sight Are like an evening gone;*
> *Short as the watch that ends the night, Before the rising sun.*
>
> O God, our help in ages past, Our hope for years to come,
> Be Thou our guide while life shall last, And our eternal home! Amen.

Scene One: How to Pass the Great American Dream Test

Cast: Mary Chilton, James Chilton, and John Alden
Set: Below deck on the seventeenth-century *Mayflower*, James rests with eyes closed, leaning against pillows on a cot. Mary, seated on a stool next to a storage barrel, is sewing, but she repeatedly raises her head to watch his breath or bows her head as if in prayer. A lighted candle sits atop the storage barrel. The candle stays lighted throughout the whole drama to represent the Pilgrims' influence on modern-day life and liberty. This heartbreaking but temporary farewell also suggests eternal life through faith in Christ.

---

99. Thacher, *History of the Town of Plymouth*, 30.

JAMES. Mary, come hither so I can see ye better; John Alden is coming soon to read the Bible, perchance our last time on the *Mayflower*.

MARY. Father, thee must rest.

JAMES. Aye; I will soon rest forever.

MARY. Father, please, thou must not say that. God is privy to thy woes and will heal thee.

JAMES. Child, verily, verily, whether I live or die, God will heal. And if I say adieu and die, I will rise.

John enters the scene and sits on the stool.

JOHN. Mary, do ye remember where that promise is in the Bible?

MARY. In Daniel 12. But I am not privy to the verse.

JAMES. Find it, brother John; the promise will comfort.

JOHN. It's verse 2: "Many of them that sleep in the dust of the earth, shall awake, some to everlasting life, and some to shame and perpetual contempt."

JAMES. I beg thee, read the next verse.

JOHN. "And they that shall rise, shall shine, as the brightness of the firmament, and they that turn many to righteousness, shall shine as the stars, for ever and ever."

JAMES. Thank ye, John. Now what have ye to say to Mary?

JOHN. Mary, thee are chosen by the elders to be the first woman to step ashore on a rock that has been sighted for landing. This is a great honor for your family, and your first step for taking the Christian faith and Scripture into the New World. I will lend ye my Bible and arm to steady thy step.

Mary slowly stands up, forcefully shakes her head, wrings her hands, then turns to her father with her hands on her hips. Seeing that they are shocked by her response, she drops her shoulders and kneels to express humbleness.

MARY. O Father, John . . . why me? Other families and women on board deserve the honor more than I do. I cannot do that.

JAMES. Mary, Mary so contrary. Thee were so brave, and humbly cared for small children and served other passengers during our lengthy voyage. Everyone on board was thankful and pleased with thee, so thee were chosen by the elders to act bravely and humbly for all the children, now and in the future, as thee step ashore.

Mary stands again, then pretends to slip and falls on the floor.

MARY. Will they be thankful and pleased, and think I act for all children, if I slip and fall?

JOHN. I will hold thy hand as we step ashore, and the Lord will send thy guardian angel to keep thee from falling.

Very dramatically, Mary pretends to eat her arm, then pull an arrow out of her heart.

MARY. Will they protect if wild animals attack and eat me, or an arrow pierces my heart?

JAMES. Then thee will be the first to die on shore for our cause. Even that is an honor.

Mary shudders, then shows her father the holes in her dress.

MARY. I am hungry, every day, and every day is colder. My clothes are threadbare and have so many holes I'm cold all the time. I'll survive without complaint, but to be sacrificed and die, and do it on purpose? That's too much to ask of me.

JOHN. Our Lord did it on purpose.

MARY. He was God. He came to earth to do it. And I believe in his humble sacrifice for me and everyone else. But I cannot believe I came here to be the first woman to step ashore, and with everyone watching me do such a prideful thing. I beg thee, don't ask this of me.

JOHN. Not in front of everyone; thou will go ashore with just a few in the small boat.

[In the full musical, Mary, John, and James would now sing a new song called "Don't Ask This of Me/You Ask Too Much of Me" or "In a Small Boat," representing both the *Mayflower* and the small boat that was used for landing. In our abridged sailing version, I ask you to imagine all singing breaks, then continue with the play.]

JAMES. We are not asking for ye or me, but for everyone on board and those who will come after. But perhaps this is God testing ye and me. If so, only his Word can guide. John, please choose something to read.

JOHN. "Moses said to the people, 'Do not be afraid. God has come to test you, so that the fear of God will be with you to keep you from sinning'" (Exodus 20:8). John 3:19–21: "This is the verdict: Light has come into the world, but men loved darkness instead of light because their deeds were evil. Everyone who does evil hates the light, and will not come into the light for fear that his deeds will be exposed. But whoever lives by the truth comes into the light, so that it may be seen plainly that what he has done has been done through God."

Mary's attitude visibly changes through softer and gentler body language as John reads. She kneels next to the cot and puts her head down next to her father's hand. He strokes her head until she raises it to look up and talk with him.

MARY. Father, God chose those verses for today. I will trust him and not be afraid.

JAMES, *tenderly touching her face.* I know, my child. And whether thee step ashore first or not, I have a surprise for thee. Thy mother and I brought along a few lengths of new cloth, woven from wool combed in Holland, because we thought that I would tailor garments in our new land as in England and Holland. Thee are right; thy dress is threadbare, and too small to wear another day. While thee cared for other children on the upper deck, down here we cut and stitched a new dress and cape as a reward for our child. The garments are wrapped in linen under my cot.

MARY *inspects and caresses the garments; she hugs them, then her father.* Father, the dress and cape are fine-looking and so well stitched. I fear thee wore thyself out for me. Thank ye father and Father God for granting mercy to thy child!

JAMES. Ye are thankful. That is good. Your mother is still stitching a new cap for thee. I pray the garments will last long and keep thee warm in the new land.

MARY. Father, when I heard read the Covenant Compact that ye signed, I asked myself how do we, sinners, even though thankful, have the right to dedicate anything to God's glory when we do not know what we will have to dedicate in the new land? Or whether we will live to see the light of another day?

JAMES. Now ye ask too much of me. I cannot say, but the Word says nations cannot bring impurities into his throne room in the New Jerusalem. So perhaps ye and our descendants will be founders of a nation that will need to be purified. John, read Revelation 21:26–27.

JOHN. "The glory and honor of the nations will be brought into it. Nothing impure will ever enter it, nor will anyone who does what is shameful or deceitful, but only those whose names are written in the Lamb's book of life."

JAMES. So Mary my sweet, it seems right that an innocent and pure young girl step ashore first. But I need to know, do thee believe, with me, that God is faithful to all generations and all people?

MARY. Yes, that promise is in Psalm 100, the psalm that expressed our joy and thankfulness when we first saw land.

[It is recorded that the Pilgrims expressed joy upon the first sight of land and that they read and probably sang psalms.]

JAMES. I'd like to sing it once more, to praise God for choosing all on board this vessel to trust him for every voyage and step of our lives and lineage. Maybe if we listen closely, we will hear the great cloud of witnesses seen in Hebrews 12 singing along with us.

[This is a cue for the audience to sing along with James, John, and Mary. *Full Sail* readers, read or sing the modern-day rendition of Psalm 100 from the Geneva Bible: "Sing ye loud unto the Lord, all the earth. Serve the Lord with gladness; come before him with joyfulness. Know ye that even the Lord is God; he hath made us, and not we ourselves: we are his people, and the sheep of his pasture. Enter into his gates with praise, and into his courts with rejoicing: praise him and bless his Name. For the Lord is good: his mercy is everlasting, and his truth is from generation to generation . . . For the Lord is good and his love endures forever; his faithfulness continues through all generations."]

JAMES. Mary, my life is slipping away. Perhaps the Spirit will comfort us if John reads verses from Psalm 139:7–12.

MARY. Father, before he reads the verses, I promise, I will step on the rock chosen for landing, as if it is the "rock of my salvation."

JAMES. I am proud of thee and shall rest assured that John's steady hands will help ye step ashore.

James and Mary hug.

JOHN [If you are acting the part of John, read both of these versions for comparison, crossing in your narrative from the seventeenth to the twenty-first century]. "Whither shall I go from thy Spirit or whither shall I flee from thy presence? If I ascend into heaven, thou art there: if I lie down in hell, thou art there. Let me take the wings of the morning, and dwell in the uttermost parts of the sea: Yet thither shall thine hand lead me, and thy right hand hold me. If I say, Yet the darkness shall hide me, even the night shall be a light about me. Yea, the darkness hideth not from thee; but the night shineth as the day: the darkness and light are both alike" [*1599 Geneva Bible*, brought to America on the *Mayflower*].

"Where can I go from your Spirit? Where can I flee from your presence? If I go up to the heavens, you are there; if I make my bed in the depths, you are there. If I rise on the wings of the dawn, if I settle on the far side of the sea, even there your hand will guide me, your right hand will hold me fast. If I say, 'Surely the darkness will hide me and the light become night around me,' even the darkness will not be dark to you; the night will shine like the day, for darkness is as light to you" [*New International Version*].

James dies while John reads; Mary kneels and weeps.

NARRATOR. Fast forward to a twenty-first-century twelfth-grade high school history class. The same actress plays the roles of seventeenth-century and twenty-first-century immigrant Mary Chilton. Andrea Williams, her family, and the drama as a whole represent Roger Williams's dramatic influence on American life and his stance between church and state.

The class teacher, Dan Adams, represents John Adams and his influence in American history, along with his John Alden ancestry. The audience is challenged to test their knowledge of history, along with the students. The Heritage Dome, worship center, and school are located in any American village, city, church campus, or community where the audience lives. The Dome represents the overarching, encircling, and widespread influence of free-style American life and liberty. Dream Test role-players and their dialogue and quotes represent the overarching, encircling, and widespread influence of Judeo-Christians in America, as well as America's diversity. The class suspects that Gabe and Michael are guardian angels. You as the audience are free to judge their suspicions.

Scene Two: How to Pass the Great American Dream Test

School bell rings to announce class beginning.

MR. ADAMS. Class, last week I told you that I'm not preparing your American history final test. You will write the test and help one another pass it. This will also convince me—or not—that you've learned something in this class. So on Friday I suggested that you present creative ideas for a test project, then vote for your choice in a democratic way. Any ideas?

After looking around and waiting, Andrea slowly raises her hand.

ANDREA. I have an idea, beginning with the *Mayflower* and progressing to making American history in the twenty-first century. I thought of it because the Heritage Dome Dedication Contest is calling for program ideas. Here's my idea: let's write and submit a musical, biblical, and historical drama to help us pass the test on the new Dome stage. That would be double use of what we've learned at Heritage High and in this class. Is that creative enough?

GABE. That's very creative. Michael and I will be happy to sing and dance.

CLASSMATE. Will you show your wings again, as you did at Christmas and Resurrection time?

MICHAEL. Can't see and sing without wings!

GABE. Oh I feel a song comin' on; can't see and sing without wings!

MR. ADAMS. Cool it, you two! We're not auditioning yet. Andrea, your grandfather is a Dome contest judge. Could you keep it a secret from him?

CLASSMATE. I have a question too. Would you be willing to roast your father the pastor in your drama?

ANDREA. Grandfather will be in Washington DC campaigning to protect church from state again while we're rehearsing the drama. About my dad, well, I guess roasting is okay, but I don't want to hurt him. Keeping it secret from him will be hard because Dad likes to talk and pray about everything that's going on in our family. He even asks for a daily teenage angst report! Do your parents do that?

[Laughter, and students groan/nod/shake their heads. Option: Some could sing and dance a "daily angst" dance while Dan tries to get control. He finally does it by accompanying the dance on the piano and bringing it to an end with something like a back-to-your-seat J. P. Sousa march or "The Saints Go Marching Back to Their Desks," a song he has used before that the students recognize as marching orders.]

MR. ADAMS. Class, you're going to get me fired, so let's cool it. (*More laughter, so Adams sits at his desk to wait for order. When things are quiet he speaks again.*) Okay, let's hear other questions, ideas, or reactions to Andrea's idea.

MICHAEL. With your family history and grandfather's campaigning, is separation a big burning deal in your drama?

Andrea purposely coughs and coughs, then pretends to gasp to talk.

ANDREA. You think you're tired of it! I live and breathe secondhand smoke.

Laughter, until Dan glares at the class.

ANDREA. I confess, though, that I agree with Grandpa. Separation is important to protect our rights, even our right to produce a drama about faith. So somehow separation should be mentioned.

CLASSMATE. Have you written a "somehow" script?

ANDREA. No. I've only made a few notes and sort of an outline, and maybe an idea for beginning, like starting with our school verse—Psalm 119:111–112.

Andrea raises and pumps her arms, and the class responds by quoting the verse.

CLASS. "Your statutes are my heritage forever; they are the joy of my heart. My heart is set on keeping your decrees to the very end."

ANDREA. Cool, that worked. Then we could quote patriotic statements by or about our forefathers. Let's try a rehearsal: a test using the quotes that you found to complete today's review assignment. As my mother says in drama class, stand up, project, and speak confidently and clearly enough to awaken the dead.

CLASSMATE. Who said this? "Is life so dear or peace so sweet as to be purchased at the price of chains and slavery? Forbid it, Almighty God. I know not what course others may take, but as for me, give me liberty or give me death!"

CLASSMATE. Patrick Henry.

CLASSMATE. "We hold these truths to be self-evident, that all men are created equal; that they are endowed by their Creator with certain inalienable rights; that among these are life, liberty, and the pursuit of happiness."

CLASSMATE. Thomas Jefferson, Declaration of Independence.

CLASSMATE. Do you know who wrote this and when? "We think good that it be established for an act: That . . . no imposition, law or ordinance be made or imposed upon or by ourselves or others at present, or to come, but such as shall be made or imposed by consent of the voters."

CLASSMATE. I have that someplace in my notes . . . wait a holy minute . . . ah, here it is, from page ten in Francis Stoddard's book, *The Truth About the Pilgrims*: "The first Declaration of Independence in America was formulated and ratified at a meeting of the General Court of New Plymouth, November 15, 1636. After reading their Compact and the Letters Patent of 1629, it was enacted: 'No imposition, law or ordinance be made or imposed, etc.'"

CLASSMATE. Who said this? "This system seems to have come directly from the hand of God."

CLASSMATE. The French political thinker and historian, Alexis de Tocqueville. He is best known for his book *Democracy in America*, which was required reading for this class.

CLASSMATE. We'd need to be very careful sourcing the quotes, because we found truth stretched during research for this class.

CLASSMATE. BOOOOOOORING, if we just recite quotes.

Silence, until . . .

CLASSMATE. Maybe we should recite in song and dance. And use today's discussion and singing and dancing as a scene.

CLASSMATE. How about a patriot's parade, with class members wearing clothing representing time periods as we quote historical people who still influence our lives?

Cruise Day Four Program

CLASSMATE. Let's include a John and Abigail love scene.
BOY CLASSMATE. I'll volunteer for his role.
GIRL CLASSMATE. I'll be Abigail.

Everyone laughs/groans at the class "pair."

CLASSMATE. I think Mr. and Mrs. Adams should do the love scene. How about it, Mr. Adams? Would your wife Gail be willing?
MR. ADAMS. Maybe. It's time to vote, beginning with a primary vote. How many want to vote now about using Andrea's drama idea for both test and contest, and about using today's discussion and review test as a scene?

Hands go up.

ANDREA. I'd like a two-thirds majority, like Congress voting for constitutional amendments, because if there is a better way to pass our test, we need to know. We also need to know if a large majority will play roles. I'll abstain from voting.
MR. ADAMS. Agree to two-thirds majority rule, without Andrea's vote?

All raise hands.

MR. ADAMS. Then vote for using Andrea's drama by raising your hand.

Hands are raised and counted.

MR. ADAMS. Okay, we're one short of a majority. Mary and Andrea didn't vote. Either of you want to break the tie, like vice presidents do in the Senate?
MARY. I want to tell you all why I didn't vote. My family and I are baby Americans. We left a nation where citizens aren't free to vote and express ideas. I carry the new citizen's oath in my Bible because it means so much to me and my family, just as God's Word does. We came here because America is a nation with good ideas and causes, and citizens defend causes during war and peace.

I wasn't exactly sure about what voting really means, until today. Voting is a privilege, and it means responsibility to do something about what you are for or against. I'd like a way to pay our school and community back for the scholarship I received to attend this school. But if I vote *yes* and choose to play a role in the drama, I'll have to find helpers. My parents and relatives work whenever they find work, so they cannot help. We have no friends, and I babysit my younger brothers and sisters and cousins, so I go home right after school. But I'm willing to defend our cause, and I really do need help passing this history test, because I don't know as much as you do. Are you willing to help me? Tell me, how should I vote?

CLASSMATE. You should vote yes so we can help your family become grown-up citizens and defend our citizenship and liberty. That's a responsibility I commit to, and I'll change my vote to yes because now I know how to help.

CLASSMATE. Me too, and I think Mary should have a major role in the play. I promise to help you learn history, study your lines, and babysit.

CLASSMATE. I think everyone in the cast and audience should recite the citizen's oath.

CLASSMATE. Good idea, because most citizens, like my family, were born citizens, and they've probably never even read it.

MARY. How many role-players will wear period clothing?

ANDREA. Those who play historical roles would need to. Why do you ask?

MARY. Sewing is how we make our living. If you want us to, my family can sew the clothing.

CLASSMATE. I've heard the school board is planning to order new school uniforms. Let's write a petition for people to sign that says to the board, "Hire Mary's family to sew the uniforms."

MR. ADAMS. They would need to bid for the job. The bid papers are in the school office. Would they have time and know how to do that?

MARY. Yes, they are all learning English, and my parents know how to bid for jobs. This is an American dream come true, and I can vote yes.

Classmates all raise their hands.

MR. ADAMS. Unanimous! I suggest that we've just experienced democracy and the American spirit in action. Let's clap for Mary and Andrea—and America!

Narrator encourages audience to clap.

CLASSMATE. Andrea, do you have a title for the drama?

ANDREA: Maybe; but it's up to all of you to decide. But first I'd like to say that this is a dream come true for me too, because I'm applying for a college scholarship to study drama writing, production, and performance. This will help a lot, and I'll take responsibility to write the drama using your ideas and research and our conversations. Thank you! So here's my title idea: How-to books are the "in" thing these days. Mary needs our help to pass our history test. So I suggest calling it, *How to Pass the Great American Dream Test.* What do you think?

[Adams moves to the piano and starts playing and humming melody lines and singing lyrics, and soon the cast and all students sing "How to Pass the

Great American Dream Test." End-of-hour bell rings, and song takes students and Adams off stage. God willing, someday we will hear, sing, dance, and dream new American music!]

Covenant and Dedications

We the Passengers covenant:
To dedicate Communities, Cities, Congregations, and Campuses
in America and all Nations to God's Glory and Honor.

Night Watch

To advance Christian faith as we rest, please review the preambles to all the constitutions of the fifty United States of America in the Cruise Library. I guarantee, you will rest better when you find God in all the preambles, and you will be better prepared for tomorrow's scenes and Dedications. Also, remember that the light shed by Mary's *Mayflower* candle is burning as our night light.

Scripture Course and Focus Points

Scripture: Numbers 12:6; Deuteronomy 4:9–10; Psalms 18:28, 19:8, 112:4; Proverbs 16:23–24; Ecclesiastes 2:13, 3:1–22; Isaiah 64:6; John 3:19–20; 1 Corinthians 2:1–5; Ephesians 5:8–11; Revelation 5:9–14.

Focus Points: Obedience, instruction, rags, power, salvation, Holy Spirit, shine, angels, glory.

We rest assured and dream about Christ the Light of the World
as he ends this day.

End of Cruise Day Four

Cruise Day Five Program
Posterity and Potential Meet

Scripture Course

Wake-Up Calls!

Fifth-Generation Introductions
Ebenezer Washburn and Patience Miles

First Briefing: Places for Posterity and Potential to Meet

Dream Test: Scene from Act Two

Free Time Intermission Options

Cruise Library Visit

Last Briefing: Patriots Parade

Dream Test: Final Scenes from Act Two

Covenant and Dedications
Theaters, Stages, Dramas, Dreams, and States

Night Watch
Scripture Course and Focus Points

Scripture Course
> *I will lead the blind by ways they have not known, along unfamiliar paths I will guide them; I will turn the darkness into light before them and make the rough places smooth.*
> Isaiah 42:16

Scripture: Psalm 78:1–2; Proverbs 2; Isaiah 58:10; Malachi 3:2–4; Matthew 13:34–43; Luke 8:16–18; John 1:50–51, 3:21, 21:16–17; Acts 17:24–28; Colossians 1; Revelation 14:6–13.

Wake-Up Calls!

Today, we are again awakened by authors who alert us to cherished, loving, and wise reasons to consider American and Judeo-Christian history relevant to our twenty-first-century lives.

> John Adams was, in the first place, a man of fierce integrity and strict Christian morality—a Puritan, at least to the extent of having unconsciously and unquestioningly accepted as his own the exacting behavioral standards of the Bible Commonwealth. If he sought fame, reputation, and success, he despised them, too, and excoriated himself in one breath for the very efforts he urged upon himself in another . . . Humor flowed naturally from Adams's dramatic objectifications of himself and the world he saw. At times, when the diarist places himself too prominently downstage and gives himself too grandiloquent a script, the humor is unintentional, and the reader ends up smiling indulgently at the overacting self-dramatist . . . But most often the humor is intentional, based squarely on Adams's dramatic imagination which exaggerated the ridiculousness of people and things: of poor Aunt Nell, who broke two teeth "at table in company, and to avoid exposing her self, swallowed them"; and above all, of JA, who found himself, to his own great relief, in comic as well as tragic roles.[100]

> Thus out of small beginnings greater things have grown by His hand Who made all things out of nothing, and gives being to all things that are; and, as one small candle may light a thousand, so the light kindled here has shone to many, yea, in some sort to our whole nation; let the glorious name of Jehovah have all the praise. (Plymouth Governor William Bradford)[101]

> It is wise for us to recur to the history of our ancestors. Those who do not look upon themselves as a link connecting the Past with the Future, do not perform their duty to the world. (Daniel Webster)[102]

---

100. Bailyn, *Faces of Revolution*, 7, 11.
101. Bradford and Paget, *Of Plymouth Plantation*, 226.
102. http://www.danielwebsterestate.org/Newsletter.php, Winter 2009.

The principle of Roger Williams is not only one of absolute justice with respect of equality before the law, but it is the essential principle of religious culture. When we look beyond form and ritual to the spiritual life of which they are the expression, it must be realized that its vital breath is the liberty of the soul in following its highest aspirations. It is only in the atmosphere of religious freedom that we may hope either for protection against error and delusion or for the maintenance of that spiritual power upon which all progress depends. (Address of Secretary Charles E. Hughes, April 27, 1922)[103]

Roger Williams wrote, "When they have opened a gap in the hedge or wall of separation between the garden of the church and the wilderness of the world, God hath ever broken down the wall itself . . . And that therefore if He will e'er please to restore His garden and paradise again, it must of necessity be walled in peculiarly unto Himself from the world."[104]

On January 9, 1872, Senator Henry Bowen Anthony delivered a Eulogy of Roger Williams in Congress: "He knew, for God, whose prophet he was, revealed it to him, that the great principles for which he contended, and for which he suffered, founded in the eternal fitness of things, would endure forever. He did not inquire if his name would survive a generation. In his vision of the future he saw mankind emancipated from . . . the blindness of bigotry, from the cruelties of intolerance. He saw the nations walking forth into liberty wherewith Christ had made them free."[105]

Fifth-Generation Introductions

Ebenezer Washburn	b. ca 1693	d. 1762
	m. 1721	
Patience Miles	b. 1704	d. after 1762

Roger Williams and my fifth-generation *Mayflower* ancestors provide us with talking and tacking points for advancing civil and Christian history, for purification, and for filling sails. Our destination, as on every Cruise Day, is the dedication of aspects of American and Judeo-Christian free-style life and liberty to God's glory.

---

103. See complete speech in Appendix Three.
104. Quoted in Federer, *America's God and Country*, 694.
105. Ibid, 51.

Ebenezer Washburn was probably born in Bridgewater, Massachusetts, about 1693 and died in Monmouth County, New Jersey, before March 5, 1762. He sold his Massachusetts land and moved to New Milford, Connecticut, where he bought land and became a blacksmith. "Patience was born in nearby Derby, Connecticut. Her father died when she was only eight and she went to live with her grandfather, Joseph Wheeler, in New Milford."[106]

Ebenezer and Patience Washburn's daughter Rebecca married Timothy Carver; their daughter Mehitable married Daniel Pierce. For years, family historians recorded that Daniel was the son of Samuel and Polly, the grandson of John and Patience and great-grandson of Michael Pierce. Today is the last time I will set this record straight, as it is possible for me to do because of twenty-first-century DNA testing: Daniel Pierce is not descended from Samuel, John, and Michael Pierce.

During Ebenezer's and Patience's lifetimes, Delaware and North and South Carolina became colonies. John Adams, Thomas Jefferson, and James Madison were born. America's first public library, in Philadelphia, was Benjamin Franklin's idea.

First Briefing: Places for Posterity and Potential to Meet

Yesterday's first *Dream Test* scene portrayed the Pilgrims bringing to New England the biblical concept of eternal life in Christ. The classroom scene portrayed our forefathers' intentions fulfilled: the freedom, advancement, and protection of Judeo-Christian faith in America as a result of our federal and state constitutions and the separation of church and state instigated by Roger Williams.

The Heritage Dome, constructed on the sturdy foundation of the civil and Christian Mayflower Compact and the separation of church from state, is therefore a meaningful covering for *Dream Test* role-players who represent *Mayflower* and Williams descendants. The audience represents the Christian community in America, then around the world through Christian missions. Angels join and speak to the cast of Revelation 14:7: "I saw another angel flying in midair, and he had the eternal gospel to proclaim to those who live on earth—to every nation, tribe, language and people. He said in a loud voice, 'Fear God and give him glory, because the hour of his judgment has come. Worship him who made the heavens, the earth, the sea and the springs of water.'"

During one scenario which is not included in today's shortened version, a *Dream Test* Jewish classmate and his family handle ticket sales to represent the first handling of God's places. The modern-day electrical system in the Heritage Dome represents Judeo-Christian faith as the light that dispels darkness.

---

106. Allan J. Warnecke, *Timothy Carver Day, May 28, 1995* program for the Town of Carmel N.Y. Bicentennial 1795–1995; "Carver-Washburn" file in the Hartford, Conn. Historical Genealogy Library.

In a scene today, Mary and Andrea will talk about the Standish cannon and uniformed guards. Their conversation represents dark scenes in North American history, mainly wars, which began with Native tribal wars and will last until the end of time in the world. When Mary dreams about catching a glimpse of demons, it is a prophetic warning—a foreshadowing—that evil does and will exist in America, as in all nations and inhabited continents.

God set foreshadowing and covering precedents. Read Genesis 3 and see that even before Adam and Eve ate the apple, God provided a covering and remedy[107] for nakedness and sin: the fig tree with leaves. The fig tree represents Israel in other Scriptures.[108] Christ used the fig-tree foreshadowing and covering as a judgment warning and call to prayer, and because we dwell under his covering and understand the foreshadowing as fulfilled, we can see Christ reconciling all things visible and invisible.[109] For example, Christ's life and victory over death is foreshadowed in Genesis. His role as the offspring of Mary and the one who brings a covering of shed blood to his family—Israel and the world—is clearly seen in God's words to the serpent: "I will put enmity between you and the woman, and between your offspring and hers; he will crush your head, and you will strike his heel."[110]

After Mary and Andrea awake from dreaming about each other, they point to one another—an act representing the potential in Mary pointing ahead to her posterity, who will glorify and honor God in the New World as Andrea points back across time to find light and faith in Mary's potential. As ancestor and descendant point at one another, posterity and potential meet and merge in the mirror of historical reflection.

The center-stage space between the girls represents and ties together the scenarios and stages between their lives and times.

To fill sails for today's *Dream Test* scenes, let's see how America's "Connecticut Time" influenced turn-of-the-century lives and made moving-ahead history.

Seventeenth-Century Democracy

English Puritans and Congregationalists began moving west to the Connecticut River Valley in the early 1630s. In 1638–9, they claimed civil independence and established a commonwealth based on the will of the people by writ-

---

107. "The fig tree was common to Palestine and employed as a remedy and as an allegory in Scripture." *Nave's Topical Bible*, 301.

108. "Well known in antiquity for its fruitfulness, sweet taste, and protective shade . . . the fig tree is a ready symbol for God in covenant relation to his people, as in the vine, with which it is often linked. Thus God is portrayed as having seen in Israel prospects of productivity as one 'seeing the early fruit on the fig tree' (Hosea 9:10 NIV), which appearing in late spring, gives promise of later fruitfulness. As covenant beneficiary, Israel could enjoy the God-given prosperity and security experience in the Solomonic ideal: 'each man under his own vine and fig tree' (1 Kings 4:25)." Ryken, Wilhoit, and Longman, *Dictionary of Biblical Imagery*, 283.

109. Matthew 21:22–24; Luke 11:20–25; Colossians 1.

110. Genesis 3:15; Romans 16:20.

ing and voting for the Fundamental Orders— recognized by many historians, though not all, as the first constitution adopted for democratic self-governing. Thus, Connecticut's nickname is "The Constitution State."[111]

The Rev. Thomas Hooker inspired the adoption of this constitution by preaching, on May 31, 1638, that "The foundation of authority is laid in the free consent of the people," and "As God has given us liberty let us take it."[112]

The U.S. Constitution and the current Connecticut Constitution declare some of the same principles, with citizens' rights assured and governmental powers stated and limited. Today's citizens of the democracy that evolved from their principles are free to consider that Connecticut's Fundamental Orders of 1638–9 were written for twenty-first-century successors who pledge, pray, and dedicate themselves to maintaining and preserving liberty:

> Forasmuch as it hath pleased the Almighty God by the wise disposition of his divine providence so to order and dispose of things that we the Inhabitants and Residents of Windsor, Hartford, and Wethersfield are now cohabiting and dwelling in and upon the River of Connectecotte and the lands thereunto adjoining; and well knowing where a people are gathered together the word of God requires that to maintain the peace and union of such a people there should be an orderly and decent Government established according to God, to order and dispose of the affairs of the people at all seasons as occasion shall require; do therefore associate and conjoin ourselves to be as one Public State or Commonwealth; and do for ourselves *and our Successors and such as shall be adjoined to us at any time hereafter,* enter into Combination and Confederation together, to maintain and preserve the liberty and purity of the Gospel of our Lord Jesus which we now profess, as also the discipline of the Churches, which according to the truth of the said Gospel is now practiced amongst us; as also in our Civil affairs to be guided and governed according to such Laws, Rules, Orders, and Decrees as shall be made, ordered, and decreed as followeth." [Emphasis mine.][113]

---

111. www.ct.gov
112. Ibid. Connecticut Chief Justice William M. Maltbie (served 1930–1950; lived 1880–1961) and various books credit Rev. Hooker for framing the Connecticut Government. The Fundamental Orders charter lasted from 1639 to 1662.
113. "The First Constitution of Connecticut," http://www.sots.ct.gov/sots/cwp/view.asp?a=3188&q=392290# HISTORICAL (Reproduction does not constitute an implied or express endorsement of this publication by the Office of the Connecticut Secretary of the State.)

Thus, to "maintain and preserve the liberty and purity of the Gospel … the discipline of the Churches … and for Civil affairs to be guided and governed"—and with gratitude to God for inspiring Reverend Hooker, Pastor Roger Williams, and other early Americans to establish precedents and a foundation for us to build on—we join Andrea, Mary Chilton, Mr. Adams, Pastor Williams, the Heritage High School senior history class, and the Heritage Dome drama team under the twenty-first-century Heritage Dome.

Dream Test: Scene from Act Two

Cast: Mary Chilton (Mary probably lived with either the Standish or Alden families after her parents died), Andrea Williams (Andrea is a Chilton and Roger Williams descendant).

Set and Opening Action: Mary exits a seventeenth-century Plymouth door. She is wearing the garments stitched by her parents. She stretches, and Andrea, in the Williams's twenty-first-century home, is seen rising from her bed, stretching. They see and point to each other. Lighted candles in a window of the Plymouth house and on Andrea's desk represent the seventeenth-century light that still shines in the twenty-first-century.

MARY, *points to Andrea.* I dreamed about thee. Who are ye?

ANDREA, *points to Mary.* I'm Andrea Williams. I dreamed about you. Who are you?

MARY. I'm Mary Chilton. What's that? (*pointing to Andrea's computer*)

ANDREA. That's a computer.

MARY. What do ye do with it?

ANDREA. Write letters, do school papers, and research on the Web.

MARY. Is that like a spider's web?

ANDREA. Sort of, because we can get caught in it. You look like a Pilgrim. (*pointing to Mary's clothes*)

MARY. I am a Pilgrim.

ANDREA. You mean, like a *Mayflower* Pilgrim?

MARY. Yes. I came across the sea to New England on the *Mayflower*. Governor Bradford said we are like the pilgrims in Hebrews 11:13: "All these died in good faith, and received not the promises, but saw them afar off, and believed them, and received them thankfully, and confessed that they were strangers and pilgrims on the earth." [1599 Geneva Bible]

ANDREA. Cool, you can recite Bible verses!

MARY. Yes, we Pilgrims are very cold, and hungry, and many are sick. My parents both died of the sickness soon after we arrived.

ANDREA. Oh, I'm sorry.

MARY. Now I live with friends. We are hungry. Might thee have something for me to eat?

ANDREA. Sure! Come on over to my house while I change.

Andrea opens a closet door, and behind it sheds pajamas that cover cut-off jeans and a T-shirt. After crossing the stage to Andrea's room, Mary points to the light on Andrea's desk.

MARY. What's that?

ANDREA. That's an electric lamp, for light to see in the dark. See? (*turns on the light*)

MARY. Do ye have a Bible, for light in the dark?

ANDREA. Yes, there, by my bed.

MARY. Can ye read it?

ANDREA. Yes, and we study it in school. My parents read the Bible a lot, and teach it too.

MARY. My friends read the Bible. I'm trying to learn. Does thy family hold fast to the Christian faith and glorify God?

ANDREA. We try to. I attend a Christian school. Mother teaches in the English and Arts Department and heads the church drama team, and Dad is the senior pastor of our church. What about your family?

MARY. Ye are blessed! My family, and the other Pilgrims, suffered greatly to be able to worship as we desired and glorify God. My father, James Chilton, and other Pilgrim men signed a Compact to promise that we will do that.

ANDREA. Oh, now I know who you are! You're history—and my ancestor, Mary Chilton.

MARY. If I'm history, and your ancestor, then I'm dead.

ANDREA. You look very alive to me!

MARY. I feel alive! (*pinches herself*) But how many generations am I dead?

ANDREA. Let's count. (*holds up a long scroll*) The genealogy chart Grandma gave me shows fifteen generations from you to me.

[On stage, this discussion might include "Genealogy Chart" or "Pinch Me," a dead-or-alive spoofing song.]

MARY. We must have many relatives. I wonder why I dreamed about thee and not the others.

ANDREA. Do you think God writes dreams?

MARY. The Bible says he spoke to Joseph and Daniel in dreams.

ANDREA. I think maybe there's another answer to your question: my parents probably prayed for something like this to happen. This is a really, really cool answer.

MARY. There ye go again, saying something is cool. I'm hot in thy house.

ANDREA. Well, I'm not surprised, considering all those clothes you're wearing. You can take off your cape and cap.

MARY. Thank ye. I'm not surprised ye are cool, considering all the clothes ye are not wearing.

(*Andrea laughs, prompting audience to laugh*)

ANDREA. You could wear shorts and a T-shirt, but your clothes are perfect for today's history test. And I have to change into my hot school uniform. The Dome is air-conditioned, so we'll stay cool. Now we'll grab something to eat, and then walk to school because it's close by.

Free Time Intermission Options

Now it is your time to foreshadow and reflect! As God guides you, write a prayer for those who are cast to play roles on dramatic stages in your state, in our union, and in other nations. If you are meeting as a group, add your prayer to those written by Heritage High students and faculty to represent the Revelation 5:8 "golden bowls full of incense, which are the prayers of the saints." (The Heritage prayer-writing scene is in the longer version of *Dream Test*, not included in this book.) Do not sign your prayers; draw to read aloud.

Cruise Library Visit

My English ancestors were Church of England members, then Separatist Pilgrims, and perhaps some were Puritans. The difference between these groups is that Puritans thought the Church of England could be purified; Separatists did not agree, so they separated from the Church.

By this time in the eighteenth century, the church established in Massachusetts by the Pilgrims and Puritans had changed—divided into two major branches, Presbyterianism and Congregationalism—a change preceded by the same division in England.

I learned about the divisions in *The Mayflower Pilgrims* by David Beale:

> Both denominations believed that true churches were formed by "voluntary covenant" among individuals, who had, through faith and repentance, experienced the new birth, by personal faith in the shed blood of Jesus Christ, the second Person of the Trinity.
>
> Many former Puritan churches became a part of this movement, which played a large role in America's Great Awakenings and religious education. On the other hand, the larger segment of eighteenth-century Congregationalism experienced gradual but gargantuan changes, from ortho-

doxy to Unitarianism, in most of the original New England churches. Major innovations would steadily bring most of New England's original Puritan, Pilgrim, and Congregational churches into Unitarianism.[114]

My Pierce forefathers were Baptists; my German and Austrian ancestors on my mother's side were Lutheran. My childhood family worshiped with a rural Evangelical United Brethren congregation, now the United Methodist denomination. My husband and I raised our children in the Reformed Church in America, and we are still RCA members. Our children worship God with other congregations in other denominations.

While living and working in the American military community in West Germany for four Cold War years, my husband and children and I worshiped with a nondenominational military chapel congregation. As Bible students and teachers in America and Europe, we used nondenominational materials. I received help with writing and publishing this nondenominational cruise logbook from gifted Jewish and Gentile authors, theologians, teachers, and missionaries, from my publisher and his editors, and from lay members aligned with various denominations. Thank you all!

My ancestors and other early Americans would not have known it then, but by looking back in history's mirror, we know that the years 1648 to 1789 were the "Age of Reason and Revival." Bruce Shelley provides an interesting point for seeing ourselves as we are now—free-style:

> Faith was less dogma and more experience. This evangelical Christianity spread rapidly by the power of preaching alone. And many Christians came to see that state support was no longer essential for Christianity's survival. Modern Christians could accept religious freedom.[115]

Last Briefing: Patriots Parade

Today's Wake-Up Call introduced John Adams's importance in American history. To move ahead through a century change, and to understand why I cast an Adams as Andrea's history teacher, our sails are filled by author and historian Michael Novak, who casts Adams as the central character on the eighteenth-century American stage:

> Few today think so deeply about the architecture of American government as Adams did, and Adams did so *be-*

---

114. Beale, *The Mayflower Pilgrims*, 152–156.
115. Shelley, *Church History in Plain Language*, 309

fore there was an American government. Without Adams, neither independence nor the Constitution or its ratification would have seen reality. More deeply than his peers, he thought through the principles of the Republic to which we this day pledge allegiance.

There is ample reason, further, to believe that this century will at last be the Adams century. The return to religious and moral education as a *sine qua non* of the survival of the Republic is as finally apparent to many as it once was to him. The intellectual and legal bankruptcy of the extreme Jefferson/Madison position on church and state has been exposed. But the deepest reason of all is that no other founder—not Washington, not Jefferson, not Madison—delved so profoundly into the practical necessities of republican governance. Alongside these three, Adams certainly deserves to be listed as one of the four giants of the founding.[116]

Dream Test: Final Scenes from Act Two
First Scene

Cast: Mary Chilton and Andrea Williams

Set and Opening Action: Girls walk to the Dome. As twenty-first-century pictures of America roll by on a revolving stage or projection screens and the audience sings "America the Beautiful," Mary points to things like cars and trucks, bicycles, street signs, sidewalks, and children playing a ball game. Andrea seems to be explaining what they are, but she's not heard.

Song
America the Beautiful

O beautiful for spacious skies,
For amber waves of grain, For purple mountain majesties
Above the fruited plain. America! America! God shed His grace on thee,
And crown thy good with brotherhood From sea to shining sea.

O beautiful for pilgrim feet, Whose stern impassion'd stress
A thoroughfare for freedom beat Across the wilderness.
America! America! God mend thine ev'ry flaw,
Confirm thy soul in self-control, Thy liberty in law.

---

116. Novak, *On Two Wings*, 173.

O beautiful for heroes prov'd In liberating strife,
Who more than self their country loved, And mercy more than life.
America! America! May God thy gold refine
All success be nobleness, And ev'ry grain divine.

O Beautiful for patriot dream that sees beyond the years.
Thine alabaster cities gleam, Undimmed by human tears.
America! America! God shed his grace on thee,
And crown thy good with brotherhood, From sea to shining sea.[117]

MARY. "America" is the name of this nation?

ANDREA. Yes; you and I are Americans. In fact, at Plymouth, you were the first American teenage girl from Europe—oh, wow, that makes you the very first American dream girl on stage!

MARY. It does?

ANDREA. Yes, because our American tradition says that ye, I mean you, were the first woman or girl to step on Plymouth Rock.

MARY. Ye have that right. I was. My father made me do it.

ANDREA. Now you're sounding like an American teenager! My parents make me do things all the time.

MARY. That sign in front of this building has a cross on it. If it's a Church of England sanctuary, I must needs leave right now.

ANDREA. No, the Heritage Worship Center and school are nondenominational. Why would you need to leave that other church?

MARY. If the pastor or members heard my name, I'd be burned at the stake because my family separated from the church. Friends say the smell is terrible.

ANDREA. No one is burned at the stake in the twenty-first century; anyway, not in America—usually, anyway, I hope.

MARY, *staggers and grabs Andrea's arm.* This is the twenty-first century?

ANDREA. Yes.

MARY. I live in the seventeenth century. In my dream, I saw and heard ye explaining my dream. That's why I wasn't afraid when I woke up and saw ye. Maybe I should go back to dreaming, because now I am afraid of those things ye call computers, television, telephones, refrigerators, cars, trucks, and air-conditioning and electricity, and everything that is happening so fast. It's like Daniel 12 coming true.

ANDREA. Maybe it is. But please don't be afraid. Stay—I dreamed that my class helped you pass an American history test in this century.

MARY. I'll try to stay, if ye stay close.

---

117. Lyrics by Katherine Lee Bates; music by Samuel A. Ward.

[Bev's Note: Mary's request is a plea for us to recognize that history and generations are closely related.]

ANDREA. I will.

MARY. Are all these people friendly? (*points to audience and people walking around*)

ANDREA. Sure. They are my friends, classmates, musicians, people who've come to see or act in a drama.

MARY. Ye mean on stage, like a Shakespeare play?

Andrea's head jerks to stare at the audience with big eyes, a prearranged signal to the narrator.

NARRATOR. We now see that even the Puritan setting is a stage where actors flipped the script, meaning that Mary ad-libbed. While Andrea regains composure, let me explain. Shakespeare lived from 1564–1616; *Mayflower* passengers and Puritans likely knew about him and didn't approve of his plays. In her mother's drama class, Andrea memorized lines from Shakespeare's *As you Like It*, Act IV.

Andrea relaxes and nods.

ANDREA. "All the world's a stage, and all the men and women merely players. They have their exits and their entrances; and one man in his time plays many parts."

MARY. Are those men and women wearing uniforms playing parts?

ANDREA. Yes, they are guards, here to protect us and the new Dome.

MARY. Captain Miles Standish wears a uniform, and the *Mayflower* brought a cannon across the ocean to protect us. Do these guards have cannons?

ANDREA. Well, sort of small cannons.

MARY. To protect them from wild animals?

ANDREA. No, not usually, unless they're hunting. Some people don't want us to pass the Dream Test and dedicate the Dome, so they cut electrical wires during rehearsals. The guards are watching for the wire cutters. They recognize us, so we are free to go in.

MARY. Wait! I see someone, no, many people who were in my dreams. Only they weren't people; they were angels wearing wings. Some were good angels wearing white robes; they were fighting with demonic angels wearing black and masks over their faces. It was horrible and evil!

ANDREA. Where, where? Point to them.

MARY. Over there . . . oh, now they have disappeared into the crowd.

[When Dream Test is set to music, this scene ends with a dark wire-cutter song and dance by demon-like characters with wire cutters lurking around on stage, even in the audience. White-robed angels hover to indicate protection if the demons get too close to the people they are assigned to watch over, a covering promised in Psalm 91:9–12. The stage is prepared for the next scenes, and Mary and Andrea enter the Dome.]

Second Final Scene

NARRATOR. This is the final scene, the Dream Test. Remember that Andrea's father, Pastor Rod Williams, and this dramatization represents the ongoing influence and history made by Roger Williams. The history students chose two questions to answer: First, looking back, did America's forefathers leave enough evidence to pass a God-and-country loyalty test? Second, can we pass the test in the twenty-first century?"

Cast: Mary Chilton, Andrea Williams, Marilyn Williams, Michael, Gabe, Dan Adams, Pastor Rod Williams, Classmates, Narrator, Audience

Set and Opening Action: On the Dome Stage. Andrea, (now wearing a school uniform) turns on her laptop computer, reads the screen, then stands and speaks to the audience.

ANDREA. We are here to test historical Americans—whether they were loyal to God and country, and established and maintained civil order—and to pass the tests ourselves. And we are here to help a classmate whose parents and other relatives are new citizens. Remember in the previous scene where Mary flipped the script, and the Narrator reminded me to quote Shakespeare about a person playing many roles? Well, during the intermission behind the scenes, my Dad said that was Providential because it wasn't scripted—but that I *should* explain why Mary plays two roles in *Dream Test*.

On our historical stage, she is the first female immigrant to step on the American stage. To stress how important it is for a twenty-first-century immigrant to know and respect American history and values, Mary has no way of knowing how or why—other than seeing or hearing what happens on this stage—to pass a twenty-first-century test. Therefore, without any prejudices or assumptions, as she learns history she will decide who passes. Listen carefully, because you will decide if you pass the test.

MARY. What if someone disagrees with my opinion?

ANDREA. Hmmm, I hadn't thought of that.

Andrea's mother Marilyn, the school drama teacher, rushes on stage to rescue Andrea from this flip.

MARILYN. Hello, Mary. Your costume is perfect for playing Mary Chilton's part.

MARY. I am Mary Chilton.

ANDREA. Mother, Mary really gets into her roles. Is everyone else here?

MARILYN. Yes. Let's begin.

MARY. I thought we had already begun. What begins now?

ANDREA. The test! The first question is this: "Did the Mayflower Compact writers pass the God and country loyalty test?"

MARY. I know the answer, and I can recite the Compact from memory.

ANDREA. Yes, I know, but we'll read the shortened version from the screen because it is in modern-day English.

MARY. I think thine English very strange. As ye wish.

ANDREA AND MARY. "Having undertaken for the Glory of God, and Advancement of the Christian Faith, and the Honour of our King and Country, a Voyage to plant the first colony in the northern Parts of Virginia; Do by these Presents, solemnly and mutually in the Presence of God and one another, covenant and combine ourselves together into a civil Body Politick, for our better Ordering and Preservation, and Furtherance of the Ends aforesaid."

MARY. The writers and signers passed. Has someone written a twenty-first-century compact for me to judge?

ANDREA. The history class asked my grandparents to write a new compact that connected the Mayflower Compact to the twenty-first century. It's in the program and on the screen for everyone to read. Let's say it together.

AUDIENCE AND CAST. "In the Name of God Almighty, Supreme Ruler of all Nations, the Alpha and Omega of Time and Events, *We the People* whose names He knows, Solemnly and Mutually Compact, Covenant, and Combine ourselves together openly and freely, without malice and with foresight, to declare our Beliefs and Pledges. Believing in the Potential of this Declaration and with a firm reliance on the Protection and Guidance of Divine Providence, We Pledge Alliance and Allegiance to the United States of America and will do all within our Power and according to God's Will to Protect and Preserve this Nation and fulfill our Duty to the World. We agree to and Dedicate this Compact for God's Glory and Honor—and for the Furtherance of the Ends aforesaid in the United States of America."

MARY. The new Compact passes. What does "United States" mean?

ANDREA. There are fifty states in our nation, the United States of America.

MARY. Is the nation near Plymouth Plantation?

ANDREA. Plymouth Plantation is in Massachusetts, one of the fifty states in America.

MARY. America is truly beautiful. The cities are larger than what I saw in my dream, and Plymouth's tiny gardens would be a speck of dust in America's fields. Now I understand why ye have so much food in thy house. Are ye ever hungry?

ANDREA. Just before meals, or when I don't allow time to eat before school. But starving, no! I can always find food. Grandma makes the best mac 'n' cheese![118]

MARY. I don't know what that is. But I know that ye in America are blessed.

ANDREA. Sounds like you are saying American farmers pass the test.

MARY. That is true. Americans might even try saying thank ye to God.

ANDREA, *stares at the audience again.* Novel idea, isn't it?— a Pilgrim suggesting that we should say thank you!

MARY. "Patriot" and "hero" were new words in my dream and in the America song. Please explain them to me.

ANDREA. Since the seventeenth century, patriotic heroes have established and fought to protect and preserve our nation and liberty. We have modern-day heroes and heroics too.

MARY. Do American patriots and heroes pass the test, giving thanks and believing in God?

ANDREA. That's for you to decide. We can sit down now to watch a Seventeenth- and Eighteenth-Century Patriots and Heroes Parade.

MARY. What's a parade?

ANDREA. Ah . . .

MR. ADAMS. Mary, today's parade is Americans walking through national history, representing the men and women who made that history.

MARY. Who leads the American nation parade?

MR. ADAMS. Class, who is considered by many to be America's founder?

ALL: Samuel Adams!

MR. ADAMS. Whoever remembers a Sam Adams quote will receive an "A" for the day.

CLASSMATE DRESSED LIKE SAM ADAMS: "May God preserve the nation from being greatly injured, if not finally ruined, by the vile ministrations of wicked men in America!"[119]

A Patriots and Heroes Parade

[*Full Sail* Passengers, the Patriots and Heroes in this parade are quoted or talked about on Cruise Days. So you will be their judge as you read the logbook. Feel free to add other patriots and heroes to the list. William Penn is a good example.]

---

118. This is more than Andrea's family trivia and taste buds speaking. According to "Cheese and Variation" by Chris Macias (*The Sacramento Bee*, June 10, 2009), "Thomas Jefferson typically gets credit for introducing pasta to the United States. Whatever the case, macaroni has been simmering around the United States since the country's earliest days."

119. September 1768, in a letter to Dennys Deberdt, agent of the American assembly in England. Quoted in Hosmer, *Samuel Adams*, 124–5.

Squanto
Roger Williams
Thomas Hooker
Noah Webster
Benjamin Franklin
George Washington
Samuel Adams
John and Abigail Adams
Benjamin Rush
Thomas Jefferson
John Quincy Adams
Patrick Henry
Francis Scott Key
Daniel Webster

MARY. Those patriots and heroes in the seventeenth and eighteenth centuries passed. Will nineteenth- and twentieth- and twenty-first- century citizens pass the God and country test? Natives helped us plant corn; some believed. Do dark-skinned people still live in America, and do they believe in God?

ANDREA. Wait, wait, you asked too many questions at once. Yes. Americans are many colors and cultures, and many are believers. Listen, and then decide if these citizens pass the test.

[Many of these patriots are quoted in *Full Sail*; other biographies and quotes can be found in books and on Web sites.]

Sojourner Truth
Abraham Lincoln
Mary McLeod Bethune
Clara Barton
Theodore Roosevelt
Franklin Roosevelt
Harry S. Truman
John F. Kennedy
Peter Marshall
Charles Evan Hughes
Rev. Billy and Ruth Graham
Dwight D. Eisenhower
Martin Luther King
Ronald Reagan

MARY. They all pass. Another question. The song "America the Beautiful" asked, "May God thy gold refine till all success be nobleness and every gain divine." Has God answered and refined thy gold in America?

ANDREA. Hmmm . . . I don't really know what that means.

MR. ADAMS. A man shaping silver and gold holds the pieces in the fire until he can see his image. God holds our lives in the refiner's fire until his pure and holy image can be seen in ours.

MARY. That sounds like Malachi 3:2–4. Who here can read or recite it?

NARRATOR. Me. "Who can endure the day of his coming? Who can stand when he appears? For he will be like a refiner's fire or a launderer's soap. He will sit as a refiner and purifier of silver; he will purify the Levites and refine them like gold and silver. Then the Lord will have men who will bring offerings in righteousness, and the offerings of Judah and Jerusalem will be acceptable to the Lord, as in days gone by, as in former years."

MR. ADAMS. Haym Salomon [1740–85] is a good example for giving acceptable offerings. Should he be added to the Patriots Parade? Does anyone in my class remember learning about him?

CLASSMATE DRESSED AS HAYM SALOMON, *Comes from offstage.* Yes, he should be added, and I remember what we learned, probably because I'm Jewish. Salomon was a Polish-Jewish immigrant and a broker and dealer in securities who gave and gave offerings from his personal fortune, and asked others to give, to General George Washington's army. Salomon died penniless, but he saved the Army and our freedoms by multiplying his financial contributions through others. Many givers were the sons of Judah and Jerusalem, meaning that they were also Jewish. They were not honored or thanked. His family never received any financial help even though they asked Congress to reimburse them.

MR. ADAMS. What should we do now?

CLASSMATE. We should finally say thanks to Haym Salomon. That would be refining, too, if citizens need to confess anti-Semitism.

MR. ADAMS. My ancestor, John Adams, expressed anti-Semitism. So now I'd like to say I regret that, and I suggest we have a few moments of silence for confession. Then I'll lead a standing ovation for the Jewish citizens who have played important roles in history, and to this day, to bless our nation. But first, know that this student purposely chose to stay off stage, out of the limelight and parade, to represent the truth that Jews like Haym Salomon are often ignored and disrespected. Let's change that today on this stage in our history, and let's give this honor student our thanks and respect!

The classmates clap; audience claps according to conscience and heart changes. Jewish student bows, and Gabe and Michael put their arms around him to represent angels' wings watching over Israel.

ANDREA. So if God is refining American citizens and our country, others should see his image in us, and we should see his image in American life and liberty.

MR. ADAMS. Yes; if God can be seen in a person or part of America, then that person or part is refined and passes the test. This value applies even to refining our money, by carefully choosing who will receive our offerings and respect. Haym Salomon was an excellent example.

ANDREA. My daddy will need to forgive me for saying so, but that was the best introduction for taking and multiplying an offering that I've ever heard!

MARY. What does "taking an offering" mean?

MR. ADAMS. We give gifts to organizations or people of our choice that need help, like hungry people. We'll do that at the end of the test.

MARY. I know about being hungry. Do ye test to see if Christ's image is seen in the organizations or people?

MR. ADAMS. Yes. And if they pass the test, they receive our gifts.

MARY. I'm glad we are "taking an offering," because Isaiah 58:10 says, "If thou pour out thy soul to the hungry, and refresh the troubled soul: then shall thy light spring out in the darkness, and thy darkness shall be as the noon day." [1599 Geneva Bible]

MICHAEL. And because Romans 12:20 says, "If your enemy is hungry, feed him; if he is thirsty, give him something to drink."

GABE. And John 21:16–17 says, "Feed my lambs; feed my sheep."

MARY. I don't have anything to give to the sheep.

MARILYN, *comes on stage holding Andrea's and Mary's candles.* Yes, you do. Mary, what is this?

MARY. My seventeenth-century *Mayflower* candle. And it is still burning! If I use it to light twenty-first-century candles, is that a gift?

MARILYN. Absolutely! After Pastor Rod prays for the offering, two Heritage musicians will sing a duet as the offering is taken, and then your class will use your candle to light their candles.

PASTOR ROD WILLIAMS. I must confess family pride tonight; citizens and God, please forgive me. But my pride is about more than family. Before we pray, let's thank the history class, Mr. Adams, and everyone who worked so hard in the congregation, school, and community to dramatize *Dream Test.* I also sense that the Williams reputation for separation of church and state is somewhat vindicated: we set a precedent tonight, so let's continue working together to relieve suffering and satisfy hungers around the world. We also share another responsibility, to "fill the earth with the knowledge of the glory of the Lord, as the waters cover the sea."[120] So let's pray about these things.

---

120. Habakkuk 2:14.

Almighty God, we praise you for patriots, who through the ages passion-ately fought for and preserved liberties in Christ in America and other free nations. Thank you for sending angels to watch over your children. Thank you for creating this rich land to satisfy physical and spiritual hunger at home and abroad. Lift the curse of greed and replace it with generosity's blessing. Use tonight's offering as seeds for a harvest of hope and health. Heal our nation as church and state work and serve together. Protect the church from the state, and bless the state through your church. Finally, we ask you to protect our children and fill them with your knowledge, biblical values, and your intent to share your love and shine your light around the world. Amen.

Lights shine on musicians. Mary is heard talking to Andrea.

MARY. Andrea, I'm sure of it. Gabe and Michael are two of the angels I saw outside and in my dream.
ANDREA. Ah-ha! Caught in the act! Maybe they'll confess in their duet.

[Gabe and Michael duet: "Can't Sing Without Wings." After they finish, the lights suddenly go out. It sounds as if a choir of angels is singing.]

NARRATOR. Everyone please stay calm and seated. We prepared for this blackout possibility, and the timing is perfect. The senior class and drama team even rehearsed in the dark, counting steps and holding hands to be in the right place to light fifty candles to represent the fifty United States. The students will light one candle for the District of Columbia and another for all United States territories. As they light their candles, they will name the states in alphabetical order. Please pray that citizens of the states, the District of Columbia, and the territories will glorify God.

The state preambles all mention God. But many dedications were written years ago. Today you can rededicate by switching on your battery-operated candle when you hear the preamble of the state where you were born. If you were born in or live in another nation, a territory governed by the United States, or the District of Columbia, turn on your candle when you hear the state where you reside now or where your relatives reside. The students will read the preambles in alphabetical order so you can anticipate when to light the candle for your state.

Lights go back on after the preambles are read and all candles are lighted. Full Sail *Passengers, see the preambles in Appendix Two in the Cruise Library.*

NARRATOR. The culprits who caused today's darkness were caught and will be prosecuted. Now we can see the dedication words in our programs.

Covenant and Dedications

Today We the Pilgrims on America's twenty-first-century stage covenant,
with thanksgiving for Light and Truth to share:
To dedicate Theaters, Stages, Drama, Dreams,
and States in America and other Nations
to God's Glory and Honor.

Night Watch

Scripture Course and Focus Points

Scripture: Genesis 6:11; Psalms 16:11; 107:8–9; 115; Isaiah 48:10–11; Jeremiah 16:18; Daniel 12:2–4; Joel 2; Habakkuk 2:14; Matthew 5:6, 17; John 3:16; Acts 17:28; 1 Corinthians 2:10–16; 15:52; Ephesians 5:8–11; Colossians 3:2; Hebrews 1, 2, 8, 13.

Focus Points: Violence, filled, fullness, tested, Israel, remember, bless, refinement, idols, dreams, visions, prophets, covers, world, yielding, angels, knowledge, wisdom, moving, Spirit, inheritance, light, submission, victory, New Covenant.

We rest assured as the Maker of heaven and earth
ends this dramatic day.

End of Cruise Day Five

Cruise Day Six Program
The Letter "L" in American History

~~~~~~~~~~~~~~~~~~

Scripture Course

Wake-Up Calls!

Sixth-Generation Introductions
Rebecca Washburn and Timothy Carver

First Briefing: Liberty, Land, Language, and Literacy

Free Time Options

Last Briefing: Lyrics, Libraries, Letters, and Lives

Cruise Library Visit

Covenant and Dedications
Liberty, Land, Language,
Literacy, Lyrics, Libraries, Letters, and Lives

Night Watch
Scripture Course and Focus Points

~~~~~~~~~~~~~~~~~~

Scripture Course
> *The heavens declare the glory of God; the skies proclaim*
> *the work of his hands. Day after day they pour forth speech,*
> *night after night they display knowledge.*
> *There is no speech or language where their voice is not heard.*
> *Their voice goes out into all the earth, their words to*
> *the ends of the world.*
> Psalm 19:1–4

Scripture: Leviticus 25:10; Deuteronomy 32:8–9; Psalms 37:3–6, 141; Jeremiah 29:4–7, 11; Hosea 10:12; Micah 5:7–8; Matthew 5:18.

Wake-Up Calls!

"I am a chief and ruler over my tribes. My influence extends to the waters of the great lakes and to the far blue mountains . . . Listen! The Great Spirit protects that man (pointing at Washington), and guides his destinies—he will become the chief of nations, and a people yet unborn will hail him as the founder of a mighty empire. I am come to pay homage to the man who is the particular favorite of Heaven, and who can never die in battle."

This story of God's divine protection could be found in virtually all school textbooks until 1934. Now few Americans have read it. Washington often recalled this dramatic event that helped shape his character and confirm God's call on his life.[121]

I always consider the settlement of America with reverence and wonder, as the opening of a grand scene and design in Providence for the illumination of the ignorant, and the emancipation of the slavish part of mankind all over the earth. (John Adams, notes for A *Dissertation on the Canon and Feudal Law, February of 1765*)[122]

The land itself must be seen to have a measure of dignity and respect and when it does not receive these accommodations, human beings who live on the land are accordingly incomplete.[123]

We the People of the United States, in Order to form a more perfect Union, establish Justice, insure domestic Tranquility, provide for the common defence, promote the general Welfare, and secure the Blessings of Liberty to ourselves and our Posterity, do ordain and establish this CONSTITUTION for the United States of America. (Preamble, the United States Constitution)

Sixth-Generation Introductions

Rebecca Washburn	b.1736/37	d. Unknown
	m. ca 1752	
Timothy Carver	b. 1728	d. before the Revolution

---

121. Toby Mac and Michael Tait, *Under God*, 12–13.
122. Quoted in Federer, *America's God and Country*, 5.
123. Nabokov, *Native American Testimony*, 19.

Welcome to the Sixth Cruise Day on board the *Mayflower*! Rebecca and Timothy Carver are my sixth-generation ancestors, direct descendants from seventeenth-century passengers. A family history indicates that their son, Timothy Carver, Jr., was born in 1753 in Bridgewater, Massachusetts, and moved to Frederickstown, now Carmel, New York, as a young child in the 1750s. "His parents, Timothy, Sr. and Rebecca Washburn Carver, established a homestead and 350 acre farm on the north side of Long Pond where they raised their family."[124]

The Native chief's Wake-Up Call, spoken in 1770, speaks of the inability of fighters to kill George Washington during the 1755 Battle of the Monongahela at Fort Dequesne during the French and Indian War. I chose the story to fill today's sails because Washington and the chief lived during the same years as Rebecca and Timothy Carver and their children.

The Carvers were probably patriots, not English loyalists. This statement is based on the documentation that Daniel Pierce fought against the British loyalists and thus for American liberty in the Revolutionary War. He married Timothy and Rebecca Carver's daughter Mehitable in 1768.

First Briefing: Liberty, Land, Language, and Literacy

Today, one "L" in our reflective history leads to another portal for reviewing American beginnings, progress, development, and struggles during the seventeenth and eighteenth centuries.

Liberty

The generation we remember today rang America's Liberty Bell. Ironically, the bell was cast, in 1752, in England. After breaking during its first ringing, it was recast in Philadelphia in 1753. The province of Pennsylvania paid about $300 for the bell.

The Liberty Bell rang on July 8, 1776, along with other church bells, to announce the adoption of the Declaration of Independence. Citizens rang the bell at each anniversary of the adoption of the Declaration until it broke on July 8, 1835, during the funeral of Chief Justice John Marshall. The last time it was struck, its tone picked up and amplified by special sound equipment, was on June 6, 1944, when Allied forces landed in France. Leviticus 25:10 is inscribed on the bell: "Proclaim Liberty throughout all the land unto all the inhabitants thereof."

Land

To trim today's sails, I explain the legitimate American application of Bible verses, such as Leviticus 25:10, which in their original context are speaking

124. Warnaecke, program for Timothy Carver Day. See Footnote 105.

to and about the citizens and land of Israel. Granted, many early Americans thought America was the new "holy land," and they used Scripture as the basis for land takeover. We confessed and repented of those takeover sins several days ago. With all due and right respect to those still suffering the consequences of those actions, let us use our spiritual and national citizenships and loyalties to sanctify whatever land we live on, maintaining our accountability to Scripture as we celebrate truth and forgiveness.

The following review moves us ahead in civil history. By and during the eighteenth century, American land was divided into New England, the Middle Colonies, and the Southern Colonies. Colonial capital cities at various times during the birth of America included Portsmouth, New Hampshire; Boston, Massachusetts; Providence, Rhode Island; Newport, Rhode Island; Hartford, Connecticut; New Haven and New Amsterdam (New York City), New York; Perth Amboy and Burlington, New Jersey; Philadelphia, Pennsylvania; New Castle, Delaware; Annapolis, Maryland; Williamsburg, Virginia; New Bern, North Carolina; Charles Town, South Carolina; and Savannah, Georgia.

Editor Carroll Calkins, in *The Story of America*, describes the division by Colonies.

New England Colonies

Massachusetts Puritans spread inland and along the coast to people this region's stony soil. Most became small farmers or artisans, dwelt in villages, and fiercely insisted on self-government. Others depended on the sea; they fished, built or manned ships, or traded with England and the West Indies. Busy ports, such as Boston and Newport, were havens for merchants who slyly evaded British attempts to tax and regulate their trade with French and Dutch Colonies.

Middle Colonies

New York, New Jersey, and Delaware, first settled by Dutch and Swedish traders, and Pennsylvania, which under William Penn welcomed many nationalities, were the most cosmopolitan of the English Colonies. Most residents were prosperous farmers, but numbers of tradesmen, mechanics, and shippers clustered around Philadelphia and New York. More genial and tolerant than New England, more energetic than the South, the Middle Colonies best represented the creative ferment of classes and cultures that would characterize America after the Revolution.

Southern Colonies

Agriculture was the heart of Southern life, and the tidal rivers were its arteries. Along their banks flourished vast, self-sufficient plantations that shipped their crops to foreign markets from their own wharves. Because plantations were scattered and isolated, development of the South lagged behind that of the other Colonies; Charleston was its only real city until after the Revolution. Along the Appalachian frontier independent backwoodsmen cultivated small farms.[125]

Language and Literacy

Some early Americans and their descendants were literate, and some recorded their faith in the English language. Today, because America's free public educational and library systems were soon to come in the eighteenth century and remain available to us today, you and I can read and use English-language books. Daniel J. Boorstin, in his book *The Americans: The Colonial Experience*, summarizes the uniqueness of our American language.

> While Englishmen along the colonial seaboard tried to cling to the familiar local ways of the different parts of England from which they had come, they founded—without meaning to—a culture which was in many ways more homogeneous in vast America than it had been in little England. The settlers clung to their mother language, and in the course of moving about the New World and in moving up and down the social scale, they made it more uniform. A single spoken language soon echoed across the continent, overcoming space as the printed word overcomes time. The American language would fulfill the Elizabethan prophecy of Samuel Daniel written in 1599:

> And who, in time, nows whither we may vent
> The treasure of our tongue, to what strange shores
> This gaine of our best glory shall be sent,
> T' inrich unknowing Nations with our stores?
> What world in th' yet unformed Occident
> May come refin'd with th' accents that are ours?

---

125. Calkins, *Story of America*, 22.

Only two centuries later when this dream had become a fact, Noah Webster foresaw that "North America will be Peopled with a hundred millions of men, all speaking the same language." Contrasted with Europe, America promised a "period when the people of one quarter of the world will be able to associate and converse together like children of the same family." . . .

The linguistic uniformity of America is geographic (without barriers of regional dialect) and social (without barriers of caste and class). Both types of uniformity have had vast consequence for the national life; they have been both symptoms and causes of a striving for national unity . . . Many other features of modern American culture—including the geographic mobility of the population, the public educational system, the mail-order catalogs, the networks of radio and television, the national mass-circulation magazines and "national advertising" (with all these have meant for the standard of living)—would have been more difficult in a nation of several languages. What would have happened to the Log-Cabin-to-the-White-House style of American politics if, as in England, a man who lacked the "proper" background betrayed himself in every word? Our common, classless language has provided the vernacular for equality in America.[126]

Free Time Options

We pause now for a Free Time break to meditate on the meaning and value of freedom of speech and of Liberty, Land, Language, and Literacy; Lyrics, Libraries, Letters, and Lyrics in our lives.

Jesus taught that every *jot and tittle*—the smallest letter, the least stroke of a pen—is important. Now it is your turn to jot down some thoughts about these subjects or to write a letter to share with someone else or with a group. I also suggest using your powers of literacy and language to share an encouraging, inspirational letter with another. Choose one or more of these options to fill and trim sails for our Last Briefing and today's Library Visit and Dedications.

Last Briefing: Lyrics, Libraries, Letters, and Lives
Lyrics

The Great Awakening of the 1700s was a heaven-sent revival to many parts of the world. In America, the preaching of George Whitefield and Jonathan Edwards renewed

---

126. Boorstin, *The Americans*, 271–272. Used by permission of the publisher.

Christian zeal and swept multitudes into the kingdom. In England, the open-air evangelism of Whitefield and the Wesley brothers did the same. In Wales, it was the electrifying preaching of Howell Harris and his convert, William Williams . . .

Williams is best remembered, however, for his hymns. Several stanzas of his hymn, "Guide Me, O Thou Great Jehovah," are seldom sung. One of the best reads:

> Musing on my habitation, musing on my heav'nly home;
> Fills my soul with holy longings: Come, my Jesus, quickly come.
> Vanity is all I see; Lord, I long to be with Thee.

When President James Garfield was dying of an assassin's bullet . . . his wife began singing this hymn, and the President, listening intently, began to cry. To his doctor, Willard Bliss, he said, "Glorious, Bliss, isn't it?"

The hymn was also sung at the funeral of England's Princess Diana.[127]

Passengers, please pray the timeless lyrics written in 1745:

Prayer Song
Guide Me, O Thou Great Jehovah

> Guide me, O Thou great Jehovah, Pilgrim through this barren land;
> I am weak, but Thou art mighty, Hold me with Thy pow'rful hand.
> Bread of heaven, Bread of heaven,
> Feed me till I want no more; Feed me till I want no more.

> Open now the crystal fountain, Whence the healing stream doth flow;
> Let the fire and cloudy pillar Lead me all my journey through.
> Strong Deliv'rer, strong Deliv'rer,
> Be Thou still my strength and shield; Be Thou still my strength and shield.

> When I tread the verge of Jordan, Bid my anxious fears subside;
> Death of death and Hell's destruction Lead me safe on Canaan's side
> Songs of praises, songs of praises,
> I will ever give to Thee; I will ever give to Thee. Amen.[128]

127. Morgan, *Then Sings My Soul*, 60–61.
128. William Williams and John Hughes.

More Lyrics

At the end of the eighteenth century, when John Adams was president, France and Britain were fighting and the American Congress was divided over supporting either nation. Another congressional battle began after Adams signed the Jay Treaty, which favored England. In 1798, Congress passed the Alien and Sedition Acts, allowing the president to banish anyone he personally felt did not meet the requirements for being a loyal American. These laws had the potential to make the nation a monarchy or dictatorship. Because of these laws and what they stood for, resentfulness and hatred were at an all-time high in the capital—until a "spontaneous musical moment in American political history":

> At a critical moment when it appeared that government "by the people and for the people" might not survive to see the 1800s, a Philadelphia singer, Gilbert Fox, and a young lawyer [and lyricist], Joseph Hopkinson, gave the country a musical peace offering. "Hail Columbia" united a divided nation and got two sides to talking about things that brought them together instead of tearing them apart. In the midst of a heated political war, Americans rediscovered a bit of this song's peace and unity. When they did, they forged ahead with a new vision of what America should and must be.[129]

Song
Hail Columbia

Hail! Columbia, happy land! Hail! Ye heroes, heaven-born band,
Who fought and bled in freedom's cause, And when the storm of war was gone,
Enjoyed the peace your valor won;

Let independence be your boast, Ever mindful what it cost,
Ever grateful for the prize, Let its altar reach the skies.

Firm, united let us be, Rallying round our liberty,
As a band of brothers joined, Peace and safety we shall find.

Immortal patriots, rise once more! Defend your rights, defend your shore;
Let no rude foe with impious hand, Invade the shrine where sacred lies
Of toil and blood the well-earned prize;

129. Collins, *Songs Sung Red, White, and Blue*, 103–104.

While offering peace, sincere and just, In heaven we place a manly trust,
That truth and justice will prevail, And every scheme of bondage fail.

Sound, sound the trump of fame! Let Washington's great name
Ring through the world with loud applause! Let every clime to freedom dear
Listen with a joyful ear;

With equal skill, with steady power, He governs in the fearful hour
Of horrid war, or guides with ease The happier time of honest peace.

Behold the chief, who now commands, Once more to serve his country stands,
The rock on which the storm will beat! But armed in virtue, firm and true,
His hopes are fixed on heaven and you.

When hope was sinking in dismay, When gloom obscured Columbia's day,
His steady mind, from changes free, Resolved on death or liberty.[130]

Letters and Lives

Many believe that the letters written by the Apostle Paul are the most inspiring literary masterpieces and challenging letters ever written. Choosing a favorite verse or passage that has touched my life is impossible; there are just too many! However, because this generation in history is growing up to make decisions that will affect life and liberty around the world for many generations, I have chosen to share Paul's letter to Titus: "Remind the people to be subject to rulers and authorities, to be obedient, to be ready to do whatever is good, to slander no one, to be peaceable and considerate, and to show true humility toward all."[131]

Two letter writers growing up during this generation were Abigail and John Adams. Their correspondence has survived as an example to touch our lives and fill sails as we visit the Cruise Library and head toward Dedications.

Abigail's letters to John during the Revolutionary War remind us that wives are on the front lines along with their husbands, fighting for just causes. In Abigail's case, John was one of five Massachusetts delegates to the Continental Congress.

Adams and his two companions arrived at Philadelphia on Thursday, February 8, 1776, fifteen days after leaving Braintree.

His first letters from Abigail did not reach him until more than a month later and were filled with accounts of thrilling

---

130. "Hail Columbia!" music is attributed to Philip Phylo, written in 1789 as an inaugural march for George Washington. The words were written nine years later by Joseph Hopkinson for a special occasion.
131. Titus 3:1–2.

events. The American bombardment of Boston had begun March 2 and 3. "No sleep for me tonight," she wrote, as the house trembled about her. On March 5 she described a more thunderous barrage: "the rattling of the windows, the jar of the house and the continuous roar of the 24-pounders."

The night before, working at great speed, Washington's men had moved the guns from Ticonderoga to commanding positions on the high Boston Harbor and the British fleet...

The British had been outwitted, humiliated. The greatest military power on earth had been forced to retreat by an army of amateurs; it was a heady realization . . .

That such had come to pass, wrote Abigail, was surely the work of the Lord and "marvelous in our eyes."[132]

A John Adams Letter

This letter from John Adams to Abigail about the Second Continental Congress delegates expresses his weariness and humor:

> This assembly is like no other that ever existed. Every man in it is a great man—an orator, a critic, a statesman, and therefore every man upon every question must show his oratory, his criticism, and his political abilities.
>
> The consequence of this is that business is drawn and spun out to immeasurable length. I believe if it was moved and seconded that we should come to a resolution that three and two make five, we should be entertained with logic and rhetoric, law, history, politics, and mathematics concerning the subject for two whole days, and then we should pass the resolution unanimously in the affirmative.[133]

As a consequence, we can no longer think that "spin" is merely a twentieth- and twenty-first-century contribution to literary entertainment and resolution making!

Cruise Library Visit
In his book *The Mayflower Pilgrims*, history professor David Beale does not spin Pilgrim history. He values and speaks truth.

---

132. McCullough, *John Adams*, 76–77.
133. Ibid.. 166.

One could create a fair-sized list of Pilgrim contributions, some originating in England, some in the Netherlands, many in the New England wilderness. Without categorizing or prioritizing, a general overview might include their stress upon character as a supreme requisite of true religion; their acceptance of civil marriages and private funerals; their simplicity in the administration of law and the enforcing of basic criminal codes; their measures designed to prevent "officialdom," such as electing officers for a term of no more than one year; their methods of recording deeds and mortgages, conveying land, probating wills, and recording births, marriages, and deaths by towns; their system of administering estates by permitting the inclusion of any children—male or female, not simply the oldest son; their emphasis on the laity, as an integral part of the church; their general practice of the autonomy and independence of the local church and freedom of religious worship, which led eventually to disestablishment, and often prompted observers of later generations to exclaim, "We are all Separatists now." But these things are not the real Pilgrim story. These are peripheral.

The real Pilgrim story is not one of governments and institutions. The Pilgrims never set out to build worldly enterprises. They did not write the Mayflower Compact for a national constitution or government. They wrote it as a measure for survival. The Pilgrim story is essentially a story of conviction and survival. It is a story of personal and ecclesiastical conviction, born in persecution, developed in exile, and based upon the Bible. It is a story illustrating the importance of sound doctrine. It is a story, not founded upon the tradition of Plymouth rock, but upon the truth of Providence. It is a story of faith, hope, charity, sacrifice, loyalty, and working together. America would be honored and blessed if those things alone were the Pilgrims' contributions. Their story reveals that Christianity is not perpetuated by the faith of the fathers; it is perpetuated by personal and present conviction, each individual and each local assembly finding the depth of biblical conviction and divine awareness which moved Pilgrim fathers and mothers to forsake all, for a cause whose purpose and reward looks beyond this present existence. It is a story of the believer's struggle against the world, the flesh, and the Devil. Its earthly conclusion is not with the "good guys winning." The Pilgrim story does not end on earth. Looking "not so much on these things," they saw with the eye of faith that there is a place where life is fair, and where every person will give an account for his own pilgrimage.[134]

American Library History

You already know that Elder William Brewster and Governor William Bradford brought their libraries, including Bibles, to America on the seventeenth-century *Mayflower*. The very presence of God's printed Word blessed Plymouth Colony.

Please join me in the twenty-first century to ask God to bless the *Full Sail* Cruise Library and your personal library, whether it is made up of this one book or a thousand others.

Library Blessing

O Lord, let the virtue of thy Holy Spirit descend on these books;
Let it purify, bless, and sanctify them -
Sweetly enlighten the hearts of those who read them;
Impart their true sense to them.

Grant us also to be faithful to the precepts emanating from Thy Light, in accomplishing them by good works, according to Thy Will.[135]

Today I quoted a book published at Harvard University, the first American university (est. 1631), which established the first American library when four hundred books were inherited from John Harvard, a Massachusetts minister. In 1731 in Philadelphia, Benjamin Franklin founded the first subscription library to make books available to everyone. Many early Americans collected personal libraries. The Library of Congress was established in 1800 as a legislative library. It purchased Thomas Jefferson's library in 1815, after the British burned the original collection during the War of 1812. Today, on its Web site, www.loc.gov, the Library of Congress modestly describes its mission as "to make its resources available and useful to the Congress and the American people and to sustain and preserve a universal collection of knowledge and creativity for future generations."[136]

America's free public school system led to a movement of free public libraries in the nineteenth century. About 1880, Scottish immigrant and then-rich

---

134. Beale, *The Mayflower Pilgrims*, 160–161.
135. "Library Blessing": Imprintur: Jeannes P. Cody, S.T.D., Episcopus Dioecesis Kansanopolitarae-Sainti Josephi, Conception Abbey Press (now known as The Printery House), Conception Abbey, Conception, Missouri.
136. Gingrich, *Rediscovering God in America*, 93.

man Andrew Carnegie began to give millions of dollars for the construction of free public libraries, eventually helping to build more than 2,500 libraries in the United States, Canada, and other countries.[137]

The first library building that I ever walked into was a "Carnegie Library." Heaven seemed to come down to earth that day, for I was a child introduced to a love of books by a school teacher and reading mother. Decades later, I still cherish books my parents purchased for me. Bill and I have a growing library, and our children and grandchildren are book readers and collectors.

Now, some libraries are offering digital books and digital audio books, useful even for people with ordinary equipment and nominal computer knowledge. Check it out!

Interesting Extra Reading About American Language

British English in America changed from the sixteenth century to form our unique "international" American language. Since my childhood in Minnesota, I have paid attention to the background and meaning of Native American words that are part of our English and geographical language. Jack Weatherford explains more about this in *Native Roots: How the Indians Enriched America*:

> No scholar of language writing in 1492 would have had reason to suspect that English might one day become an international language used throughout the world and spoken by far more people outside England than within it. The changes necessary to make this happen did not occur automatically. Before English could become an international language, it needed a tremendous expansion and revitalization that it never could have received in England. That change began in North America, where the provincial language of England was filled with new words, phrases, and concepts. The changes continued as English became the language of British colonial administration in India, Africa, and the South Pacific, but none of these other areas inspired the extensive changes brought about by the native languages of the Americas . . .
>
> When the language came to America, the Choctaw, Ojibwa, Cherokee, Muskogee, Seminole, and dozens of others added to the European tribal language of the Angles, Jutes, Saxons, Celts, Vikings, and Normans.

To end today's Library Visit, please join me in prayer.

---

137. *World Book Encyclopedia*, s.v. "Libraries."

Prayer

Almighty Master:

With praise for guidance and full-sail power, we ask you as the world's librarian to place *Full Sail* and other "jot and tittle" books in American and other libraries worldwide. Use the words to help us find and reflect the Pilgrim way, conscience, and cause again; to heal broken hearts and homes; to open eyes to see and claim heritages either forgotten or disregarded as myth and fantasy; to introduce and strengthen free-style life and liberty in many lands; and to replace books on shelves that are not blessed and intended for your glory and honor. —*Amen*

Covenant and Dedications

Today We the Passengers covenant:
To dedicate Liberty, Land, Language, and Literacy,
Lyrics, Libraries, Letters, and Lives
in America and all Nations to God's Glory and Honor.

Night Watch

Today's intent was to raise appreciation for the many important words in our language, history, and lives that begin with the letter "L." The main "L" words are, of course, the *Lord's Love Language*, to be found in God's Library for free-style Life and Liberty in the Land:

Do not seek revenge or bear a grudge against one of your people, but love your neighbor as yourself. I am the Lord. (Leviticus 19:18)

Scripture Course and Focus Points

Before retiring, rest assured and fill sails by spending more time in God's Library listening to *his* Love Language. Remember, the verses and passages below could be assigned for weekly discussions, perhaps with group members taking leadership turns. Also, today I encourage you to find focus points of your own in God's language in the Scripture.

Scripture: Exodus 20:4,12; Deuteronomy 6:4–8; Leviticus 25:10; Psalms 19:1–4, 14; Zephaniah 2:3–11; Matthew 22:37–38; Romans 12:9–21; 13:8–10; 1 Corinthians 13; 1 John 2–3.

We rest assured in Christ's Love as he ends this day.

End of Cruise Day Six

Cruise Day Seven Program
Wars, Veterans, and the Military

~~~~~~~~~~~~~~~~~~~

Scripture Course

Wake-Up Calls!

Seventh-Generation Introductions
Daniel T. Pierce and Mehitable Carver

First Briefing: The Ongoing Fight for Freedom

Free Time Options

Cruise Library Visit

Last Briefing: Twenty-First-Century Deployment
The Soldier's Creed

Cruise Bonus
Serving Our Country in Time of Need

Covenant and Dedications
Veterans and Active Military

Night Watch
Scripture Course and Focus Points

~~~~~~~~~~~~~~~~~~~

Scripture Course
Gird your sword upon your side, O mighty one; clothe yourself with splendor and majesty. In your majesty ride forth victoriously in behalf of truth, humility and righteousness; let your right hand display awesome deeds. Let your sharp arrows pierce the hearts of the king's enemies; let the nations fall beneath your feet.
Your throne, O God, will last for ever and ever; a scepter of justice will be the scepter of your kingdom.
Psalm 45:3–6

Scripture: 1 Samuel 17:47; 2 Chronicles 20:15; 32:8; Psalm 34:14; Isaiah 2:4; Ezekiel 13:5; Daniel 9:26–27; Micah 5:5; Matthew 5:9, 44; 24:6; John 16:33; Romans 7:23; 2 Corinthians 10:3–6; Ephesians 6:10–24; James 3:18; 1 Peter 2:11; Revelation 16:14, 19:11, 20:6, 21:4.

Wake-Up Calls!

The U.S. military has long made it safe for men and women to sail ahead in history.

The Military history of the United States spans a period of less than two and a half centuries . . . In 2005, the U.S. military consists of an army, navy, air force and marine corps under the command of the United States Department of Defense. The United States Coast Guard is controlled by the Department of Homeland Security. In each of these branches of military, the President of the United States is the commander in chief of the armed forces.

In addition, each state has a national guard commanded by the state's governor and coordinated by the National Guard Bureau. The President of the United States has the authority during national emergencies to assume control of individual state national guard units.[138]

The physical and emotional pain that combat veterans endure is something that cannot be measured. (Richard Van Regenmorter, *Because He Loves Me, There Is Life Beyond Trauma*)

To the Congress of the United States: "Yesterday, December 7, 1941—a date which will live in infamy—the United States of America was suddenly and deliberately attacked . . . " (President Franklin Delano Roosevelt, *Mayflower* descendant)

During the Second World War, nearly everyone in the United States was mobilized in one way or other . . . From collecting scrap metal to fighting on the front lines to gathering intelligence to working in factories, men, women, and children served in an enormous variety of capacities. There was a place for every kind of contribution on both the war front and

---

138. www.wikipedia.org.

the home front. In the spiritual war over eternal destinies of men and women, there is an even greater cause for mobilization and an even wider range of abilities needed. Christ has distributed gifts to every member of his body, and all of us are called to use them in obedience to his purpose on the front lines and in support of one another behind the lines.[139]

From Valley Forge to Vietnam, from Kuwait to Kandahar, from Berlin to Baghdad, our veterans have borne the costs of America's wars—and they have stood watch over America's peace. The American people are grateful to the veterans and all who have fought for our freedom. (President George W. Bush, November 11, 2006, Arlington National Cemetery Veterans Day Observance)

Seventh-Generation Introductions

Daniel T. Pierce I	b. 1742 or 1745
	d. 20 April 1812 Putnam Co. NY
	m. 1768
Mehitable Carver	b. 12 December 1753
	or 13 December 1751 Bridgewater, MA[140]
	d. 16 April 1837 Putnam County, NY

First Briefing: The Ongoing Fight for Freedom

Daniel and Mehitable Pierce were eighteenth-century Revolutionary War veterans. The war began on April 19, 1775. The Declaration of Independence was written in 1776; the war ended in 1783; our Constitution was written and ratified by the States in 1787 and 1788; the Bill of Rights was written by James Madison in 1787; and Francis Scott Key wrote our national anthem in 1814—all in Mehitable's lifetime!

God's power and involvement were expected and requested:

With no way of knowing the significance of the day he chose, Jonathan Trumbull, governor of the Connecticut Colony, chose April 19th, 1775 to be a day of prayer and fasting. The proclamation remains relevant as a 21st century request. That . . .

---

139. Kaiser, *Winning on Purpose*, 87.
140. The 1751 date is probably correct because, according to family historians, Mehitable's brother Timothy Carver, Jr. was born October 1753. My Mayflower Society lineage lists both dates.

"God would graciously pour out His Holy Spirit on us to bring us to a thorough Repentance and effectual Reformation that our iniquities may not be our ruin; that He would restore, preserve and secure the Liberties of this and all the other British American colonies, and make the Land a mountain of Holiness, and Habitation of Righteousness forever."[141]

To win and preserve liberty, many nations ask or order citizens to serve in the military. Only men served as state militia on the Revolutionary War front lines, and usually just in their own region. Now, American women also serve and sacrifice around the world. After wars, militia and military men and women are called "veterans."

Quite likely, you, as I do, have many deceased or living military and civilian veterans in your family and among your relationships. American veterans served in many wars, and the numbers are increasing as wars continue until the *end*, as prophesied by Christ and recorded in Matthew 24:6–7. Some Americans fought one another—as in the wars with Natives and in the Revolutionary and Civil Wars—and immigrants from former enemy nations are now American citizens and our neighbors.

Today's sails are set to express respect and appreciation for our veterans. We'll fill sails by saying prayers for both veterans and today's military, and for their families, whose front-line fight for freedom is ongoing, sacrificial, and sometimes terrifying. We who no longer safely reside at home—because terrorists purposely attack civilians—have more reasons than ever to spend serious time in prayer today, for America and for all nations.

Each of us for various reasons—related to war and peace—may need to tack, to come about for setting a new course before today's prayers and Dedications. If so, perhaps reviewing Ephesians 6:10–24 will help.

Prayers

O God our Father, by whose gracious Providence our forefathers won our
liberties of old, we give you thanks for all the men and women of our
country who in the day of decision ventured much to preserve those same
liberties which we now enjoy. More especially, we thank you for those who
served our country in the past wars to defend and protect our way of life.
Holy Father, we commend to your gracious care and keeping all of
the men and women of our armed forces presently serving at home
and abroad—on land, on sea, and in the air.
Defend them, we pray; give them courage to face the perils that beset them,
and let them each be strengthened by a sense of your presence in their lives.

---

141. Hall, *Christian History of the American Revolution*, 407.

We also ask you for strength and wisdom to overcome evil with good. We pray this in the name of our precious Saviour, Jesus the Christ.—*Amen*[142]

The National Day of Prayer Web site also calls us to pray and review war history:

> As American troops stormed the beaches of Normandy, President Franklin Roosevelt called for our nation to unite in prayer. He also offered a prayer to prepare each citizen for the road ahead. "Let our hearts be stout, to wait out the long travail, to bear sorrows that may come, to impart our courage unto our sons wheresoever they may be. And, O Lord, give us faith. Give us faith in Thee." The victory that followed on June 6, 1944—also known as D-Day—began the march to Berlin. Eighteen months later, WWII was over and one of the world's greatest evils had been defeated. The prayers of a nation had been a powerful force.
>
> Prayer has always been used in this country for guidance, protection and strength—even before we were a nation or a handful of colonies. The Pilgrims at Plymouth relied on prayer during their first and darkest winter. Our founding fathers also called for prayer during the Constitutional Congress. In their eyes, our recently created nation and freedoms were a direct gift from God. And being a gift from God, there was only one way to ensure protection—through prayer.
>
> President Abraham Lincoln knew this well. It was his belief that, "It is the duty of nations as well as men, to owe their dependence upon the overruling power of God." When it came to the fate of the nation, he practiced what he preached. Before the battle of Gettysburg, he turned to God in prayer. "I went to my room one day and I locked the door and got down on my knees before Almighty God and prayed to him mightily for victory at Gettysburg." Won by the Union, Gettysburg was one of the turning points in the war that ended slavery and kept the states united. Today the need for prayer is as great as ever. Our nation again faces battlefields, along with an epidemic of broken homes, violence, sexual immorality and social strife. As the heroes of our nation did in the past, we must again bow our heads in prayer. We must ask the Lord to bless our leaders with wisdom and protection, and that we will have the fortitude to

---

142. Rev. John H. Case, quoted in Teal and Folger, *Pilgrims at Prayer*, 40.

overcome the challenges at hand. If Roosevelt, the Pilgrims and Lincoln never underestimated the power of prayer, neither should we. [143]

The next prayer is from a 1942 American Army and Navy Hymnal. I changed "Army" to "military" in the third line.

> Lord of Hosts whose power is from everlasting to everlasting,
> and whose Name is above every name in heaven and earth:
> Keep, we pray Thee, under thy protecting care the [military]
> of our country and all who serve therein. Defend them amid violence
> on land or sea or in the heavens, and grant that they may be a sure defense
> and a safeguard for the people of the United States and a security
> for such as come and go in peaceful and lawful pursuit. In time of
> peace keep them from evil, and in the day of conflict suffer not
> their courage to fail: that they may guard the American heritage
> against those who would destroy or straiten the liberties of government
> by the people, and to the end that the blessings of religion and law
> may be preserved to posterity. Through Christ our Lord. —*Amen*[144]

Song

Power to tap into for today's Dedications can also be found by singing a favorite, and famous, American song, written during our Civil War. The third verse, usually not found in songbooks, was in the original version published in 1862 in the *Atlantic Monthly*.

Battle Hymn of the Republic
by Julia Ward Howe

> Mine eyes have seen the glory of the coming of the Lord;
> He is trampling out the vintage where the grapes of wrath are stored;
> He hath loosed the fateful lightning of his terrible swift sword:
> His truth is marching on. *Refrain.*
>
> I have seen him in the watch-fires of a hundred circling camps;
> They have builded him an altar in the evening dews and damps;
> I can read his righteous sentence by the dim and flaring lamps;
> His day is marching on. *Refrain.*

---

143. www.nationaldayofprayer.org: promotion for the May 2005, 54th annual National Day of Prayer.
144. Bennett, *Hymnal Army and Navy.*

I have read a fiery gospel, writ in burnished rows of steel:
"As ye deal with my contemners, so with you my grace shall deal;
Let the Hero, born of woman, crush the serpent with his heel,
Since God is marching on." *Refrain.*

He has sounded forth the trumpet that shall never call retreat;
He is sifting out the hearts of men before his judgment-seat;
Oh, be swift, my soul, to answer him! be jubilant, my feet!
Our God is marching on. *Refrain.*

In the beauty of the lilies Christ was born across the sea,
With a glory in his bosom that transfigures you and me:
As he died to make men holy, let us live[145] to make men free,
While God is marching on. *Refrain.*

Refrain: Glory! Glory! Hallelujah! Glory! Glory! Hallelujah!
Glory! Glory! Hallelujah! His truth is marching on!

Free Time Options

Wars will continue, then *end,* as Christ promised in Matthew 24:6: "You will hear of wars and rumors of wars, but see to it that you are not alarmed. Such things must happen, but the end is still to come."

Someday, on earth or in heaven or both, we will likely face former enemies. Certainly we will face people we do not agree with. To fill and trim sails, let's test ourselves.

★ Are my cultural, faith, and national traditions fighting on Christ's side?

★ Am I willing to enlist and wear Christ's armor to serve the Prince of Peace on his front line?

★ Am I willing to reconcile, repent, and love and pray for my enemies?

★ Am I willing to let God avenge evil and to overcome evil with good? (Guidelines are in Romans 12:17–21.)

★ Am I willing to add my peacemaking energy to fill sails and dedicate spiritual power to God's glory and honor?

Cruise Library Visit

Today, I recommend Korean War veteran Richard Van Regenmorter's book, *Because He Loves Me, There Is Life Beyond Trauma* in the Memoirs and Letters category in our Cruise Library.

---

145. *Die* was the original word in 1862.

Last Briefing: Twenty-First-Century Deployment

Following the tragic terrorist attacks in the United States on September 11, 2001, we sensed that the world would never again be the same. How can we be deployed to make a difference in this new world?

Involvement

With U.S. soldiers deployed throughout the globe defending our nation's freedoms, the Department of Defense launched the Defend America outreach program in the wake of 9/11 to offer Americans the most up-to-date information on the Global War on Terrorism and the successes of our heroic men and women in uniform. The civilian deployment program is described on the DoD Web site, www.defense.gov. By visiting the site, we can update our prayers.

Honor

Bill and I were touring Italy with friends and other tourists from the Allied countries on German Unification Day, October 3, 1990. Sensing patriotism on board, the French tour director and the bus driver detoured to the Florence American Cemetery and Memorial to honor 4,402 Americans who lost their lives during World War II—including many Japanese-Americans who fell fighting fascism.

Our friend, Tatsuo Suzuki, walked slowly by the white crosses and Stars of David until he found a friend's grave. The tears traveling down many cheeks whispered *thank you* for the sacrifice louder than words could have done, as Tats bowed his head and touched the cross-shaped headstone.

President Roosevelt also honored Tatsuo Suzuki and all who served in the 442nd within the 100th Battalion:

> No loyal citizen of the United States should be denied the democratic right to exercise the responsibilities of his citizenship, regardless of his ancestry. The principle on which this country was founded and by which it has always been governed is that Americanism is a matter of the mind and heart; Americanism is not, and never was, a matter of race or ancestry.[146]

As a World War I soldier, Bill's father, Harold C. Stroebel, walked across France to Verdun. For the remainder of his life, he wondered what war was all

---

146. President Franklin D. Roosevelt, February 1, 1943, upon activating the 442nd Regimental Combat Team. The 442nd was the Nisei—Japanese-American—Infantry Regiment.

about. But he and others served valiantly. After his death at age 86, we found this "Soldier's Creed" in a box he had filled with military memorabilia. Let's review the Creed to honor him and others who served during the war that President Woodrow Wilson expected "to end all wars":

Soldier's Creed

> In this victory for Democracy, and world wide fray, I've tried my best, to not betray;
> The honor of our nation's flag, and live the traits of which I brag;
> Of being an American, in mind and deed and serve my country in time of need.
>
> I've tried to be ready for honest toil, That would protect our nation's soil;
> I've kept in mind the debt I owe, To those who died that I might know,
> Our country prosperous and ever free, A heritage that was passed to me.
>
> I've always tried in trouble's hour To answer the call of our nation's power;
> To defend our country that we may live, In a land which always freedom give.
> I've tried to avoid the acts that scan, The pride and name American.
>
> I've done my best that we may be, A nation of freedom on land and sea;
> I'll always try to bravely stand To guard the glory of our land;
> I'll be an American in mind and deed: God grant me strength to keep this creed.

—A Soldier's Creed by E.C. Morris Pvt, Fourth Army Corps A.E.F.
American Expeditionary Forces 1917–1919
Third U.S. Army, Army of Occupation
Lieut. General Hunter Liggett, Commanding General
Brig. General Malin Craig, Chief of Staff

Cruise Bonus
Serving Our Country in Time of Need

Dwight D. Eisenhower is a twentieth-century American hero, the soldier whom President Franklin D. Roosevelt chose to lead the Allied forces to defeat Hitler. As with Ulysses S. Grant after the Civil War, "Ike" was elected after World War II to serve his nation as president. Still yearning for peace at the end of his presidency in 1961, this "old soldier" said the task belonged to "statesmanship to mold, to balance, and to integrate these and other forces, new and old, within the principles of our democratic system—ever aiming toward the supreme goals of our free society . . . In the councils of government, we must guard against the acquisition of unwarranted influence, whether sought or unsought, by the military-industrial complex."

Eisenhower's whole farewell speech can easily be found on the Internet. I pray that every statesman reading this logbook will heed the timeless warnings and fearless faith advancement in the speech of the thirty-fourth president of the United States.

To balance our thanks to veterans with such warnings, today's bonus begins with General Eisenhower's "D-Day Letter" and ends with President Eisenhower's prayer.

Soldiers, Sailors and Airmen of the Allied Expeditionary Force!

> You are about to embark upon the Great Crusade, toward which we have striven these many months. The eyes of the world are upon you. The hopes and prayers of liberty-loving people everywhere march with you. In company with our brave Allies and brothers-in-arms on other Fronts, you will bring about the destruction of the German war machine, the elimination of Nazi tyranny over the oppressed peoples of Europe, and security for ourselves in a free world.
>
> Your task will not be an easy one. Your enemy is well trained, well equipped and battle hardened. He will fight savagely.
>
> But this is the year 1944! Much has happened since the Nazi triumphs of 1940–41. The United Nations have inflicted upon the Germans great defeats, in open battle, man-to-man. Our air offensive has seriously reduced their strength in the air and their capacity to wage war on the ground. Our Home Fronts have given us an overwhelming superiority in weapons and munitions of war, and placed at our disposal great reserves of trained fighting men. The tide has turned! The free men of the world are marching together to Victory! (D-Day Letter, June 6, 1944)

President Eisenhower's Farewell Address to the Nation - Excerpt
January 17, 1961

So—in this my last good night to you as your President—
I thank you for the many opportunities you have given me for
public service in war and peace. I trust that in that service you
find some things worthy; as for the rest of it, I know you will
find ways to improve performance in the future.

You and I—my fellow citizens—need to be strong in
our faith that all nations, under God, will reach the goal of
peace with justice. May we be ever unswerving in devotion
to principle, confident but humble with power, diligent in
pursuit of the Nations' great goals.

To all the peoples of the world, I once more give expression to America's prayerful and continuing aspiration:

We pray that peoples of all faiths, all races, all nations,
may have their great human needs satisfied; that those now
denied opportunity shall come to enjoy it to the full; that all
who yearn for freedom may experience its spiritual blessings;
that those who have freedom will understand, also, its heavy
responsibilities; that all who are insensitive to the needs of
others will learn charity; that the scourges of poverty, disease
and ignorance will be made to disappear from the earth, and
that, in the goodness of time, all peoples will come to live together in a peace guaranteed by the binding force of mutual
respect and love. —*Amen*

Song

Wherever we are advancing Judeo-Christian faith, whatever battle we're
fighting or front line we're on to prepare the way of the Lord and bring glory to
him, God will take care of us.

God Will Take Care of You

Be not dismayed what e'er betide, God will take care of you;
Beneath His wings of love abide, God will take care of you.
Refrain
Through days of toil when your heart doth fail, God will take care of you;
When dangers fierce your path assail, God will take care of you.
Refrain

All you may need He will provide, God will take care of you;
Nothing you ask will be denied, God will take care of you.
Refrain

No matter what may be the test, God will take care of you;
Lean, weary one, upon His breast, God will take care of you.
Refrain

Refrain:
God will take care of you, Through every day, o'er all the way;
He will take care of you. God will take care of you.[147]

Covenant and Dedications

Today We the Passengers covenant:
To dedicate the Veterans and their Descendants,
Deployed Peacemakers, and the Military and their Families
of the United States of America and her Allies
to God's Glory And Honor.

Night Watch

Remember to take your time reading and searching for the focus points in these many passages, or divide them to share for filling sails until we meet again.

Scripture Course and Focus Points

Scripture: Joshua 1, 24; Psalms 24:8, 46:8–10; Joel 2; Zechariah 4:6, 9:10, 10:4–5; Matthew 10:34–36; Luke 6:27–35; Romans 12:20; 1 Corinthians 15:25–26; Ephesians 2:14–18; 1 Peter 5:8.

Focus Points: Courage, battles, do good, love, pray, peacemakers, feed, death, warriors, tactics, wall, hostility, rescue, trains, armor, power, devil, leadership, wrath, last enemy.

We rest assured in the Prince of Peace as he ends this day.

End of Cruise Day Seven

---

147. Lyrics by Civilla D. Martin, alt., 1904.

Cruise Day Eight Program
Matchmaking

Scripture Course

Wake-Up Calls!

Eighth-Generation Introductions
Timothy Pierce and Katie MacDonald

First Briefing: Matching Relatives, History, and the Bible

Free Time Options

Last Briefing: Matchmaking Blessings

Cruise Library Visit

Cruise Bonus
Guidelines for Establishing a Hearts for Israel Prayer
and Awareness Group

Covenant and Dedications
Covenants and Marriages

Night Watch
Scripture Course and Focus Points

Scripture Course
My heart is stirred by a noble theme as I recite my verses for the king;
my tongue is the pen of a skillful writer. You are the most excellent of men
and your lips have been anointed with grace, since God has blessed you forever.
Gird your sword upon your side,
O mighty one; clothe yourself with splendor and majesty.
Psalm 45:1–3. *A wedding song.*

Scripture: Genesis 1:27, 2:24; Ezekiel 36:23–26; Luke 22:20; John 17:20–23; Acts 9; Ephesians 5:29–33; Hebrews 13:4-5; Revelation 19:5–10, 22:20.

Wake-Up Calls!

I need the favor of that Being in whose hands we are, who led our fathers, as Israel of old, from their native land and planted them in a country flowing with all the necessaries and comforts of life; who has covered our infancy with His providence and our riper years with His wisdom and power, and to whose goodness I ask you to join in supplications with me that He will so enlighten the minds of your servants, guide their councils, and prosper their measures that whatsoever they do shall result in your good, and shall secure to you the peace, friendship, and approbation of all nations. (Thomas Jefferson, Third U.S. President, Second Inaugural Address, March 4, 1805)[148]

Be my wife according to the practice of Moses and Israel, and I will cherish, honor, support and maintain you in accordance with the custom of Jewish husbands who cherish, honor, support and maintain their wives faithfully.[149]

I hear a fish break the water's surface, and the Lord begins to share His passionate longing for His Body to "Arise." He ministers Isaiah 60 to my heart, and I start to journal. Take a look with me, and see yourself (YOUR name and YOUR face) in this scripture and my paraphrase . . .

"Arise, shine; For your light has come!" Isaiah 60:1 (NKJV)

Come on, My beautiful Bride! Wake up! Stir yourself from the sleepiness, the depression and frustration in which circumstances have bound you. Get up to a new day, a new life! Shake off the worldliness and procrastination which has captured you, and drugged you. You have been held back for too long from your full-bloomed loveliness, your undiminished strength, your all inclusive potential.

"And the glory of the Lord is risen upon you." Isaiah 60:1.[150]

---

148. Quoted in Weiss, *God in American History*, 58.
149. Beginning words of the Jewish marriage contract, the *ketubahm*. Quoted in "Marriage in the Time of Joseph and Mary," *The Chosen People Newsletter*, Dr. Mitch Glaser, Volume XIII, Issue 10, 12/07: 4.
150. Butel, *Overshadowed*, 19.

Eighth-Generation Introductions

Timothy R. Pierce   b. 8 February 1775 Dutchess County, NY
                              d. 30 April 1839   Putnam Co., NY
                              m. unknown

Katie MacDonald   b. Scotland
                              d. Pauling, NY after 1795

First Briefing: Matching Relatives, History, and the Bible

Today's sails are set to dedicate covenants and marriages to God's glory and honor—but not because Timothy and Katie's marriage was long or because I recommend Timothy's widower lifestyle. Katie died young, and their children, Daniel II and Mary, were raised by grandfather Daniel I, my seventh-generation ancestor. A Southern California history book containing Pierce biographies describes Daniel I: "The paternal great-grandfather is recalled with particular pride, because of his personal worthiness and his military services during the Revolutionary War."

If Timothy was paying attention, what an interesting time his was in which to live! During his lifetime, George Washington, John Adams, Thomas Jefferson, James Madison, James Monroe, John Quincy Adams, Andrew Jackson, and Martin Van Buren were presidents of the United States. America won the war with Britain, and Francis Scott Key wrote "The Star-Spangled Banner" during the War of 1812–1814. The Lewis and Clark Expedition was successful. Adams and Jefferson both died on July 4, 1825, exactly fifty years to the day after signing the Declaration of Independence.

Those are just a few of the important people and power-filled American events that matched with Timothy's lifetime. The first family records I found about Timothy said that he died without issue, or else he remarried and was never heard from again after moving to western New York. A family genealogist found the truth in a March 1828 court case record ordering Timothy to pay support for his children born out of wedlock, and in his will, dated April 27, 1839, in Putnam County, New York. Timothy left money and land to his later children; none to his and Katie's.

"Grandfather" Timothy expressed faith in God in his will. However—rather than support his widower's life-style to fill and trim sails for advancing Judeo-Christian faith today—we'll tap into God's standard and style for matchmaking and purity before, during, and after human marriage.

The released matchmaking energy for today's Dedications could save marriages and solve biblical mysteries. I really mean these bold statements, and I share them because I know that God advances faith through marriage. I speak from experience and through knowing Christ, God's Living Word, in a personal way.

For example, I know that way back in Israel's history, God told Hosea to take his adulterous wife Gomer back and love her. Hosea and Gomer's relationship mirrors the relationship God had—and still has—with his chosen people, Israel, and with Christ's bride, the Jewish and Gentile believing church.

Hosea was the first prophet to proclaim God's covenant by comparing it to the human covenant of marriage. Other prophets such as Jeremiah, Ezekiel, and Isaiah also used images of marriage and infidelity to describe God's covenant of grace and the sin of covenant breaking. In their writings, Israel's apostasy was often expressed in the language of divorce. But the final word through the prophets was always one of grace and eternal love, not abandonment.[151]

Dr. Moishe and Ceil Rosen, Jewish believers and the founders of Jews for Jesus, are excellent examples of the truth that God is still loving and wedding the church through Christ (see Ephesians 5:22–33). Today, the Rosens explain the divine marriage relationship and restoration plan:

> God put into motion the restoration of His relationship with man through His people, Israel. He proposed to Abram in Ur. He betrothed Himself to Israel at the Passover, and He married the nation at Sinai. But Israel was no stronger in spiritual resoluteness than the rest of humanity around her. At times she strayed and became an unfaithful wife to Jehovah. Despite this, He looks upon her with compassion and love and has promised to restore her once again, and with her, all other nations who are willing. Therefore, when the Messiah of Israel came as the Word made flesh, He proposed that loving relationship with God to all humanity. He betrothed Himself to those who would believe and accept Him at Calvary. The consummation of that marriage is yet to take place when He returns for His beloved, the Bride called out from among believing Jews and Gentiles.[152]

In other words, at Passover, Christ the Bridegroom offered his body for marriage. At Calvary, he gave his life as a payment for his bride. On Resurrection Day, he fulfilled Isaiah 52:13–15. He promised to build a house for his

---

151. Lowery, *Covenant Marriage*, 50.
152. Rosen and Rosen, *Christ in the Passover*, 100.

new-covenant bride, as recorded in John 14. He sent Paul to court the Gentiles (Acts 9, 26). In Romans 15:1–13, quoting Isaiah 11, Paul promoted unification and said that Gentiles would praise and glorify the Lord and hope in him and that the Root of Jesse would spring up to rule over the nations.

Christ established the new covenant during communion at his last Passover, also called the "Last Supper." His Jewish followers would have recognized the betrothal context when he lifted the third cup and said, "This cup [of salvation] is the new covenant in my blood, which is poured out for you" (Luke 22:20). Jewish bridegrooms-to-be offer a symbolic cup of wine representing provision, or redemption, when asking a father or family for permission to marry their daughter. You can think of Christ's redemptive betrothal act this way as well: Jesus spoke for his heavenly Father as the divine, heavenly Husband, saying the Bride should prepare herself for marriage. In this way he also revealed the Father to us in a new way.

I will explain God's rich matchmaking metaphor to fill and trim sails, and we will stay on course if you read Isaiah 62. Thank you! "As a bridegroom rejoices over his bride, so will your God rejoice over you."

After a Jewish betrothal, the bride prepares herself and her trousseau for marriage while waiting for her bridegroom to return. The bride must be properly clothed in pure faith and righteousness—the white linen garment trousseau as pictured in Revelation 19:8.

> The bride does not know when her groom will come; neither do we know when Christ our bridegroom will return to feast with his bride. Through the months of waiting, brides grow restless and impatient. Sound familiar? If not, begin to pray with me, "Come, Lord Jesus, come."[153]

As I indicated, Christ's bride is the united Jewish and Gentile church. Years ago, I thought unity like that would never happen. I was wrong! God pushed aside my doubts and united Bill and me with Jewish believers. We are Gentiles. We are not the only ones; the amazing, mysterious matchmaking between Jews and Gentiles is happening all over the world. Messianic Jewish believers in Jesus endorsed this *Full Sail* cruise and lead Disembarkation Prayers for Israel and other nations. Credible counters report that hundreds of thousands of Jewish people now believe Christ is the Messiah. God is softening Jewish hearts around the world, as promised in Ezekiel 36:24–26, before celebrating the marriage feast with the Bridegroom Jesus Christ. Each fulfilled promise surely deserves a star!

---

153. Revelation 22:20. In Hebrew, *Bo Adonai Yeshua Bo.*

★ I will take you out of the nations;
★ I will gather you from all the countries and bring you back into your own land.
★ I will sprinkle clean water on you, and you will be clean;
★ I will cleanse you from all your impurities and from all your idols.
★ I will give you a new heart and put a new spirit in you;
★ I will remove from you your heart of stone and give you a heart of flesh.

Why did I say earlier that our knowing about the Jewish marriage covenant would improve and save marriages? When I understood the symbolic and spiritual relationship between Christ and his people, I realized and respected the truth that Christ was loving me through my husband. We both became more accountable to live with Christ's presence and love in our lives and marriage. As Paul says in Ephesians 5:22–33, this is a profound mystery. I add that it is also a very passionate and spiritually romantic reality.

Today, in the twentieth-first century, there are many ways to fill sails by holding hands with each other and promoting the marriages of minds, hearts, and hopes. I hold hands across land and sea, via e-mail and telephone, with a U.S. military wife. Before praying with Christ for Jews and Gentiles, please wed your hearts with ours as you read Julie's award-winning, sail-filling poem:

Poem
The Grace of His Love

(Poetry Award presented to Julie R. Jones on April 28, 2009 by Turnbull Memorial Library, U.S. Army Garrison Post, Hohenfels, Germany)

Love's precious gift through His eyes.
Beautiful, magnificent.
God's perfect plan, for man.
From the dust of the ground.
Breathed life all around.
Living stones beautifully made.
With every color and shade.
Diamonds, Sapphires, Emeralds, and Rubies.
Weaved by His hands that will never fade.
Consumed with the wind of fire.
His heart so desperately desires.
You've never forgotten how valuable we are.
You named each one and placed every star.
Purest gold love with abundance of healing rain.

From heaven's sea of glass, clear as crystal grain.
God's grace touches the human vein.
Red Scarlet threads that forever remain.
Radiant hands of gold, hugs and true kisses.
God touches the hearts of many wishes.
Out of the belly flows living water.
A price He paid for all, by the Father.
God's most beloved Son.
Who came to die for everyone.
Wedding feast, life's eternal share.
You too can receive His loving arms of care.

Prayer

Almighty Master,
"My prayer is not for them alone. I pray also for those who
will believe in me through their message, that all of them may be one,
Father, just as you are in me and I am in you. May they also be in us so that
the world may believe that you have sent me. I have given them the
glory that you gave me, that they may be one as we are one:
I in them and you in me. May they be brought to complete unity to let
the world know that you sent me and have loved them even as you loved me"
(John 17:20–14).
God, we are available and ready for marriage. Unite what was
separated. Rejoice over us! —*Amen*

Song
The Church's One Foundation

The Church's one foundation Is Jesus Christ her lord,
She is His new creation By water and the word;
From heaven He came and sought her To be His holy bride;
With His own blood He bought her, And for her life He died.

Elect from every nation, Yet one o'er all the earth,
Her charter of salvation, One Lord, one faith, one birth;
One holy name she blesses, Partakes one holy food,
And to one hope she presses, With every grace endued.

'Mid toil and tribulation, And tumult of her war,
She waits the consummation Of peace for evermore;

Till with the vision glorious, Her longing eyes are blest
And the great Church victorious Shall be the Church at rest.
Yet she on earth hath union With God, the Three in One,
And mystic sweet communion With those whose rest is won;
O happy ones and holy! Lord, give us grace that we
Like them, the meek and lowly, On high may dwell with Thee.[154]

Free Time Options

Option for today's free time: reflect on God's love for us, as Jews, Gentiles, and individuals, and the reality that we are truly and already one with our Bridegroom, the Lord Jesus Christ.

If your heart is empty and open, consider this second option: ask his passionate love to come into your heart.

Last Briefing: Matchmaking Blessings

Our sails need trimming and filling, and the only way that comes to mind is to tell another personal story—this time about writing a "wedding" story.

My first writings, after writing for my college newspaper and penning letters for many years to friends and family, were short pieces for church newsletters. In 1987, after a journalism teacher challenged a friend and me to write about our faith, we self-published a holiday anthology written by us and our friends and family. I loved the challenge and the process of writing a book!

The publication, *In the Spirit of Christmas*, motivated me to enroll in writing classes. For an assignment in a class about writing for children, I developed a story about a boy and a girl and their families moving to Germany and living in the American military community, as my family had done.

Much to my surprise, after the class ended, I could not stop writing the story. I dreamed story, and I woke almost every morning knowing the day's writing assignment. Eventually, I realized that the coming-of-age boy and girl in the tale represented the church as the Bride and Christ as the Bridegroom at his second coming.

Then, my meetings with Jewish believers in Jesus were obviously Providential, confirming that Christ's bride was both Jewish and Gentile. Eventually, after our church missions team leader heard me talk enough about my heart for the Jewish people and Israel, she suggested that Bill and I start a group that would pray for and raise awareness about Jewish believers. So we did, in the year 2000.

Did I—do I—know enough to write about the Jewish and Gentile bride and her Bridegroom? Evidently not, because God continues to bring Jewish believers into my life. Now I can say without reservation that we live in an amazing time

---

154. Lyrics (1866) by Samuel J. Stone; music (1864) by Samuel S. Wesley.

on God's prophetic calendar. That is the personal story to explain why today's Cruise Bonus is a set of guidelines for establishing a "Hearts for Israel" group.

Where am I now with the bride and groom story? As you cruise with me, I am still dreaming and waking to write daily assignments. To prepare to understand the story, search the Bible for the word "cut," beginning with Matthew 25 and Romans 11, and you will learn that "cut" can mean separation from God, from fellowship with his sheep grazing on green pastures, from nourishment by the original olive tree root.

Cruise Library Visit

Every day is a *new day* for pilgrimage, but today is special because God is awakening his bride to understand that we are a match made in heaven. With *new* thinking for motivation, I did a *new* thing for me—I purchased on the Internet and downloaded an e-book to use as a Wake-Up Call and recommendation: *Overshadowed* by A. J. Butel. This Australian author, according to the promotion for the book, "looks at how the Holy Spirit is searching for those TODAY whom He can come upon, to envelop in His Glory, impart His supernatural influence, and advance His Kingdom purpose."

I also recommend Dr. Fred Lowery's book, *Covenant Marriage.* He writes, "The concept of covenant is the key to understanding all relationships—with God, our families, our friends, and especially our mates. God loves us by covenant. He provides for us by covenant. He blesses us by covenant. He operates in our lives by covenant. In reality, every truly valuable thing in life is ours because of covenant."[155]

While still in the library, to advance matchmaking and awaken the potential for God's overshadowing presence, power, passion, and protection—especially if you live in a metropolitan area—look in the phone book for a Messianic Jewish synagogue to worship with.

Here are a few more suggestions for awakening matchmaking power:

★ Attend a Messianic Passover *Seder*
★ Start a Hearts for Israel Group (see the guidelines in today's Cruise Bonus)
★ Jewish believers are now writing books that add matchmaking energy to our understanding. I recommend Dr. Bob Fischer's books and his DVD about Jewish roots (available in bookstores and at www.olimpublications.com), Edith Schaeffer's *Christianity is Jewish*, and books by Dr. Moshe and Ceil Rosen, David Brickner, Sam and Miriam Nadler, Joel Rosenberg, Sandra Teplinsky, Gerrie Mills, and Russell Resnik, among others listed in the Cruise Library.
★ If you are a Gentile married (or considering marriage) to a Jewish person, or to a Gentile if you are Jewish, view *Joined Together*, a DVD available on the Chosen People Ministries Web site. See the Library for more information.

155. Lowery, *Covenant Marriage*, 54.

Cruise Bonus
Guidelines for Establishing a Hearts for Israel Prayer
and Awareness Group

Sandra Teplinsky introduces today's bonus:

> Jews and engrafted Gentiles must serve one another in a reciprocal flow of life not only to survive, but to bear "fruit that will last" (John 15:16). To put it more practically, Messianic Jews represent today's original, once-broken-off but now re-grafted, branches. We need loving reciprocal relationships of integrity with Gentile Christians. Just as much, Gentile churches need relationship with Messianic congregations and ministries. To produce fruit pleasing to the Master, we must learn (if that is what it takes) to serve one another in humility, for our destinies in Him are inextricably intertwined as one body.[156]

Messianic Rabbi Russell Resnik, Executive Director of the Union of Messianic Jewish Congregations (www.umjc.org) presents guidelines for prayer, the primary Hearts for Israel calling.

Why, How, and When to Pray for Israel and the Jewish People

Despite the troubling and disappointing news that we often hear from Israel, the Lord is up to something there. How should we pray?

> *Pray for shalom in Yerushalayim; may those who love you prosper.*
> Psalm 122:6

1. Pray. Sha'alu in Hebrew means to seek or request. Our prayer is a matter of seeking God to do what he has promised. It also means seeking the good of Jerusalem, and Israel and the Jewish people.
2. Shalom. This is peace and more, not the absence of hostility, but the restoration of a right standing with God and with one's fellow man. It won't come to Israel through military or political efforts. These may be necessary at times, but God is after the heart of his people and the shalom that Yeshua brings comes to a changed heart.

---

156. Teplinsky, *Why Care About Israel?* 120.

3. Those who love you. Prayer support must reflect God's own love for his people. Some Christians have to repent of anti-Jewish attitudes and preconceptions, and of praying for Israel just because it fits into a theory of the end times. Yeshua went after the lost sheep because he valued them greatly—read the whole of Luke 15 in its context.

The High Holy Day season between Rosh ha Shannah and Yom Kippur is the time of year for spiritual awakening and renewal among the Jewish people.

Pray:

1. For a move of God's spirit among the Jewish community that would bring many to faith in Messiah.

2. For Messianic Jewish congregations to observe this season in the name and spirit of Yeshua, and to open their doors wide to Jewish visitors.

3. For us all to respond to the message of return to God and his ways that resounds throughout the High Holy Days.

Hearts for Israel History

The Hearts for Israel group was founded at a California church in 2000 by Jewish and Gentile believers in Jesus. The nondenominational group meets monthly and hosts annual events at churches or at a local Messianic synagogue. Offerings received are dispersed through the churches and synagogue to Messianic missionaries and humanitarian aid needs. Please feel free to use the following guidelines for establishing other groups.

Hearts for Israel Group Guidelines

★ Pray for Israel and all nations.
★ Pray for Jews and Gentiles.
★ Love, serve, and pray for the church—the body of Christ comprised of Jewish and Gentile believers in Yeshua the Messiah.
★ Pray for and reconcile with Messianic believers and synagogues.
★ Prayerfully read Scripture's promises to the Jews back to the Lord.
★ Serve as peacemakers and matchmakers between Jewish and Gentile congregations, ministries, and individuals.
★ Raise awareness about God's Messianic movement in the world today.
★ Pray for and raise support for worldwide Messianic Jewish missions and for humanitarian aid in Israel.

★ Host Messianic Jewish feasts.

★ Raise awareness that God keep his promises to the Jewish people.

★ Act as a tangible witness that Jews and Gentiles, praying, serving, reconciling, and worshiping together, are co-heirs in Christ.

Hearts for Israel Scriptural Foundation

I will make you into a great nation and I will bless you;
I will make your name great, and you will be a blessing.
I will bless those who bless you, and whoever curses you I will curse;
And all peoples on earth will be blessed through you.
(Genesis 12:2–3)

Pray for the peace of Jerusalem: May those who love you be secure.
May there be peace within your walls and security within your citadels.
For the sake of my brothers and friends, I will say, "Peace be within you."
(Psalm 122:6–9)

For the sake of the house of the Lord our God, I will seek your prosperity.
(Isaiah 62:1)

I am not ashamed of the gospel because it is the power of God for the salvation of everyone who believes; first for the Jew, then for the Gentile.
(Romans 1:16)

There will be glory, honor and peace for everyone who does good: first for the Jew, then for the Gentile. For God does not show favoritism.
(Romans 2:10–11)

There is a remnant chosen by grace.
(Romans 11:5)

Accept one another, then, just as Christ accepted you,
in order to bring praise to God.
(Romans 15:7)

For if the Gentiles have shared in the Jews' spiritual blessings, they owe it to the Jews to share with them their material blessings.
(Romans 15:27)

He has committed to us the message of reconciliation.
(2 Corinthians 5:19)

> This mystery is that through the gospel the Gentiles are heirs
> together with Israel, members together of one body, and sharers
> together in the promise in Christ Jesus.
> (Ephesians 3:6)

Hearts for Israel Doctrinal Beliefs

★ The Bible is the inspired, only infallible, authoritative Word of God.

★ God is one, and eternally existent in three persons, Father, Son, and Holy Spirit.

★ The Lord Jesus Christ [*Yeshua* in Hebrew] is the divine and promised Messiah.

★ All humans are sinners.

★ Yeshua willingly sacrificed his life for Jews and Gentiles.

★ The New Covenant body, the Church, is comprised of Jews and Gentiles who accept Yeshua's atoning sacrifice for sin.

★ Jews are physically descended from Abraham, Isaac, and Jacob.

★ Rather than losing it, Jews fulfill their Jewish identity when accepting Yeshua.

★ Gentiles are the peoples and nations not descended from Abraham, Isaac, and Jacob.

★ Israel was and is a sovereign nation created by God to be a light to all nations, and that light is the Lamb of God, the Messiah Yeshua.

★ We are one body reconciled to God through the cross.

★ Jews and Gentiles are to unite and accept one another, just as Yeshua accepted us, in order to bring praise and glory to God.

Hearts for Israel Questions

Q: How do we schedule or attend a Messianic Passover Seder or other festival?

BEV: Chosen People, Jews for Jesus, and Word of Messiah are Messianic ministries that schedule Passover Seder demonstrations. Messianic congregations or churches in your local area may also host Seders.

Q: How does HFI fit into the Messianic family?

BEV: Sam Nadler answers: "Hearts for Israel is committed to pray for Israel and for the Jewish people to come to know their Messiah. It is my prayer and desire that the Lord will move hearts among believing communities in every city to pray for and seek the salvation of Jewish people." (Sam Nadler, President, Word of Messiah Ministries; author listed in Cruise Library.)

Jews and engrafted Gentiles must serve one another in a reciprocal flow of life to survive and bear "fruit that will last" (John 15:16). We must serve one another for our destinies in Him are inextricably intertwined as one body. (Sandra Teplinsky, Light of Zion Messianic ministry leader, author of *Why Care About Israel?* and *Israel's Anointing*, www.lightofzion.org.)

Hearts for Israel Prayer

Yeshua ha Mashiach—Jesus the Messiah
We pray as one body
For you to reign on David's throne with power and majesty.
For the peace of Jerusalem. May they prosper who love you.
May peace be within your walls.
For Jews and Gentiles to reconcile and share your love and Word
with friends, family, neighbors, and nations.
For Jews and Gentiles suffering persecution around the world.
For Jews and Gentiles in all nations to repent and
humbly ask you to heal their lands.
For Jews and Gentiles in all nations to prepare
the Way of the Lord with praise in their hearts.
For you to prepare all nations and peoples to hear Jews in Jerusalem shouting,
Baruch Haba B'SHEM Adonai
Blessed is he who comes in the name of Adonai, the King of Israel.
The Spirit and the bride say, Bo Adonai Yeshua Bo
Come, Lord Jesus, come
Hesed Adonenu Yeshua ha Mashiach eemahchem
May the grace of the Lord Jesus Christ be with you
We dedicate Hearts for Israel Groups
to God's glory and honor. —*Amen*

Covenant and Dedications

Today We the Passengers covenant:
With our One God in a Marriage of Heart and Mind:
To Protect and Preserve Families and Marriages.
Give us Passion for Your Loving Ways, the Desire to Teach and
Obey Your Word,
and Invitations and Acts that Lead to Blessings and Praise.
We dedicate Covenants and Marriages in America
and in all Nations to God's Glory and Honor.

Night Watch

Scripture Course and Focus Points

Scripture: Psalm 19; Hosea; Mark 10:5–9; Romans 9–12; Ephesians 2:11–22; 3:1–13, 5:22–33; 1 Peter 3:1–7; Revelation 19:6–11; 21.

Focus Points: Marriages, creation, male and female, joined, adultery, love stories, wedding, respect, brides, bridegrooms.

We ask for full sails to rest assured
in Christ our Bridegroom.

End of Cruise Day Eight

Cruise Day Nine Program
Finding Our Niche on the Ninth

~~~~~~~~~~~~~~~~~~~~~~~

Scripture Course

Wake-Up Calls!

Ninth-Generation Introductions
Daniel Pierce II and Mary Reynolds

First Briefing: A Lifetime of Change

Free Time Options

Last Briefing: Chap and Coop Comment on Change

Cruise Library Visit

Cruise Bonus
Finding Your Volunteer Niche

Covenant and Dedications
Industry and Volunteerism

Night Watch
Scripture Course and Focus Points

~~~~~~~~~~~~~~~~~~~~~~~

Scripture Course
May your deeds be shown to your servants, your splendor to their children.
May the favor of the Lord our God rest upon us; establish the work of our hands
for us—yes, establish the work of our hands.
Psalm 90:16–17
Scripture: Leviticus 25:35; Psalm 72:12–13; Ecclesiastes 4:9–12; Matthew
6:19–24; Acts 20:32–35; 1 Corinthians 3:8–9; James 1:27, 2:26; 3:17–18,
4:17.

Wake-Up Calls!

The Louisiana Purchase that cost about $15 M was arranged in 1803 during Thomas Jefferson's first administration. Borders were established with Canada and Spain in 1818 and '19. Florida was gained and Texas surrendered during a 1819 treaty with Spain. The purchase and border treaties increased the economic resources of the United States, and cemented the union of the Middle West and the East. Eventually all or parts of 15 states were formed out of the region.[157]

"The President in Washington sends word that he wishes to buy our land. But how can you buy or sell the sky? the land? The idea is strange to us. If we do not own the freshness of the air and the sparkle of the water, how can you buy them?" (Chief Seattle)[158]

According to an AP report, a study by the Corporation for National and Community Service shows a rise in volunteering, putting participation at a 30-year high. The research found that more than 1 in 4 adults—or 27 percent—currently volunteer their time for their communities, an increase from 20.4 percent in 1989.

One of the most exciting aspects of the study was the evident rise in young people volunteering. Sixteen to nineteen-year-old teens averaged the biggest increase with 28.4 percent participating, compared to a low of only 13.4 percent in 1989. (*Christian Breaking News*, December 6, 2006)

Nonprofits offer help and hope, a way for someone who is personally hurting to reach out to help others and, in the process, ease that pain. With individual acts comes the opportunity, nay the obligation, for us all to push beyond our comfort zone . . . The collective focus becomes something unstoppable, a shared responsibility to make sure that our community not only survives challenging times, but emerges on the other side ready to thrive. (Jane Hagedorn)[159]

---

157. *World Book Encyclopedia*, s.v. "Louisiana Purchase."
158. www.barefootsworld.net/seattle.html. Chief Seattle surrendered his tribal lands in the 1800s.
159. CEO of Breathe California of Sacramento-Emigrant Trails for more than thirty years, Hagedorn has served in board leadership roles with numerous organizations.

Ninth-Generation Introductions

Daniel Pierce II	b. 1795/6	Dutchess Co, NY
	d. 1874	Walton, NY
	m. 1821	Dutchess County
Mary Reynolds	b. 1796 or 1800	Dutchess County NY
	d. 1840	Meredith, NY

First Briefing: A Lifetime of Change

Daniel II was raised as a farmer by his grandfather and namesake, Daniel I. He worked hard, saved his money, and purchased a farm in Andes, Delaware County, New York. He and Mary had eight children. Mary died in 1840, so stepmother Elizabeth Lockwood most likely raised the youngest, my great-grandfather Marcus Pierce, who was born in 1838.

As America purchased land from other colonial nations or took over Native land, Daniel's generation and their children moved west. Daniel and Mary moved from Dutchess to Delaware County. Marcus migrated from New York to Minnesota in the nineteenth century. Some of his siblings and cousins moved from New York to California. Bill and I moved from Minnesota to California in the twentieth century, seeking employment and a place to live as in previous family migrations.

Today, we will dedicate American industry and volunteerism to God's honor and glory. I chose industry as the first topic for this generation because it was during Daniel II's lifetime that my family began to move away from their New England colonial roots and America, as a nation and agricultural economy, headed into the Industrial Revolution.

Back in the seventeenth century, ten Pilgrims were America's first well-known volunteers. Myles Standish, John Carver, William Bradford, Edward Winslow, John Tilley, Edward Tilley, John Howland, Richard Warren, Stephen Hopkins, and Edward Dotey left the *Mayflower*, setting out in a shallop to find a place to settle. Now volunteerism is often called America's way to express her heart and soul.

In this generation in my family history, Daniel II was raised by a volunteer father, his grandfather, who was also a Revolutionary War volunteer. Several of Daniel II's sons, including Marcus, were Civil War volunteers. Moving ahead and to advance Christian and civil history, many Pierces were and are church and community volunteers. My daughter Carrie Grip's Master's Degree thesis topics were non-profit organizations and volunteerism. She is the executive director with the nonprofit Rebuilding Together in northern California. Friends and members of our church volunteer with Rebuilding Together. A Pierce cousin and his family volunteer around the world. A close friend is a

United Way executive director. A couple we know well and their family have volunteered as church musicians for decades. Other friends are Gideon volunteers. A Jewish friend volunteers by leading Shabbat (Sabbath) worship services at a U.S. veteran's home.

Powerful and meaningful American history was made during Daniel II's lifetime and in the nineteenth-century decades that followed, which today is power for progressing with full sails. In 1808, slave importation from Africa ended. In 1825, the Erie Canal opened, leading to New York City's financial magnitude. Abraham Lincoln was elected to serve as an Assemblyman in the Illinois legislature in 1834; he was elected sixteenth U.S. president in 1860. Lincoln signed the Emancipation Proclamation on January 1, 1863, and was assassinated on April 14, 1866. The first telegraph line was strung by Samuel F. B. Morse from Baltimore to Washington, D.C., in 1844; the first transatlantic telegraph cable was laid in 1866.

In 1870, "The main trends of the Industrial Revolution were clearly marked."

> Industry advanced faster than agriculture. Goods were made by power-driven machinery, and were assembled in factories where management planned operations and the workers were little more than tenders of machines. Capital controlled industrial production, but labor was being allowed to organize to fight for higher wages, shorter hours, and better working conditions. The railroad, the improved sailing ship, the steamship, and the telegraph had reduced the cost and time factors in transportation and communication. Living standards of the masses in industrial countries were higher than they had ever been. Populations, growing at a high rate, were denser than ever before.[160]

Prayer

> We think it is incumbent upon this people to humble themselves before God on account of their sins—[And] also to implore the Divine Blessing upon us, that with the assistance of His grace, we may be enabled to reform whatever is amiss among us, that so God may be pleased to continue to us the blessings we enjoy. Amen. (John Hancock, American Revolutionist, first signer of the Declaration of Independence)[161]

---

160. *World Book Encyclopedia*, s.v. "Industrial Revolution."
161. Quoted in Harrison House, *Pray for Our Nation*, 67.

Free Time Options

To progress under full sail during this relaxing and optional time, volunteer your heart, mind, body, and soul to Christ. Then record the date in your journal and/or tell someone about your action.

You might also try these options:

List and discuss changes in the world during your lifetime.

List and pray about changes you would like to see made during your lifetime.

Begin a search for your volunteer niche.

Last Briefing: Chap and Coop Comment on Change

Just as American culture changed dramatically before and during the Industrial Revolution, lives on board this cruise have also been changing. Let's listen to Chap and Coop comment on the changes.

CHAP. Coop, you look puzzled. What's on your mind?

COOP. The Passengers are changing. Passengers who carried heavy baggage on board are lighthearted and happy. Very private Passengers are making friends. People wearing sad faces when they boarded are smiling. High snooty attitudes are now down to earth. The rich are serving the poor. The sea is smoother than yesterday. What is going on?

CHAP. Can you hear the Passengers reading Scripture and singing?

COOP. Yes.

CHAP. Then listen closely; the words will answer your question.

PASSENGER. "'What must I do to inherit eternal life?' Jesus answered, 'No one is good—except God alone. You know the commandments: 'Do not murder, do not commit adultery, do not steal, do not give false testimony, do not defraud, honor your father and mother'" (Mark 10:17–19).

PASSENGER. "Do not store up for yourselves treasures on earth, where moth and rust destroy, and where thieves break in and steal. But store up for yourselves treasures in heaven, where moth and rust do not destroy, and where thieves do not break in and steal. For where your treasure is, there your heart will be also" (Matthew 6:19–20).

PASSENGER. "The word is near you; it is in your mouth and in your heart, that is, the word of faith we are proclaiming: That if you confess with your mouth, 'Jesus is Lord,' and believe in your heart that God raised him from the dead, you will be saved. For it is with your heart that you believe and are justified, and it is with your mouth that you confess and are saved. As the Scripture says, everyone who calls on the name of the Lord will be saved" (Romans 10:8–13).

COOP. Now I understand why I have such a long list of sins to hurl into the sea!

CHAP. Why are you keeping a confession list?

COOP. Just doing my baggage control job! Most sins were confessed by many. These are the sins that caused high waves and rocked the boat the most: racism, discrimination, prejudice, injustice, abuse, adultery, lust, lie-telling, stretching the truth, vanity, anger, revenge, complacency, insensitivity, pessimism, doubt, laziness, pride, unfaithfulness, jealousy, stinginess, mean temper and tongue, disbelief, giving in to addictions, arrogance, stealing, rudeness, critical nature, greed, snobbery, hate, meanness, ridicule, slander, gossip, greed, selfishness . . .

CHAP. Throw the list overboard!

COOP. Why?

CHAP. Listen to the hymn the Passengers are singing, and you will know why.

Song
And Can It Be That I Should Gain?

And can it be that I should gain An interest in the Savior's blood?
Died He for me, who caused His pain? For me, who Him to death pursued?
Amazing love! How can it be That Thou, my God, shouldst die for me?

He left His Father's throne above, So free, so infinite His grace!
Emptied Himself of all but love, And bled for Adam's helpless race!
'Tis mercy all, immense and free, For, O my God, it found out me.

Long my imprisoned spirit lay Fast bound in sin and nature's night.
Thine eye diffused a quickening ray; I woke— the dungeon flamed with light!
My chains fell off, my heart was free. I rose, went forth, and followed Thee.

No condemnation now I dread: Jesus, and all in Him, is mine?
Alive in Him, my living Head, And clothed in righteousness divine,
Bold I approach the eternal throne, And claim the crown, through Christ
my own.[162]

COOP. They are free! No heavy chains. Their sins are washed away. With their baggage hurled into the sea, the ship is safer on the waves, and our sails are filled!

CHAP. Right! Free-style Christians don't need your list, or any list of sins made by anyone else, to save their souls.

COOP. I've made another list. I suspect you won't tell me to throw it into the sea.

CHAP. Try me.

COOP. It's a list of volunteer, charity, and missions organizations that Passengers serve with or support.

CHAP. You're right again. Now, I suggest you post the list in the Cruise Library for free-style Passengers looking for organizations and individuals to support.

COOP. Speaking of free-style Passengers, here comes the Host. She's wearing her prayer face.

CHAP. What's a prayer face look like?

COOP. Spacey, like she's off in another world . . .

HOST. I heard that, Coop, and I confess that sometimes I look and act holier than thou. Please forgive me. Let's pray.

Prayer

Almighty Master,
Forgive personal and national sins such as ego and snootiness.
Thank you for ways to sincerely love and serve one another through
industry and volunteerism. With Christ at the helm, use the changes
in us for your honor and glory. —*Amen*

---

162. Words: Charles Wesley (1738/39), Lyrics: Thomas Campbell (1825/35).

Cruise Library Visit

Check out other libraries for books about the westward migration of American settlers and the Industrial Revolution that Daniel II's generation and century paved the way for. In the Cruise Library, William Bennett, page 423, in *America The Last Best Hope*, Volume I, and using statistics from *Time Almanac, 2004*, explains the changes that occurred during and after the Civil War in the 1860's:

> In material terms, America's wealth and power would have astonished even such visionaries as Franklin and Jefferson. Everywhere, sail gave way to steam. Canal building—which had so strongly appealed to future-oriented leaders like Washington—was rapidly eclipsed by railroad construction. Americans followed up the Golden Spike of the Transcontinental Railroad with a rush of tributary lines to bind the country together with rails of steel. Immigrants flocked to the country. Even with 540,000 deaths in the Civil War, America in the 1860s showed a robust *26 percent increase* in population. The population in 1860 was 31,443,321, one-seventh of whom were slaves and 13 percent of whom were immigrants. By 1870, with slavery abolished, the U.S. population was 39,818,449. Immigrants accounted for 14.2 percent of these.
>
> For all the criticisms of a materialistic age, the material changes in American life were stunning. Civil War veterans said that it seemed they had grown up in a different *country* than the one to which they returned from the battlefield...
>
> Breakthroughs in agriculture and industry made it possible to feed more people than at any time in history. America became an important *exporter* of foodstuffs throughout the world. Refrigeration and canning created a continental market for meats and vegetables. Most Americans wanted a greater share of the material abundance that freedom made possible.

Song
Joy to the World!

Joy to the world! The Lord is come:
Let earth receive her King; Let every heart prepare Him room,
And heaven and nature sing, And heaven and nature sing,
And heaven and nature sing.
Joy to the world! The Savior reigns
Let men their songs employ; While fields and floods, rocks, hills, and plains

Repeat the sounding joy, Repeat the sounding joy, repeat the sounding joy.
No more let sins and sorrows grow, Nor thorns infest the ground;
He comes to make His blessings flow Far as the curse is found,
Far as the curse is found, Far as, far as the curse is found.

He rules the world with truth and grace, And makes the nations prove
The glories of His righteousness, And wonders of His love,
And wonders of His love, And wonders, wonders of His love. Amen.[163]

Cruise Bonus
Finding Your Volunteer Niche

Volunteering is *philanthropy* in the sense of giving time, energy, and funds from God's investment in each of us. He has a storehouse filled with treasures ready to disperse that were prepared for blessing. According to Malachi 3:8–12, our responsibility is to tithe from the investment.

The amount we return to his storehouse is of little concern to God. The poor widow who gave all she had to live on, recorded in Luke 21:1–4, made volunteer philanthropic history. Matthew 6:19–24 says we "cannot serve both God and Money." The Web site www.dictionary.reference.com defines philanthropy:

> 1. altruistic concern for human welfare and advancement, usually manifested by donations of money, property, or work to needy persons, by endowment of institutions of learning and hospitals, and by generosity to other socially useful purposes.
> 2. the activity of donating to such persons or purposes in this way: to devote one's later years to philanthropy.
> 3. a particular act, form, or instance of this activity: The art museum was their favorite philanthropy.
> 4. a philanthropic organization.

These organizations are among thousands of niche examples and opportunities for volunteering time, energy, and funds:

Rebuilding Together

Across the country, two hundred Rebuilding Together affiliates provide a variety of home improvement services. The annual National Rebuilding Day, where thousands of volunteers across the country join together in the old-

---

163. Lyrics (1719) by Isaac Watts, based on Psalm 98; music partially by George Friedrich Handel.

fashioned barn-raising tradition of neighbor helping neighbor, occurs on the last Saturday in April.

Affiliates may offer other services. Sacramento's staff and Safe at Home volunteers install safety devices, such as wheelchair ramps and bathroom grab bars, to increase the homeowner's mobility and independence. Some affiliates also hold Fall rebuilding days. Energy efficiency, home maintenance workshops, year-round repairs, and home modifications for veterans are services offered at various affiliates throughout the country.

Powerhouse Ministries

Established for the underprivileged in a California community, the Powerhouse staff and volunteers refresh lives and rejuvenate spirits. The services provided by this faith-based ministry are food and clothing closets, youth and children's ministries, community referrals, resources, assistance for people needing help such as rental assistance, and prayer and personal support. www.powerhouse-ministries.org

NGO Global Resource Services (GRS)

GRS works inside the country helping with food distribution, agriculture, children and families. http://mail.grsworld.org

Heifer Project International

HPI is a non-profit organization whose goal is to help end world hunger and poverty through self-reliance and sustainability. www.heifer.org

Senior Gleaners

This California non-profit alleviates hunger among the poor and elderly by gleaning surplus foods, at low or no cost, from every available source, for distribution among the 501(c)(3) qualified charitable organizations. www.seniorgleaners.org

Compassion International

This niche is an opportunity to share your love, prayers, and support with a boy or girl who lives in poverty. Children are waiting now. www.compassion.com

For more waiting opportunities, type "volunteer organizations" into your search engine and find niches abroad, for high schoolers and teens, cross-cultural work, disaster response, and many other ways to tithe and fulfill our duty to the world and our nation.

Ultimately, only God will know if *Full Sail* is philanthropically profitable—by We the Passengers giving money, volunteering time, and agreeing to dedicate industry and volunteerism to God's glory and honor.

Covenant and Dedications

Today We the Passengers covenant:
To dedicate Industry and Volunteerism in America
and all Nations to God's Glory and Honor.

Night Watch

Fellow Pilgrims on this journey through life and liberty, if we give a penny or more than most—spiritually or materially—God will bless: "As the rain and snow come down from heaven, and do not return to it, without watering the earth and making it bud and flourish, so that it yields seed for the sower and bread for the eater, so is my word that goes out from my mouth: It will not return to me empty, but will accomplish what I desire and achieve the purpose for which I sent it" (Isaiah 55:10–11).

As this day ends, we can rest assured by reading Scriptures and their matching Focus Points to stay on course and sustain sailing power until we meet for another Cruise Day.

Scripture Course and Focus Points

Scripture: Psalms 37:3–11, 92:12–14, 112; Proverbs 18:9, 22:6, 29; 28:19; Matthew 7:1–2; 1 Corinthians 2; Hebrews 10:26–39, 12; James 5:16.

Focus Points: Causes, justice, compassion, power, work, serve, sincere love, prophesy, power, prosperity, goodness, knowledge, self-control, perseverance, kindness, watchfulness.

End of Cruise Day Nine

Cruise Day Ten Program
Health, Healing, and Hope

Scripture Course

Wake-Up Calls!

Tenth-Generation Introductions
Marcus Pierce and Adelaide Cramer

First Briefing: Practicing Medicine

Free Time Options

Last Briefing: Personal Cases

Cruise Library Visit

Cruise Bonus
"Coming Alongside" Prayer Card and Prayer for Practicing Medicine

Covenant and Dedications
Medicine, Caregiving, and Recreation

Night Watch
Scripture Course and Focus Points

Scripture Course
Praise the Lord, O my soul; all my inmost being, praise his holy name.
Praise the Lord, O my soul, and forget not all his benefits—who forgives all
your sins and heals all your diseases, who redeems your life from the pit and
crowns you with love and compassion, who satisfies your desires with
good things so that your youth is renewed like the eagle's.
Psalm 103:1–5

Scripture: Deuteronomy 30:11–20; Psalm 139, 147; Proverbs 15:13; 2 Corinthians 12:7–10; James 5:13–16; Revelation 21.

Wake-Up Calls!

We hold these truths to be self-evident, that all men are created equal; that they are endowed by their Creator with certain inalienable rights; that among these are life, liberty, and the pursuit of happiness. (The Declaration of Independence)

Religion my Friend does not forbid us to weep and to mourn for our departed friends. But it teaches us to cast our Sorrows upon that Being in whose hands and at whose disposal we are and who can heal the wounded bosom and bind up the broken heart. (Abigail Adams to —, January 19, 1811)[164]

This life is not forever, nor is it the best life that will ever be. The fact is that believers are headed for heaven. It is reality. And what we do here on earth has a direct bearing on how we will live there. Heaven may be as near as next year, or next week; so it makes good sense to spend some time here on earth thinking candid thoughts about that marvelous future reserved for us. (Joni Eareckson Tada)[165]

Robert Frost (1874–1963), one of America's most esteemed poets, underlined the country's fascination with sports when he said, "Nothing flatters me more than to have it assumed that I could write prose—unless it be to have it assumed that I once pitched a baseball with distinction." Whether poet or politician, carpenter or cardiologist, Americans from all walks of life share an abiding interest in athletic games and contests.[166]

Louise Ann was four when she died. We dressed our little girl in a play dress and laid her to rest in a little white casket. Sulfa, available just a few years after she died in 1928, might have saved her life. (Rose Stroebel)

---

164. Quoted in Hutson, *The Founders On Religion*, 111.
165. Tada, *Heaven Your Real Home*, 15.
166. From *Sports in America*, an electronic journal of the U.S. Department of State, Volume 8, Number 2, December 2003.

Promote spiritual, physical, and emotional health and wellness through education programs and support groups. (A Church Health Ministry Mission Statement)

During the Civil War, The New York 144th Regiment lost during service 2 Officers and 37 Enlisted men killed and mortally wounded and 4 Officers and 174 Enlisted men by disease. Total 217.[167]

Graduating from undergraduate and medical schools, helping patients heal, Shirley and I raising a family, and keeping my legs strong for climbing all the major mountains in the Northwest USA seemed like utmost accomplishments for life—until while going through cancer treatments, I learned what the Lord required of me in Psalm 147:10–11: "His pleasure is not in the strength in the horse, nor his delight in the legs of a man; the Lord delights in those who fear him, who put their hope in his unfailing love." (Gordon L. Pierce, M.D., 1929–1953)

Tenth-Generation Introductions

Marcus P. Pierce   b. May 11, 1839   Delaware County, NY
                                 d. April 22, 1892   Blue Earth County, MN
                                 m. May 18, 1865   Delaware County, NY

Adelaide Cramer   b. September 4, 1845   Delaware County, NY
                                 d. September 18, 1917   Blue Earth County, MN

First Briefing: Practicing Medicine

Life and death are real to children growing up on farms. Animals are born and die; crops are planted, mature, and die; seasons begin and end. The country school that my brother Gordon and I attended was located across a county road from the community's cemetery. We watched grave digging and burial services during class recesses, and we could see our grandparents' graves through school windows.

Because we tended graves and observed Memorial Day with our family and community, decades later I can still go directly to our and our classmates' grandparents' and parent's graves, and some siblings' too.

Several aunts and uncles rest in the same cemetery. My great-grandparents, Marcus and Adelaide Pierce, rest in a cemetery nearby. Born and married in

---

167. www.itd.nps.gov/cwss. National Park Service Web site.

New York State, they moved their family to Minnesota in the 1890s. The reasons for the move are only supposed—perhaps they went because Minnesota land was available, or perhaps it was because Marcus had tuberculosis and they were looking for a different climate. They lived in Mankato, Minnesota, for a while before purchasing farmland.

Marcus's lung disease, contracted while serving with the New York 144th Regiment during the Civil War, is the reason we are focusing on medicine during his generation. I have combined medicine with caregiving and recreation dedications today because Marcus's great-grandson—my brother Gordon, who was a licensed medical physician—hiked, ran, biked, and climbed mountains to stay healthy. Sadly, multiple myeloma caused his death of cancer at age fifty-three, a death that was painfully slow because his heart and lungs were healthy.

Even though Gordon found peace, love, and hope in Psalm 147, I grieved deeply until facing my own mortality and relating to the words of Ecclesiastes 3:11: "God has set eternity in the hearts of men; yet they cannot fathom what God has done from beginning to end."

Therefore I can say with peace, please do not think about skipping or denying this day! God told Adam and Eve that they would die and return to dust, and so deterioration, disease, and death are unavoidable—like seasons, our bodies are terminal from birth to death. The saddest part is watching a child die. Bill's parents, Rose and Harold C. Stroebel, grieved for Louise Ann all their lives.

Be assured, though—I am not sounding a morbid alarm to warn that we are sinking down to a watery grave on this Tenth Cruise Day! Just the opposite. Our sails are set for tacking and coming about into the wind for filling to review medicine and recreation in history; in the twenty-first century, to consider ways to practice medicine for staying alive, well, happy, and active—spiritually, physically, and emotionally; and to prepare for heaven's eternity as faith and facts advance.

Practicing Medicine on the *Mayflower*

Records reveal that Dr. Samuel Fuller was the only known medical doctor on board the *Mayflower* in the seventeenth century. Possibly, William Brewster, Stephen Hopkins, and Dr. Fuller's apprentice William Butten were trained in some medical arts and qualified to treat various illnesses or injuries. Wives and mothers on board were most certainly familiar with home remedies.[168]

But even with practitioners on board, before leaving the ship on March 21, 1621, several passengers and crew members were ill with a contagious mix

---

168. Duane A. Cline, "Medical Arts on the Mayflower," 2000, www.rootsweb.ancestry.com.

of scurvy, pneumonia, and tuberculosis. Only fifty-three survived. The victims included two of my ancestors, Mary Chilton's parents.

Although progress to control and cure has been made, these three diseases are still threatening and claiming lives. For example, "Scurvy is a disease that accompanies malnutrition, and is alive and well in people who eat just junk food."[169]

Moving Ahead in Medicine and Recreation

Several historic organizations fill today's sails, beginning with the Young Men's Christian Association (YMCA), founded in London, England, in 1844. In 1855, the first American YMCA was founded in Boston, Massachusetts—during Marcus and Adelaide's lifetime. This first YMCA may have touched Marcus's life as a Civil War soldier. Originally established to unite Christian young men, the Y's mission is now to "build strong kids, strong families, strong communities," although groups will differ according to leadership and location.

Although America's Civil War is remembered for its high death rate and terrible battlefield suffering, medical progress was made during that time. Ambulances were on the battlefields, and the Army Nurse Corps and other organization and practices were started.

The American Red Cross has also touched many lives for many years, since Clara Barton and a circle of acquaintances founded the organization in Washington, DC, on May 21, 1881. The Red Cross received its first congressional charter in 1900 and a second in 1905, the year after Barton resigned from the organization. This charter—which remains in effect today— includes giving relief to and serving as a medium of communication between members of the American armed forces and their families and providing national and international disaster relief and mitigation.[170]

The American Cancer Society was established by New York physicians in 1913 as a voluntary health organization. Local offices and the ACS Web site provide detection information and combat false information about cancer. Dedicated to helping everyone who faces cancer, through research, patient services, early detection, treatment, and education, the ACS provides information for patients and families at www.cancer.org.

Medical associations play an important role in research, teaching, and practicing medicine. The Christian Medical and Dental Associations Web site presents the ethics and morality of the historic Hippocratic Oath. You may find this article review interesting:

---

169. Stone, "Eight Decades of Scurvy," http://www.spearsmacleod.com/links/s/scurvy/index.htm
170. For more history and support information, see www.redcross.org/museum.

"The Moral Basis for Medical Science," D. Elton True-blood. CMDS Journal Winter/Spring 1988; XIX(1):5–7: Science is important in our culture, but science depends on ethical integrity. The moral basis of medical science is the recognition of a "real right and a real wrong" which is wholly consistent with theism. Hippocrates recognized this as he dealt with questions of medical practice such as abortion. Such ethical realism leads to a humility and a reverence for life which ultimately leads to a reverence for persons. For these reasons, the spiritual life of the medical scientist is more important than his technical ability.

The same spiritual intent and oath can apply to any profession and to all pilgrimages heading toward dedicating medicine and recreation to God's honor and glory.

Christian Physician's Oath

With gratitude to God, faith in Christ Jesus, and dependence on the Holy Spirit, I publicly profess my intent to practice medicine for the glory of God.

With humility, I will seek to increase my skills. I will respect those who teach me and who broaden my knowledge. In turn, I will freely impart my knowledge and wisdom to others.

With God's help, I will love those who come to me for healing and comfort. I will honor and care for each patient as a person made in the image of God, putting aside selfish interests, remaining pure and chaste at all times.

With God's guidance, I will endeavor to be a good steward of my skills and of society's resources. I will convey God's love in my relationships with family, friends, and community.

I will aspire to reflect God's mercy in caring for the lonely, the poor, the suffering, and the dying.

With God's direction, I will respect the sanctity of human life. I will care for all my patients, rejecting those interventions that either intentionally destroy or actively end human life, including the unborn, the weak and vulnerable, and the terminally ill.

With God's grace, I will live according to this profession.[171]

---

171. Passed by the Christian Medication and Dentistry House of Delegates, May 3, 1991. Chicago, IL. Amended by the CMDA House of Representatives, June 10, 2005, Denver, Colorado. Used by permission.

Song

This sail-filling song reminds us that there is more to life than physical life and death. God created in us a soul—a space to sense his companionship and comfort and prepare for eternity in heaven.

Be Still, My Soul

> Be still, my soul! The Lord is on thy side; Bear patiently the cross of grief or pain;
> Leave to thy God to order and provide; In every change He faithful will remain.
> Be still, my soul! Thy best, thy heavenly Friend Through thorny ways leads to a joyful end.
>
> Be still, my soul! Thy God doth undertake To guide the future as He has the past.
> Thy hope, thy confidence let nothing shake; All now mysterious shall be bright at last.
> Be still, my soul! The waves and winds still know His voice who ruled them while He dwelt below.
>
> Be still, my soul! The hour is hastening on When we shall be forever with the Lord.
> When disappointment, grief, and fear are gone, Sorrow forgot, love's purest joys restored.
> Be still, my soul! When change and tears are past, All safe and blessed we shall meet at last.[172]

Free Time Options
Spend a few moments reflecting upon, and/or listing in a journal, ways that God *has* and *is* loving and caring for you and me.

Commit to taking better care of yourself and others.

Find a friend or family member to share accountability in accomplishing consistent personal caregiving.

Make or update your will.

Tell a disabled person about Joni Eareckson Tada's programs for the disability community throughout the world. Check them out at www.joniandfriends.org.

---

172. Lyrics (1752) by Katherina A. Von Schlegel, translation (1855) by Jane L. Borthwick; sung to the tune of "Finlandia" (1899) by Jean Sibelius.

Last Briefing: Personal Cases

I was not sure that my family's personal health and caregiving histories would add power to fill today's sails and advance faith until my first editor praised God in the margin next to our early-detection stories—now told to encourage you to seek early detection at routine check-ups. Please tell others to do the same to add power for raising praises to our Master.

Bill

Bill and I can count sixteen inside and outside surgical scars. His first of eight cuts was a mastoid operation at age six. When he was near death, a father-to-son blood transfusion probably saved his life, but it could not prevent partial hearing loss in the infected ear. Years later, bone implants by surgeons at the House Ear Institute in Los Angeles partially restored the loss.

In 1999, rising PSA counts indicated, and a biopsy confirmed, the presence of cancer cells in Bill's prostate gland. He injured his back while moving garden rocks soon after cancer surgery was scheduled. Cancer surgery was postponed and back surgery was scheduled, preceded by X-Rays on Good Friday.

Nervously paging through a magazine in the X-Ray waiting room, I spotted familiar names and pictures in an article about the Scottish game of curling, played since the 1850s in our hometown in Minnesota. One picture in the story was a high-angle shot of the curling rink and its members. Beyond the rink I could see the village cemetery and the cedar tree that hovers over the Stroebel family monument and headstones.

When I saw the cemetery picture in the waiting room on Good Friday in 1999, I asked, "God, are you warning me that Bill will die soon?"

Then I remembered that Acts 17:28, "In Christ we live," had been engraved, at our request, on the face of the granite cemetery monument just a few months before the cancer diagnosis. Truly, remembering made that Friday good!

Our friends and family applied prayer prescriptions to Bill's back. Therapy began on Resurrection Sunday. A week later, back surgery was canceled, and cancer surgery was rescheduled. The cancer was still there, barely contained in the gland. This probably would be a very different story about tapping into power through early detection if cancer surgery had been postponed. Today Bill is cancer-free, his PSA count 0. Please praise our Providential and life-giving Lord with us.

Bev

Early detection of cancer probably saved my life at age thirty-two, and by choosing surgery, a simple mastectomy, we may have chosen life for our third baby girl, born three years later. When her older sisters heard warnings in the 1960s about smoking, they knelt in front of the family smoker—*me*—and prayed that I would stop. I had previously tried to quit smoking several times. This time, accountability—to loving children and to God —prevailed. I remain cancer- and smoke-free.

The U.S. Surgeon General provides warnings: "Smoking harms nearly every organ of your body . . . The list of diseases caused by smoking has been expanded to include abdominal aortic aneurysm, acute myeloid leukemia, cataracts, cervical cancer, kidney cancer, pancreatic cancer, pneumonia, and stomach cancer."[173]

Long after my surgery and lifestyle change, and even before Bill's cancer scare, we joined the health ministry team at our church out of gratitude for our physical, emotional, and spiritual well-being. Most of the church health ministry team members are medical professionals, but some are nonprofessionals who, like us, connect spiritual and medical perspectives for healing and health. Health ministries, parish nurses, and pastoral caregivers use Scripture, prayer, support groups, and education to promote spiritual and physical wellness.

Bill's mother and several friends have died of breast cancer. Promoting the American Cancer Society's October breast cancer events has comforted our souls and contributed to our wellness. Today's Cruise Bonus contains reminders for "Coming Alongside," along with a prayer for practicing medicine.

Dedicating Recreation

Sports are a huge American and family pastime. Bill and other family members enjoy golfing. Some are skiers, swimmers, walkers, and joggers. A Pierce cousin runs in marathons. My brother and his wife chose physical exercise and outdoor sports for their family's recreation. Years later, their children and grandchildren are running, climbing mountains, and competing in gymnastics and basketball. Their son was in the climbing accident on Oregon's Mount Hood in May 2002. Jeff is a seasoned climber and trained in emergency medical procedures. In his words, he was "a victim for about five seconds." Also following in his father's footsteps, Jeff is still climbing mountains and training novices.

Power to Fill Sails Through Caregiving

Bill and I cared for my mother in our home for the last four years of her life. Her lifespan was almost a century, from 1900 to 1996. We were good friends and deeply loved one another.

---

173. Find more information about smoking at www.cdc.gov/tobacco.sgr.

Caregiving can be full-time. In our case, other family members were available to occasionally spend time with Mother. She was a loving and companionable person who enjoyed playing games, reading, and watching favorite television programs until she became too ill and aged.

We made mistakes during those years, but we also made wonderful memories together, learned more about the best and worst in ourselves, and discovered how to pray for the elderly—even for God to call home a person who is suffering—and for exhausted caregivers.

Senior hotlines and state and private agencies provide services, warnings, and guidelines for caring for seniors. Here are a few personal suggestions and power sources:

★ Be accountable to Exodus 20:12 for parental caregiving: "Honor your father and your mother, so that you may live long in the land the Lord your God is giving you."

★ To avoid abuse by the caregiver or the cared-for person, tempers and habits absolutely need to be under control. If not, find other help.

★ Pray for the nursing home and other caregivers.

★ Watch for and report signs of abused seniors.

★ Before dementia or illness takes over, seniors should carefully choose their caregivers—remembering that a Durable Power of Attorney for financial and health care decisions can give license for paying bills as well as for stealing, along with other life-and-death matters.

★ Ask a spokesperson from state or private agencies to speak to your seniors group or several groups at a congregational or other facility.

★ Ask for help with caregiving, and if a life is ending, contact a hospice service. A doctor's referral may be needed.

★ Gather information for obituaries while your family member is still lucid. Asking a senior to tell stories will often provide the information, and it is more fun.

★ Shower your loved one with love and with the reassurance that he or she is not going through this time of life alone.

★ Make burial and funeral plans before death is eminent, if possible, including speakers, songs to be sung, and Scriptures to be read.

★ Read the Bible and songs aloud with care receivers. "What a Friend We Have in Jesus" is a comforting example.

Cruise Library Visit

Rather than recommending books during this library visit, I encourage you to visit Web sites or find someone to search for you. Search for the Declaration of Geneva, first adopted by the General Assembly of the World Medical

Association in Geneva, Switzerland, in September 1948. Then read the 1968, 1970, 1971, and 2005 versions. Look specifically at the pledge: "I will maintain the utmost respect for human life . . . " and see how it changed from 1948 to 2005.

Then, after reading the following compassionate challenge for the common good, ask God if he wants you to give *Full Sail* to your physician(s), local politicians, or judges.

Early in life, Gordon and I learned through caregiving parents that God disciplines those he loves (1 John 3; Revelation 3:19–20). Judgment Day is coming, when we will face the Witness who sees and hears everything on earth and in heaven. That is just one reason for dedicating this Cruise Day on your behalf, dear doctors and medical professionals whom I respect and thank for saving Bill's and my life many times.

Yes, this day is dedicated on your behalf—but it is also dedicated to you out of gratefulness for my four adopted grandchildren, to speak for my brother who loved and worked to preserve life, and for the thousands of women who will grieve aborted babies and infertility all their lives. For all these, I voice a caring and compassionate complaint to the worldwide medical profession and to politicians and judges.

As parents in my generation often said, "Behave yourself!", or, if it applied, "You should be ashamed of yourself!" Does it apply? You bet! You know very well that life begins at conception, and yet you discard God's sacred creation in his image and his Providential plan for the lives that you abort. You not only abort a baby, you abort the peace and well-being of a mother. Perhaps most grievous, you abort potential to praise God and bless nations.

You often hear patients say "Ouch!" Now it's your turn if this hurts, because, according to Proverbs 3:11–12, Hebrews 12:5–6, and 1 John 3, God disciplines those he loves. He has gifted and called you to heal, not destroy; to bless when you are legislating and playing with equal rights. Do not lay this curse further, but use the following prescription to lift the heavy curse of unused baby blankets over our nation and the whole earth.

Prescription for Physicians, Politicians, Government Officials, and Judges: Kneel, confess, and ask God to forgive and hurl your sins into the sea.

Personal and Professional Prognosis: God controls winds and waves, so you will survive even if a kneeling multitude rocks your medical, political, official, and judicial boats.

National and International Prognosis: If just one or a God-size handful of physicians, politicians, and government officials will publicly express regret to mothers and tell others about this new prescription for preserving life, then peace, love, justice, and the laughter of saved children will flow like a mighty river around the world.

Cruise Bonus
"Coming Alongside" Prayer Card and Prayer for
Practicing Medicine

Support groups, health ministries, friends, families, and neighbors, please feel free to print this two-sided bookmark and prayer card, and be encouraged to place them in get-well cards and into hands that need hope to hold onto when suffering. If you are printing this card for use, any disease could be substituted for "cancer."

If you need specifics, you may choose to share my concerns for those dealing with heart disease, Fibromyalgia, Alzheimer's, arthritis, osteoporosis, emphysema, depression, cystic and pulmonary fibrosis, kidney disease, Parkinson's, autism, various syndromes, chronic fatigue, diabetes, allergies, anxiety, obesity, cancer, multiple sclerosis, lupus, aggressive pain, neuropathy, asthma, and infertility.

COMING ALONGSIDE

Jesus walked along with them
Luke 24:15

TO PRAY

TO HOLD HANDS

TO WIPE TEARS AWAY

TO FIGHT BACK

TO REMEMBER

TO REMIND

There will be no more tears,
death, mourning, crying or pain.
Revelation 21:4

CANCER IS SO LIMITED

It cannot cripple love

It cannot shatter hope

It cannot corrode faith

It cannot minimize peace

It cannot destroy friendship

It cannot supersede family

It cannot overcome confidence

It cannot shut out memories

It cannot impair courage

It cannot invade the soul

It cannot silence God's spirit

It cannot reduce the worth

of redemption

It cannot attack resurrection power

It cannot shorten eternal life

It cannot extinguish foreseen

GLOW OF GLORY!
—original source anonymous

Prayer for Practicing Medicine

Praise the Lord, O my Soul;
Forget not all his benefits—
who forgives all your sins
and heals all your diseases.
Psalm 103:2–3

You have made known to me the
paths of life; you will fill me with
joy in your presence. Acts 2:28

LORD OF HEALING, we praise your presence in the power of prayer. We ask you to avenge and cure the ravages of cancers and other diseases on the bodies, minds and souls of lives, marriages, families, workplaces, ministries, communities, nations.

LORD OF HOPE, we praise your presence in medical advances, expertise, and compassionate personal care. We ask for advocacy, medical, and faith groups to hold hands to heal humankind's hurts, grief, and diseases.

LORD OF MERCY, we praise your presence as tears are wiped away and we partner to pray in waiting, exam, hospital, and prayer rooms. We ask for your intervention to stop the silent growth of diseased cells in our bodies and the seeds of sin embedded in our souls.

LORD OF JOY, we praise your presence in the strength given to overcome and embrace our grief, weaknesses, and suffering. We ask for enough comfort, confidence, and courage to tell your love story to men, women, and children. Then fill us with your joy.

LORD OF PEACE, we praise your presence in the progress of research to reveal disease. We ask for more ways to successfully fight and survive assaults on our bodies.

LORD OF JUSTICE, we praise your presence in the light of your glorious star and sacrifice. We ask for your vision and touch on our dark and painful nights. We praise and ask in the power and promise of your names and work.
—*Amen*

—Beverly Pierce Stroebel, Full Sail, 2009

Covenant and Dedications

As we recap at the end of this tenth day on board, let us look back to the beginning and remember that the day's Scripture Course was set to redeem us from the pit, dispel darkness, and crown us with love and compassion (Psalm 103:1–5).

Today We the Passengers covenant
To dedicate Medicine, Caregiving,
and Recreation in America
and all Nations to God's Glory and Honor.

Night Watch

Scripture Course and Focus Points

Scripture: Genesis 2:26; 50:19–21; Psalms 30:1–5, 139:16; Isaiah 25:7-8, 26:19; Lamentations 2:19; John 3; Mark 1, 2; Romans 8:38–39; 1 Corinthians 15:54–55.

Focus Points: Tears, dust, saving lives, labor, kindness, choose life, disease, days, love, rise, victory.

Song

To honor Civil War veterans like my great-grandfather Marcus Pierce and advance Christian faith to another generation, today's cruise ends with these comforting words. "It remains a very sad historic irony that when each Civil War battle was finished, 'Taps' would unite men from the North and South in death, even if nothing could bring them together in life."[174]

Taps

Fading light dims the sight,
And a star gems the sky, gleaming bright.
From afar drawing nigh—Falls the night.

Day is done, gone the sun.
From the lake, from the hills, from the sky.
All is well, safely rest, God is nigh.

Then a good night, peaceful night.
Till the light of the dawn shineth bright.
God is near, do not fear—Friend, good night.

Do not fear: sails are filled for tomorrow's callings, causes,
and citizenship—Friend, good night.

End of Cruise Day Ten

---

174. Collins, *Songs Sung, Red, White, and Blue*, 168, 172.

Cruise Day Eleven Program
Callings, Causes, and Citizenship

Scripture Course

Wake-Up Calls!

Eleventh-Generation Introductions
Lewis Grant Pierce and Bertha Anna Moore

First Briefing: Grandpa

Free Time Options

Last Briefing: Grandma

Cruise Library Visit

Cruise Bonus
The American's Creed

Covenant and Dedications
Civil and Church Governments, Denominations,
Elections, and Individual God-Given Gifts

Night Watch
Scripture Course and Focus Points

Scripture Course
Shout for joy to the Lord, all the earth. Worship the Lord with gladness;
come before him with joyful songs. Know that the Lord is God.
It is he who made us, and we are his; we are his people, the sheep of his pasture.
Enter his gates with thanksgiving and his courts with praise;

give thanks to him and praise his name. For the Lord is good and his love endures forever; his faithfulness continues through all generations.
Psalm 100:1–5

Scripture: Lamentations 3:22–24; Psalm 37:3–6; John 14:1–6; 1 Corinthians 14:1; Ephesians 4:1–6; Philippians 3:20, 4:5.

Wake-Up Calls!

Here is the strength of idealism which prompted the Pilgrims: they took with them what they had lacked in their native country and had found in Holland: freedom of conscience, civil liberty, possibility, under the guidance of God, of being loyal to their calling and gifts. And they possessed from the beginning what is the real strength of a nation: a religious conviction that only in submission to God's ordinances and by walking in His ways personal and national welfare can be found.[175]

Let each citizen remember at the moment he is offering his vote that he is not making a present or a compliment to please an individual—or at least that he ought not so to do; but that he is executing one of the most solemn trusts in human society for which he is accountable to God and his country. (Samuel Adams, Father of the American Revolution. Samuel and John were second cousins.)[176]

I pray to heaven to bestow the best of blessings on this house and all that hereafter inhabit it. May none but honest and wise men ever rule under this roof. (President John Adams to his wife Abigail after moving into the White House in November 1800. The words are now inscribed on the White House dining room mantel.)

The choice before us is plain: Christ or chaos, conviction or compromise, discipline or disintegration. I am rather tired of hearing about our rights and privileges as American citizens. The time is come—it now is—when we ought to hear about the duties and responsibilities of our citizenship.

175. Plooji, *Pilgrim Fathers from a Dutch Point of View*, 30–31.
176. *Boston Gazette*, April 16, 1781. Quoted in http://www.revolutionary-war-and-beyond.com/samuel-adams-quotes-3.html

America's future depends upon her accepting and demonstrating God's government. (Rev. Peter Marshall, Chaplain of the United States Senate, January 13, 1947)[177]

The right of citizens of the United States to vote shall not be denied or abridged by the United States or by any State on account of race, color, or previous condition of servitude. The Congress shall have power to enforce this article by appropriate legislation. (Article XV [1870] Amendment to the Constitution of the USA.)

The right of citizens of the United States to vote shall not be denied or abridged by the United States or by any State on account of sex. Congress shall have power to enforce this article by appropriate legislation. (Article XIX [1920] Amendment to the Constitution of the USA.)

Friday morning Lewis Pierce was a caller in town. A few hours later, as he rose to speak at a meeting of the McPherson town board, he collapsed and died. His death was a distinct shock to everyone. A large group of neighbors and friends gathered at the church to pay their last respects to the memory of a real citizen. (*Good Thunder Herald* Obituary: "Death Takes L. G. Pierce, April 26, 1940")

In this way we are reaffirming the transcendence of religious faith in America's heritage and future; in this way we shall constantly strengthen those spiritual weapons which forever will be our country's most powerful resource in peace and war. (President Dwight D. Eisenhower, speaking about adding "under God" to America's Pledge of Allegiance)[178]

Eleventh-Generation Introductions

Lewis Grant Pierce	b. 9 August 1868	Delaware Co. NY
	d. 26 April 1940	Blue Earth Co., MN
	m. 23 December 1891	Blue Earth Co., MN
Bertha Anna Moore	b. 5 February 1873/4	Canada
	d. 16 December 1940	Blue Earth Co., MN

---

177. Quoted in Federer, *America's God and Country*, 418.
178. Ibid., 226.

Finally, today we'll sail with people I knew. I wonder, though, if my Grandmother Pierce was overjoyed when the Nineteenth Amendment to the Constitution became law in July 1920. Nor do I know if she ever voted as an American citizen.

These uncertainties and the Nineteenth Amendment itself are reasons why today we, both men and women, will dedicate voting, elections, and church and state governments to God's glory. To begin, we fast-forward technology from the twentieth to the twenty-first century, because during my grandparents' lifetimes, other worlds than their small world of ideas were lifting citizens to new heights in ways that began to affect even my life.

The larger world of ideas advances history from the Wright Brothers' first flight in 1903 to Charles Lindbergh's transatlantic flight in 1927; from the USSR's Sputnik blast-off into orbit in 1957 to Surveyor 1 landing on the moon in 1966, all the way to the in-orbit construction of the International Space Station that began in 1998 and is scheduled to be completed by 2011. See www.spaceflight.nasa.gov/realdata/tracking to know where the station is at any given time in orbit.

First Briefing: Grandpa

My Pierce grandparents lovingly "ruled the family roost" until their deaths in 1940 at ages 67 and 71. Grandpa was a highly respected church and state citizen, the son of a Civil War veteran. From him I inherited a love and appreciation for singing, a gentle spirit, a huge example for faith in my heart, an example of service in the church, and loving concern for family, friends, neighbors, church, community, and country.

Three early childhood memories describe Grandpa: he read newspaper "funnies" to grandchildren, he was important at our church, and he prayed long dinnertime prayers. I learned later in life that he was elected by the same congregation to serve as an elder for forty-two consecutive years.

As loving, dignified, and respected for integrity as Grandpa Pierce was, I doubt that he ever contemplated a calling in politics or was asked to consider running for public office. Church leadership was the calling he received and accepted. Ironically, he suffered a heart attack and died while attending a civic meeting concerning a controversial subject that he cared deeply enough to speak about.

Today, if he could speak to his family, his neighbors, and the citizens of all free nations about civic responsibility, I believe he would say, "Your voice and vote are important. If you have not done so before, please register and vote in civil elections."

Speaking about faith and church, he would begin with Scripture reflecting his life: "As a prisoner for the Lord, then, I urge you to live a life worthy of the calling you have received. Be completely humble and gentle; be patient, bearing with one another in love. Make every effort to keep the unity of the Spirit through the bond of peace. There is one body and one Spirit—just as you were called to one hope when you were called—one Lord, one faith, one baptism; one God and Father of all, who is over all and through all and in all."[179]

Next, from his heart he would say, "Your decision about faith and God is the most important vote that you will ever make. I pray, if you haven't, that you will choose to follow Christ, the way and the truth and the life. No one comes to the Father except through him. He has a place prepared for you in heaven.[180] If you are not in church fellowship, seek to find God's choice for you. Then be baptized, join the church, and become an active member. By taking those actions, you are voting for God's way and strengthening and empowering Judeo-Christian and American life and liberty."

By setting these examples, Grandpa advanced Christian faith through the eleventh generation from his ancestors on the *Mayflower*.

If you sat at Grandpa and Grandma's table, no matter how hungry you were for her good cooking, you ate after he said a long prayer. After family dinners, we sang hymns. May God bless his house and yours, through every generation, as we sing.

Song
Bless This House

> Bless this house, O Lord we pray
> Make it safe by night and day;
> Bless these walls so firm and stout,
> Keeping want and trouble out;
> Bless the roof and chimneys tall,
> Let Thy peace lie over all;
> Bless this door, that it may prove
> Ever open to joy and love.
>
> Bless these windows shining bright,
> Letting in God's heav'nly light;
> Bless the hearth ablazing there,
> With smoke ascending like a prayer;
> Bless the people here within,

---

179. Ephesians 4:1–6.
180. Based on John 14:1–6.

Keep them pure and free from sin;
Bless us all that we may be
Fit, O Lord, to dwell with Thee,
Bless us all that we one day
May dwell, O Lord, with Thee.[181]

Free Time Options

Think and talk about those who have filled your life with love, truth, prayer, music, and grace.

To fill sails for today's last briefing and activities, praise God for the legacies of grandparents or others who influenced your life.

Last Briefing: Grandma

Grandpa and Grandma said their marriage vows in a Baptist church in the southern Minnesota village where she lived and in the county where they both lived. Years later, Bill and I said our marriage vows at the same church altar in the same village and county—though at the time, we didn't know the family history behind the location!

Today's First Briefing was about Grandpa, but Grandma was important in my life, too. I even learned through her about competition between mothers-in-law and daughters-in-law when Dad said that his mother's tomato soup was better than Mother's. Grandma made quilts for every grandchild, served in the church and community, and cared for her mother the last years of her life.

My grandparents raised their family on a farm and belonged to a country church. I was raised on a nearby farm and in the same United Brethren church, now a United Methodist church. In 1961, in California, Bill and I joined the Reformed Church in America (RCA), to which we still belong.

The RCA was founded in New Amsterdam (now New York City) in 1628, an outgrowth of the Reformed church in the Netherlands. ("Holland" refers to just two provinces in the Netherlands.) The Netherlands sheltered the English Separatists—our Pilgrims—for over a decade before sailing to New England. With thanks in mind, we will pray for the Netherlands as we disembark.

Denominations govern in various ways. Methodist pastors are assigned to churches by bishops. Church leadership and congregations choose Reformed church pastors. Each local RCA church is within a classis, and each classis is within a synod. The area synods are part of the RCA's General Synod. Both the Methodist and Reformed free-style systems work well and are respected by those within them.

---

181. Lyrics by Helen Taylor; music by May H. Brahe. Boosey & Hawkes Music Publishers, 1927. Used by permission.

The same can be said about America's democratic, free-style governmental system. Daniel Webster's great speech celebrating the Pilgrim's bicentennial gives good reasons to combine the energy and dedication of religious and civil governments to God's honor and glory.

> We would leave for the consideration of those who shall then occupy our places, some proof that we hold the blessings transmitted from our fathers in just estimation; some proof of our attachment to the cause of good government, and of civil and religious liberty; some proof of a sincere and ardent desire to promote every thing which may enlarge the understandings and improve the hearts of men.
>
> Advance, then, ye future generations! We would hail you, as you rise in your long succession, to fill the places which we now fill, and to taste the blessings of existence where we are passing, and soon shall have passed, our own human duration. And when, from the long distance of a hundred years, they shall look back upon us, they shall know, at least, that we possessed affections, which, running backward and warming with gratitude for what our ancestors have done for our happiness, run forward also to our posterity, and meet them with cordial salutation, ere yet they have arrived on the shore of being.
>
> We greet your accession to the great inheritance which we have enjoyed. We welcome you to the blessings of good government and religious liberty. We welcome you to the treasures of science and the delights of learning. We welcome you to the transcendent sweets of domestic life, to the happiness of kindred, and parents, and children. We welcome you to the immeasurable blessings of rational existence, the immortal hope of Christianity, and the light of everlasting truth![182]

My Pierce grandparents probably never read Daniel Webster's 1820 speech, but their love and faith still run forward—on our *Mayflower* platform—to invite their posterity to promote the power of immortal hope and the light of truth.

---

182. Daniel Webster's Plymouth Speech, "The First Scene of our History," December 22, 1820, commemorating the bicentennial of the landing of the Pilgrims at Plymouth Rock in Plymouth, Massachusetts.

Cruise Library Visit

Today's choice in our Cruise Library is David Larsen's *Jews, Gentiles & The Church*, an author and a book that God used to call, gift, and confirm my "posterity" causes.

> A final duty is incumbent on believers everywhere. In the light of Christ's commands to live in constant readiness for His return and in view of the constellation of signs of the approaching end of the age, particularly in relation to Israel, we need a strong and growing sense of spiritual urgency in the mission and ministry our Lord has entrusted to us . . .
>
> Although warned, American forces were unready when the Japanese attacked Pearl Harbor. Many Christians today live unprepared lives. A zeal in witness, holiness in life, living on the tiptoes of eagerness characterized the early believers. We are to be a "Marantha" people who exude hope— "The Lord is coming!" . . .
>
> His coming is imminent, and we must assist others in boarding the ark of safety before the deluge of judgment falls. The promise stands: "The Lord swore an oath to David, a sure oath that he will not revoke: 'One of your descendants I will place on your throne'" (Psalm 132:11).[183]

Prayer

Voting is a privilege taken for granted by some citizens and ignored by others, but usually not by African-Americans, women, or citizens in newly freed or oppressed nations. Peter Marshall, the U.S. Senate Chaplin during my grandparents' generation, leads us in prayer about voting (called "franchise" in his prayer). Please apply the prayer to America, to your ancestral nation(s), or to nations that come to mind.

> Almighty Master:
> Lord Jesus, we ask Thee to guide the people of this nation as they exercise their dearly bought privilege of franchise. May it neither be ignored unthinkingly nor undertaken lightly. As citizens all over this land go to the ballot boxes, give them a sense of high privilege and joyous responsibility.

---

183. Larsen, *Jews, Gentiles & The Church*, 23.

Help those who are about to be elected to public office to come to understand the real source of their mandate—a mandate given by no party machine, received at no polling booth, but given by God; a mandate to represent God and truth at the heart of the nation; a mandate to do good in the name of Him under whom this Republic was established.

We ask Thee to lead our country in the paths where Thou wouldst have her walk, to do the tasks which Thou hast laid before her. So may we together seek happiness for all our citizens in the name of Him who created us all equal in His sight, and therefore brothers. Amen. (Prayer Before a National Election by Peter Marshall, U.S. Senate Chaplain)[184]

To express our praise for God's faithfulness, please join me as we meditate on and sing my Grandpa Pierce's favorite hymn.

Song
Great is Thy Faithfulness

Great is Thy faithfulness, O God my Father,
There is no shadow of turning with Thee;
Thou changest not, Thy compassions they fail not;
As Thou hast been Thou forever wilt be.

Summer and winter, and springtime and harvest,
Sun, moon and stars in their courses above
Join with all nature in manifold witness
To Thy great faithfulness, mercy and love.

Pardon for sin and a peace that endureth,
Thy own dear presence to cheer and to guide;
Strength for today and bright hope for tomorrow,
Blessings all mine, with ten thousand beside!

Chorus
Great is Thy faithfulness! Great is Thy faithfulness!
Morning by morning new mercies I see;
All I have needed Thy hand hath provided—
Great is Thy faithfulness, Lord, unto me![185]

---

184. Quoted in Catherine Marshall, *Prayers of Peter Marshall*, 108.
185. Thomas O. Chisholm, Hope Publishing Company, 1951. Used by permission.

Full Sail

Cruise Bonus

We progress today's pilgrimage through time with a creed for participation by Americans only. Written during my grandparents' generation, the American's Creed is presented with no intent to discriminate, intimidate, or be condescending toward others, but so that citizens from other nations will better understand the American mind, heart, soul, and history.

The American's Creed

I believe in the United States of America as a Government of the people by the people, for the people, whose just powers are derived from the consent of the governed; a democracy in a Republic; a sovereign Nation of many sovereign States; a perfect Union, one and inseparable; established upon those principals of freedom, equality, justice, and humanity for which American patriots sacrificed their lives and fortunes.

I therefore believe it is my duty to my Country to love it; to support its Constitution; to obey its laws; to respect its flag, and to defend it against all enemies.[186]

History of the American's Creed

The Creed contains passages and phrases from the Declaration of Independence, the Preamble to the Constitution, Lincoln's Gettysburg Address, and Daniel Webster's reply to Robert Y. Hayne in the Senate in 1830.

America's involvement in World War I was a difficult and divisive issue for our Nation. President Wilson had struggled for three years since the outbreak of hostilities in August, 1914 to maintain a position of American neutrality towards the European conflict. This effort to distance our Nation from European affairs was disturbed on May 7, 1915 when a German U-boat sank the unarmed British liner Lusitania killing more than 1,000 people including 128 Americans.

By 1917 it was becoming increasingly apparent that American neutrality could no longer be maintained. President Wilson went before Congress to request a Declaration of War with these words:

"The world must be made safe for democracy. It is a fearful thing to lead this great peaceful people into war, the most

---

186. Doug Sterner, http://www.homeofheroes.com.

190

terrible of wars. But the right is more precious than the peace, and we shall fight for the things that we have always carried nearest our hearts . . . for democracy . . . for the rights and liberties of small nations, for a universal dominion of right by such a concert of free peoples as shall bring peace and safety to all nations and make the world itself at last free."

President Wilson's view of the United States as the stalwart of world democracy wasn't shared by everyone, however. Six of the 96 U.S. Senators voted against the declaration of war. The House of Representatives passed the resolution April 6, 1917, but only after 13 hours of emotional and heated debate. Forty-nine Congressmen and the only Congresswoman (Helen Rankin of Montana), voted against the declaration.

By mid-summer General John J. Pershing's American Expeditionary Force was landing in Europe. But even as Colonel Charles E. Stanton stood before the tomb of Revolutionary War hero Marquis de Lafayette's tomb in France to proclaim, "Lafayette, we are here"; trouble was brewing at home. Congress' new program of conscription under the Selective Service Act was mandating registration for military service by every American man between the ages of 21 and 30. Not since the Civil War had an issue arisen to so divide our Country.

While George M. Cohan wrote patriotic songs like "Over There" (actually penned on April 6, the same day Congress finally passed the Declaration of War), other citizens began to protest American involvement in "Europe's troubles" and the forced recruitment of soldiers under the Selective Service Act. By the summer of 1918 the war in Europe had forced the Government to take control of industry, railroads, and food and fuel production. Taxes were raised to fund the war, postal rates went up, and censorship of some mail was being officially conducted. In May Congress passed the Sedition Act which allowed war and draft protesters to be jailed. More than 2,000 Americans were already behind bars for interfering with the draft, including one former United States Congressman (Victor Berger of Wisconsin).

In the midst of all this domestic turmoil and dissension, a Nation-wide essay contest was held to develop an American's Creed. The winning entry was submitted by William Tyler Page of Friendship Heights, Maryland. Mr. Page was a descendant of President John Tyler and former Congressman John Page who served in the House of Representatives from 1789–1797. William Tyler Page himself had also served in Congress—as a Congressional Page in 1881.

The American's Creed defines what it means to be American, both the need for faith in who and what we are as a Nation, and the responsibility we all have to love and respect our Nation and its Flag. Its message is appropriate for each generation of Americans, but becomes even more meaningful when we understand the historical context of its origin . . . written during a time of conflict and turmoil at home and abroad."[187]

Covenant and Dedications

Today We the Passengers covenant:
To dedicate Civil and Church Governments,
Elections and Individual God-Given Gifts in America and
all Nations to God's Honor And Glory.

Night Watch

Scripture Course and Focus Points

Scripture: Psalm 37; Isaiah 41:4, 48:12; Lamentations 3:22–23, Mark 11:22–26; John 8:31–33, 13:16–17, 17:23; Romans 11:25, 12, 15:14–22; Revelation 16:16, 22:13.

Focus Points: Fear, faithfulness, authority, cause, commit, service, sacrifices, truth, test, approve, unity, will, govern, citizenship, faith, heart, stand, instructions, respectable, guard, coming, beginning, end, first and last, compassions.

We rest assured in Christ and Civil Freedoms as he ends this day.

End of Day Eleven

---

187. Ibid.

Cruise Day Twelve Program
Legacies

〜〜〜〜〜〜〜〜〜〜〜〜

Scripture Course

Wake-Up Calls!

Twelfth-Generation Introductions
Ray Harold Pierce and Lillian May Weaver

First Briefing: Love At Home

Free Time Options

Last Briefing: Love Away from Home

Cruise Library Visit

Cruise Bonus
One Yarmulke: A Holocaust Story

Covenant and Dedications
Occupations, Transportation, Technology, Communication,
Science, and Traditions

Night Watch
Scripture Course and Focus Points

〜〜〜〜〜〜〜〜〜〜〜〜

Scripture Course
*Honor your father and your mother so that you may live long in the land
the Lord your God is giving you.*
Exodus 20:12

Scripture: Genesis 12:1–3; Isaiah 9, 11:9b, 40:1–5; Matthew 9:37; Luke 2:14; John 14:1–4, 17:15–19; Acts 15:7–9, 11; 1 Corinthians 15:45–49, 58; Colossians 4:23–24; Ephesians 4:12–13; 2 Timothy 2:15, 3:1–6; Revelation 1:5–6, 21:26–27.

Wake-Up Calls!

We shall not . . . finally achieve the ideals for which this nation was founded so long as any American suffers discrimination as a result of his race, or religion, or color, or the land of origin of his forefathers. (President Harry Truman, Message to Congress, 1948)

On May 14, 1948 . . . Israel was officially recognized as a sovereign state by the United Nations! Though there are a variety of views among believers as to whether or not the events of 1948 were a fulfillment of prophecy, I am personally persuaded that the birth of the modern state of Israel was nothing short of a miracle, which I will continue to praise God for the rest of my days. However, the independence of Israel will only be fully realized when the people of Israel recognize their complete dependence on Jesus the Messiah. This is our hope, and what our Mission to the Jewish people longs to see more than anything. (Dr. Mitch Glaser, President, Chosen People Ministries)[188]

Israeli army leaders warned the nation today that the operation launched this morning against Hamas will be prolonged and intense. In an indication that a major ground operation will probably be forthcoming into the Gaza Strip in the coming days or weeks, media reports say some reserve army units are already being called up. This may also be partly in anticipation of a possible missile response from Hizbullah and/or Syria.

All this to say, another serious chapter is apparently beginning to unfold in Israel's long and difficult struggle to survive and thrive in the mainly Muslim Middle East. Whatever occurs, it is definitely an appropriate time to get down on our knees in prayer. (David Dolan, December 28, 2008)[189]

---

188. Glaser, *The Chosen People Newsletter*, Volume XII, Issue 5, May 2006.
189. David Dolan is a Jerusalem-based author and journalist who has lived and worked in Israel since 1980. 2009 e-mail newsletter quote used by permission. To order Dolan books, visit www.ddolan.com.

The missile took off in a beautiful launching. It rose slowly at first in a huge splash of flame with a roar that could be heard for miles . . . (Associate Press account of the launch of the Explorer satellite, America's first earth satellite, January 1958)

You were . . . designed for discovery—and the greatest discovery of your life awaits you. So I hope you'll pursue scientific knowledge, but that you won't stop there. Don't let its allure become a destination; instead, allow it to guide you beyond itself to the incredible implications it offers for your life and eternity. (Lee Strobel, *The Case For A Creator*)[190]

Bev's and my relatives came to North American shores from Europe, then migrated to the Native Americans' "Land of the Sky-Blue Waters"—the state now known as Minnesota—by way of Pennsylvania, New York, and Wisconsin states. Farmers, they learned that adequate rainfall satisfied thirsty crops planted in the deep black Minnesota soil, washed by sunlight and moderate temperatures long enough to produce wheat, corn, barley, and rye during spring, summer, and fall seasons.

The soil that rested and was renewed during long cold winters was produced over the centuries by grass growing, dying, and decaying one season after another to develop soil several feet deep. Some forests had to be cleared for farming and lumber, but the prairie grasslands on flat, rolling fields only needed plowing to plant crops for local consumption and commercial shipping to other sections of the country and world. This farm-based economy evolved and later spawned commercial, manufacturing, and financial institutions as well.

Our parent's generation prospered from the work, discipline, and ideals of their pioneering grandparents and parents; now our generation explores, loves, prays, and works to benefit our children and grandchildren. How they choose to honor, produce, and leave legacies remains to be seen. (William Stroebel, born and raised in Blue Earth County, Minnesota)

190. Strobel, *The Case for a Creater*, 292.

Song
Work for the Night Is Coming

> Work, for the night is coming, Work thro' the morning hours;
> Work while the dew is sparkling; Work 'mid springing flower.
> Work when the day grows brighter, Work in the glowing sun;
> Work, for the night is coming, When man's work is done.
>
> Work, for the night is coming, Work thro' the sunny noon;
> Fill brightest hours with labor, Rest comes sure and soon.
> Give every flying minute Something to keep in store;
> Work, for the night is coming, When man works no more.[191]

Twelfth-Generation Introductions
My Parents: The Twelfth Generation from the *Mayflower*

Ray Harold Pierce	b. 13 April 1899	Blue Earth County, MN
	d. 20 December 1958	Blue Earth County, MN
	m. 27 October 1925	Blue Earth County, MN
Lillian May Weaver	b. 19 September 1900	Blue Earth County, MN
	d. 12 September 1996	El Dorado County, CA

First Briefing: Love At Home
Welcome, now, to my childhood home—and my parents' generation. To-day's Wake-Up Calls containing significant mid-twentieth to twenty-first century news are shared to advance history and because my parents read newspapers, listened to the radio, and watched television when TV became available. To advance faith, and fill sails, Dad and I often sang the end-times hymn, "Work for the Night is Coming."

From living at home with my parents until I left for college and marriage, I know that my parents loved God, each other, and their two children—Gordon and me. Both parents spanked us—but seldom with love, and only when necessary to discipline and help us survive childhood on the farm and reach adulthood—like the time Daddy spanked us one spring day when we walked our cousin home through Grandpa's woods and stayed too long playing by the Cobb River, which was running high and swift.

Their plans for Gordon and me were sacrificial. During the Great Depression and into our high school years, all savings were for college. Savings were only

---

191. Lyrics by Annie L. Coghill (1836–1907); music by Rev. Lowell Mason (1792–1872).

spent down when a new tractor or car were absolutely necessary. Following the example of Mother's parents, Mother and Dad planned to educate both of us.

Our parents taught my brother and me how to work, as their parents had taught them. Mother imparted storytelling to me from her family legacy. Growing up, Dad was more "churched" than Mother, but together they "churched" Gordon and me.

Dad suffered his first heart attack in 1949, when Gordon was a college junior and I was a freshman. He lived ten years with a severely damaged heart, probably surviving that long because he obeyed doctor's orders. He and Mother sold the chickens and pigs, but with hired help he still ploughed, planted, cultivated, and harvested. During his last decade, Dad saw us graduate from college and marry, and he was there when Gordon graduated from medical school. He also lived long enough to welcome posterity—the first two grandchildren in the family. Mother would welcome all seven, as well as six of her eight great-grandchildren.

The country store where my parents purchased groceries was also a farmers' gathering place to discuss politics and catch up on the news. Dad came home from the store one 1945 summer morning and sat down at the kitchen table, and we knew something was terribly wrong. The World War II Holocaust was the *wrong*—the heartbreaking news that prompted personal, family, national, and international introspection, discipline, and accountability—twentieth-century responsibilities and legacies we pray will never go away.

I remember no specific words said, but Dad's face and body language communicated sorrow and guilt. Yes—deep sorrow and head-bowing guilt, relating to what I now know God hates: disrespectful, abusive, ungrateful, unholy, slanderous, and ungodly attitudes toward the Jewish people his Son came to redeem and to use to bless all nations.

When I remember that day in the kitchen, it reminds me that Judeo-Christian survival days are upon us. The devil is restless, because now King David's descendants and remnant are rebuilding. The "house of Israel" is among the nations—shaking, sifting, and sorting, lifting curses for legacy blessings to flow, and cutting citizens, families, and nations like sheep and goats.[192]

That seventeenth- to twenty-first-century advancement and sail-filling connection of civil facts and Christian faith can be a comforting legacy for both Jews and Gentiles, if we so choose. Please praise and pray or sing Dad's favorite hymn as we often did in our Minnesota farm home, and as his family and friends sang at his funeral.

---

192. Matthew 25:31–46.

Song
He Leadeth Me, O Blessed Thought

> He leadeth me, O blessed thought! O words with heav'nly comfort fraught!
> What-e'er I do, where-e'er I be, Still 'tis God's hand that leadeth me.
> *Refrain.*

> Lord, I would clasp Thy hand in mine, Nor ever murmur nor repine;
> Content what-ever lot I see, Since 'tis my God that leadeth me.
> *Refrain.*

> And when my task on earth is done, When by Thy grace the vict'ry's won,
> E'en death's cold wave I will not flee, Still God through Jordan leadeth me.
> *Refrain.*

> *Refrain*
> He leadeth me, He leadeth me, By His own hand He leadeth me;
> His faithful follower I would be, For by His hand He leadeth me.[193]

Free Time Options

I was raised in a Christian home, a blessed and predictable path to come to know God's love through family love and legacies. If your memories and traditions are missing family and godly love, peacemaking, sweet-talk, and other ways to survive when the devil rages, please feel free to use my family as your role model—a blessed thought for me as love and legacies flow from my heart and home to yours.

If you need to add fun and mischievous times to your mental images of family love, picture in your mind egg-throwing fights between brother and sister when we were expected to stay occupied in the summer by cleaning chicken eggs before they were crated for sale.

Write on your calendars so you will remember to pray: Holocaust Memorial Day takes place annually on January 27, the anniversary of the liberation of the concentration camp at Auschwitz-Birkenau.

For memoir-writing examples, check out the Memoirs and Letters category in the Cruise Library.

Last Briefing: Love Away From Home

My dad did not know that he was a *Mayflower* descendant, or that the seventeenth-century Pilgrims and Puritans did not celebrate Christmas at home or

---

193. Joseph H. Gilmore

away from home. They did not follow Christmas traditions as they had probably observed them in England and the Netherlands, believing these traditions had pagan origins and were timed according to the winter solstice for sun worship.

They were right. To this day, every year as my family celebrates the traditional ways, I am challenged to remember that Christ was born into Jewish culture and according to the Jewish calendar. He was probably born in the fall, not during a northern-latitude winter when life on Judean hills was cold for shepherds and sheep. If our Passover Lamb, the King of the Jews, was born in the end of September, the angel Gabriel's Annunciation to Mary may have been December 25 on our Gregorian calendar. If you are inclined to know more, or to verify or contest the preceding timings, ask your Internet search engine, "When was Christ born?" and about the "Winter Solstice."

Whether they fell at the right time or not, my memories and legacies from December Christmastimes are precious. One Christmas Eve during a blizzard, Daddy bundled up, lighted a lantern to guide his way, and walked over a mile from home to church. Yes, he walked through a storm to worship Jesus. But more important to Gordon and me when he came home—the pockets in Daddy's big, snow-covered coat contained boxes of hard Christmas candy. You know the kind: the crunchy hard candy that comes in different shapes, sizes, colors, and even curls to delight a sweet tooth and create a loving memory long after children have moved away from home.

Mother and Dad stayed on the farm until his death. Then she moved to Mankato, Minnesota, to live until she moved to California to live with Bill and me from 1992 to 1996—the last four years of her long life.

To pass time on lonely Mankato days, Mother wrote stories about her teddy bear collection. I have embellished her Christmas story as a legacy for our children and grandchildren.

Bear Bickering and Christmas Peace
by Lillian Weaver Pierce and Beverly Pierce Stroebel

Lil was sick and tired of bear bickering. So she stuffed her bears into a shopping bag, called a driver who took seniors wherever they wanted to go, and told him she wanted a ride to the mall. "Last minute Christmas shopping?" he asked over the phone.

"Yes, sort of."

"How many people?"

Lil looked down at the bears in the bag, before answering, "One person, carrying a bag of . . . oh, just come as soon as possible, please."

A little later, as Lil grasped the driver's arm so she wouldn't slip on the icy street as they walked to his car, he caught a glimpse of the bear in the bag.

"Are you going to the mall to donate the brown teddy bear to the Christmas toy collection?"

Lil took a deep breath before answering, "Maybe; we'll see."

"Good idea, if you are. Tomorrow is Christmas Eve, so today is the last day to donate. Some child who won't get a present would really love to befriend that bear! And remember that the angel said, "Glory to God in the highest, and on earth peace to men on whom his favor rests." [Luke 2:14]

At the mall, Lil didn't even pause to window shop. She walked swiftly, straight to the center of the mall, found a bench, brushed it off with her gloved hand, and sat down. After placing the bag of bears at her feet, she slowly looked at the large decorated Christmas tree from the bottom to the top. Then she leaned over and said, "Oh dear bears, if I dared, I would take you out of the bag and hold all of you on my lap to see what I see. Maybe enjoying the beauty of the lights and the ornaments on the mall tree would take away so much of your breath and time, you'd stop bickering. And we'd all remember and enjoy peace on earth and good will."

Lil was startled when a little girl, whom she hadn't seen when she sat down, asked, "May I see your bears?"

When Lil gasped and put her hand over her mouth, the little girl giggled. When Lil giggled too, the little girl asked, "Does that brown bear have a name?"

Lil leaned over and pulled the bear out of the bag. "Yes, this is Chipper. He looks like the brown bear cubs I saw in Yellowstone Park in 1922. It's safe to hold him, if you tell him your name."

"Hello, Chipper. My name is Sally." Then petting and hugging the bear, she exclaimed, "Oh, Chipper, you are so beautiful and cuddly and soft!"

"Yes, but because he's the biggest, he's so, so bossy, too"

"Bossy?"

"Yes, he bosses the other bears around."

"Chipper, you better learn to behave yourself. Now sit still." Sally plunked Chipper on the bench, stood up and leaned over the bag. "May I meet the smaller bears?"

"Yes." Lil lifted a black-and-white bear out of her bag. "This is Randy. He's my daughter's childhood bear."

"Why did she name him Randy?"

"If she had been a boy, her . . . his name would have been Randy. She always wished she was a boy, so she gave the bear that name."

"She must have played with Randy a lot. He's kind of worn out."

"Oh, but he was such a good friend to my daughter, who was sick a lot when she was a child. She lives far away now."

"Do you miss her?"

"Yes."

Sally reached for the white bear Lil was holding. "Tell me about this cute little white bear."

"Crystal was a gift from a friend, to remember our trip way north to Alaska. She's a polar bear."

"And the black bear?"

"I found Peter in Europe, across the ocean. When he tries to speak English, the other bears tease him. And they bicker with one another, so I'm thinking of giving them away. Separation may be the only way to have peace and for them to make new friends."

"Oh, I don't think you should do that."

"Why not?"

"Because you'll miss them, like missing your little girl."

Lil sighed. "You're right, I would." Then she looked around before asking, "Are you alone? Where are your parents?"

Sally pointed as she answered, "Momma is working in that shop, over there. Daddy is a soldier far away this Christmas. I miss him a lot. I'm to stay here, near the tree, and check in with Momma every little while. She waves at me when she can. The mall security guard who watches the tree is watching me too. See, Momma is waving at me now. Excuse me, she wants me to come to her. I'll be right back."

Soon Sally's mother came and stood in front of Lil. "Excuse me, you were talking to my daughter. May I ask why?"

"For no reason, except that we were sitting here alone on the bench."

"Where do you live?"

"In the retirement home."

"The home that used to be the hospital?"

"Yes. I used to work in the hospital, as a nurse's aid on the floor where the babies are born, so I asked for an apartment on that floor."

"What years did you work on the obstetrics floor?"

"In the 1960s and 70s."

"Do you mind if I ask, what is your name?"

"I don't mind. I'm Lillian Pierce."

"Mrs. Pierce, you signed your name in my baby book."

"I did?"

"Yes, and Mother wrote that you were kind to her because she was alone. My Dad was in Vietnam. Thank you."

"You're welcome."

"You're right about Sally; she's lonesome, and her babysitters were all busy today."

"Can't your mother take care of her?"

"Mother died a few months ago. My baby book was in her things; I just looked at it last night when I was missing her and wishing she was here for Christmas because she loved the season."

"I used to, too, but now it's hard being away from family."

"Sally misses Granny Shirley so much. I need to work another hour. Do you mind talking to Sally again? And may she call you Granny Pierce?"

"Your mother's name was Shirley?"

"Yes."

"I almost named my baby girl Shirley, and now my daughter-in-law's name is Shirley."

"Lots of Shirleys in those days, because of Shirley Temple."

"She touched so many hearts with her curls and singing and dancing. So yes, of course, Granny Pierce will be happy to talk to a Shirley's granddaughter."

When Sally came back to the bench, Lil asked, "What do you want for Christmas?"

The little girl looked way up at the treetop star, and then at Lil. "I want what Mommy and Daddy want, so Daddy can come home—no fighting in the world under the star. That's what the Christmas carols are about, too, the peace on earth we sing about, and I'd like a granny like you to talk to again."

Lil smiled, and clasped Sally's outstretched hand. "You sound very grown-up for such a little girl. Do you have any brothers or sisters or cousins?"

"No, just Mommy to talk to and big stuff like stars to think about and words of songs to listen to, and I make up pretend stuff all by myself."

Lil laughed. "Me, too. Sometimes I tell stories to the bears so they'll stop bickering. I'll tell them a story now, if you'd like me to."

"Yes, and can we invite other children to hear the story?"

Lil had barely nodded when Sally stood on the bench and shouted, "Come, Granny Pierce is going to tell a story."

Almost immediately the security guard tried to hand a microphone to Lil. When she looked at it with fear and shook her head, a young boy stepped forward and said, "I'll hold it for her. I'm supposed to recite the Bible verses I memorized to introduce my church choir. Okay if I use the microphone after the story?"

"Sure. When you're through reciting, put it on the mic stand for the choir."

Lil held Chipper close, cleared her throat, closed her eyes for a few seconds, and then said to Sally and everyone listening, "Once upon a long time ago two sisters went on a long driving and camping trip out west with their father and brother. I see a hand up. Do you already have a question?"

"Yes. How far west did the sisters go on the trip?"

"All the way to the state of Colorado, to climb a high mountain named Pike's Peak. On the way they stopped in Yellowstone Park to see the scenery."

"Did they see bears?"

"Yes, and they fed the bear cubs they saw. They didn't see signs to not feed the bears. Now there are lots of warnings, and if you go there, please don't feed the bears. It's very dangerous, and the sisters shouldn't have done it. Fortunately, they were not injured by the mother bear. But they could have been."

Sally held the white and panda bears up so they were facing her. "Do you hear that, Crystal and Randy, that attacking and fighting is dangerous?"

"That's right, Sally; be stern and serious when warning others about the danger of fighting. You never know when it will get out of hand and where it will lead."

The young boy asked, "Like people wars?"

"Yes, sadly, like people wars."

"Is that the beginning, the middle, or the end of the story?"

"It could be whatever God and you, the bears, and these friends gathered around us want it to be. It could be the beginning, the middle, or the end of wars, fighting, and bickering."

A little boy came to the microphone and said, "A boy I know wants to fight all the time. So I want it to be the end."

A little girl said, "The family who lives upstairs in our apartment house fight all the time. I want it to be the end, too."

Sally held hands filled with bears up for everyone to see. "My wish for Christmas is what I think God wants it to be—for these bears and people to stop fighting and bickering!"

"And as the angel promised when Christ was born, we have peace on earth." Signaled by his church choir that they were ready to sing, the boy with the microphone continued, "Thank you, Granny Pierce, for the story. It was a perfect introduction to the verses I memorized: 'The wolf will live with the lamb, the leopard will lie down with the goat, the calf and the lion and the yearling together; and a little child will lead them. The cow will feed with the bear, their young will lie down together, and the lion will eat straw like the ox. The infant will play near the hole of the cobra, and the young child put his hand into the viper's nest. They will neither harm nor destroy on all my holy mountain, for the earth will be full of the knowledge of the Lord as the waters cover the sea.'"[194]

As if on cue, more shoppers gathered around, and Sally's mother came to sit by Lil and hold her daughter on her lap as the church choir sang the Isaiah 9:6 and 40:11 lyrics [abbreviated here] from Handel's *Messiah*: "For unto us a child is born, a son is given, and the government shall be upon his shoulder, and his name shall be called Wonderful Counselor! The Mighty God! The Everlasting

---

194. Isaiah 11:6–9.

Father! The Prince of Peace! . . . He shall feed his flock like a shepherd, and he shall gather the lambs with his arm, and carry them in his bosom, and gently lead those that are with young. Come unto him, all ye that labour, that are heavy laden, and he will give you rest."

On the way home, Lil's driver said, "I see you still have your bear."

"Yes, and the others in the bag. We met a new friend who needs friends to visit. She and her mother are coming to my apartment for a tea party after Christmas."

And they came, again and again, with Sally's Christmas bear named Prince to have tea with their new friends, Chipper, Randy, Crystal, and Peter.

Prayer

Wonderful Counselor! Mighty God! Everlasting Father! Prince of Peace!
Please bless all the little children everywhere who believe and
memorize Scripture and sing Christmas songs about angels, wise men,
shepherds, and the shining star that points to Bethlehem and to Baby Jesus,
the Legacy and Light of the world. Bless children and families who light and
use the Servant candle to light the other eight candles on the
Hanukkah menorah. May their faith grow, glow, and glare so brightly
that children of all ages will see and follow the Light through snow and
sunshine to worship Jesus.
Comfort those who relate to sweet, sad, and sentimental family memories.
Use the sail-filling power generated by your Spirit to energize parents,
grandparents, teachers, preachers, and elders to open your Word to the
right places at the right times for understanding and explaining
history-making events in our nation and throughout the world.
To bring peace on earth and end suffering and holocausts,
we plead with you to "carry out your sentence on earth with speed
and finality" as you reveal that "there is no difference between Jew and
Gentile—the same Lord is Lord of all and richly blesses all who call
on him, for, everyone who calls on the name of the Lord will be saved."[195]
We pray in the Name of Jesus our Savior. —*Amen*

Cruise Library Visit

Although this Cruise Day largely focuses on positive legacies, we can see legacies of "bickering"—much like Lil's bears—as well. One topic for scientific bickering that heated up in our parents' generation is whether to believe in Intelligent Design or Darwin's evolution theory. If you need to resolve the issue in your mind, I recommend checking out Lee Strobel's *The Case for a Creator* and viewing the documentary *Expelled: No Intelligence Allowed*, hosted by Ben Stein.

---

195. Romans 9:28, 10:12–13.

COOP. Chap, why are you and the Host staring at each other?

CHAP. Because we've been bickering about if and how to mention centuries of church bickering over a divisive question.

COOP. Why are you bringing that up in the Library?

CHAP. Because the Pilgrims brought Bibles to America, and the bickering began as denominations formed and interpreted the Bible differently.

COOP. Have you reached a resolution?

CHAP. Yes and no. Yes, in that we've decided that I, representing spiritual leadership, am free to admit that once again, after being trapped in blindness for centuries, the Jewish people are being released by God from bondage to evangelize and bless both Jews and Gentiles! We have seen and heard it said again and again on this *Mayflower* platform. That peacemaking, resolution, unification, and reconciliation process is promised over and over: in Isaiah, the Old Testament minor prophets, Matthew 24–25, Romans 9–15, John 15–17, 1 Corinthians 12, 2 Corinthians 5:11–21, and Ephesians.

COOP. I resolved that issue in my mind when Rabbi Rubinstein said the Messianics would sanctify the whole. So what is the unresolved "no"?

CHAP. "No" unresolved means that the bickering about when and how the Lord will return will not end until "the glory of the Lord will be revealed, and all mankind together will see it" (Isaiah 40:5). Thank God that *he* knows, but humans don't know when that will be!

Another bickering point and legacy from the twentieth-century generation, when the pace of busyness and technology advanced beyond comprehension, capability, and accessibility for many people, is choosing between quality and mediocrity. Bill was so concerned and interested in the topic that in the 1980s he purchased a book about it. Amusingly, considering the title and topic, several pages were missing. The publisher sent another copy, but without an explanation; we could only guess that a fast printing and bookbinding machine had broken down.

Editors, my publisher, our guest speakers, and I trust that every machine and way of communication used to produce and promote *Full Sail* will work perfectly—so there will be no bickering about the quality of the *Mayflower* Pilgrims' legacy in your hands. The Apostle Paul charted the course in the first century:

Rejoice in the Lord always. I will say it again: Rejoice! Let your gentleness be evident to all. The Lord is near. Do not be anxious about anything, but in everything, by prayer and petition, with thanksgiving, present your requests to God. And the peace of God, which transcends all understanding, will guard your hearts and your minds in Christ Jesus.

Finally, brothers, what is true, whatever is noble, whatever is right, whatever is pure, whatever is lovely, whatever is admirable—if anything is excellent or praiseworthy—think about such things. Whatever you have learned or received or heard from me, or seen in me—put it into practice. And the God of peace will be with you. (Philippians 4:4–9)

Cruise Bonus
One Yarmulke: A Holocaust Story

My husband's career placed our family on the front lines during the tense time in American and world history known as the Cold War. This post-World War II war was both an ideological and a military war, much like the Korean and Vietnam Wars, fought between free and communist nations.

From news heard at the end of World War II, we were prepared to see no Jewish people while living in West Germany and connected to the military communities of the North Atlantic Treaty Organization (NATO) and the United States.

We were wrong. From 1976 to 1980, we saw one yarmulke on one man's head. As Gentiles who worshiped God in churches, we didn't know that a traditional yarmulke, or *kippah* (Hebrew for covering), was a skullcap usually worn by devout Jewish men during reverent times in synagogues and homes—and sometimes in public, like the one yarmulke we saw in four years.

A search for worship sanctuaries in German villages and cities ended in many churches and cathedrals, but only a wall plaque in a West Germany city indicated a former synagogue site.

After we found a Jewish cemetery dating back to the 1100s in Worms, an elderly man told us an unusual story of mercy during the Holocaust. He recalled that when SS troops came to destroy the Jewish cemetery, local citizens told them that Himmler did not want the burial ground disturbed. The "Himmler" they spoke of was a Worms City Council member—not the infamous Heinrich Himmler! The ruse was successful, and the ancient Jewish cemetery was preserved.

While we looked for other memorials, more than thirty years after the World War II Holocaust—when six million Jews and millions of other innocent victims were murdered by Nazi tyranny—we saw artifacts and pictures of starving and murdered Jews and the *Never Again* memorial at Dachau Concentration Camp near Munich.

We walked on grassy knolls at Munich's 1972 Summer Games Olympic Park that covers city debris from church ruins and other bombed rubble. Silent white crosses and Stars of David in U.S. military cemeteries said more than we wanted to hear about tyranny's lust for conquest on the European landscape.

William L. Shirer, in *The Rise and Fall of the Third Reich*, writes, "The guns in Europe ceased firing and the bombs ceased dropping at midnight on May 8–9, 1945, and a strange but welcome silence settled over the Continent for the first time since September 1, 1939."[196]

This proof of the battle waged between good and evil caused us to wonder why a nation and citizens steeped in centuries of logic, science, arts, theology, and civilized cultural advantages forgot how to obey God's commands: "Do not seek revenge or bear a grudge against one of your people, but love your neighbor as yourself." And believe that "When the Most High gave the nations their inheritance, when he divided all mankind, he set up boundaries for the peoples according to the number of the sons of Israel. For the Lord's portion is his people, Jacob his allotted inheritance."[197]

People believe and obey the command to love in different ways. Jan Karski, a Holocaust eyewitness who reported to Allied leaders during World War II, obeyed when she told Holocaust liberators, "This sin will haunt humanity to the end of time. It does haunt me. And I want it to be so."[198]

We can believe and obey by listening as silent, haunting voices speak truth more deafening than sight or words. We can add our tears to God's, because laughter, cheering, clapping, weeping, music, stories, poetry, prayers, and footsteps are not heard—now by heaven and earth for over half a century. We can shout and live by truth to drown the voices of those who discredit, distort, or deny historic and biblical truth and devalue Holocaust sacrifices, victims, and lessons.

I must ask: In the twenty-first century when Holocaust survivors and first-hand observers of Nazi tyranny are gone, will disobedience, ignoring, and denying be easier for us? With unrighteous alliances forming and determined criminals again planning "final solutions," will we still taunt God's faithful counsel and mock his anointed? What can or should we do to solve our collective dilemma—to prevent forgetting and recurrences of the twentieth-century tragedy?

---

196. Shirer, *Rise and Fall of the Third Reich*, 1139.
197. Deuteronomy 32:8; Leviticus 19:18; Matthew 22:37–38; Mark 12:29–30; Luke 10:27; Romans 12:17–21; Galatians 5:14; James 2:8
198. Elaine Woo, "Holocaust eyewitness Jan Karski, 86, reported slaughter to Allied leaders," *Sacramento Bee*, July 15, 2000. Woo quoted Karski's 10/81 speech at the International Liberators Conference in Washington DC.

We can begin with serious intentions and paced steps. During the finite time the Holocaust survivors still live on earth with us, we can choose to overcome evil with good and rehearse for reconciliatory conversations in heaven: "Jewish friends and neighbors, God of Israel, please forgive us for closing our eyes, ears, hearts, and minds to tyranny and evil."

Our forefathers set eye-opening precedents. During American Revolutionary days, the liberty written on Patrick Henry's heart became freedom's vision when he established the "live free or die" attitude toward tyranny: "Is life so dear, or peace so sweet, as to be purchased at the price of chains and slavery?" he asked. His answer was clear: "Forbid it, Almighty God! I know not what course others may take; but as for me, give me liberty, or give me death!"[199]

As peoples, nations, and we ourselves are challenged by history's civil conscience, clamor, choices, and chaos, believing as we do that liberty's victory over evil is on God's righteous and always relevant agenda, we attach our courageous and zealous souls to a soaring breeze on this fresh-air day. Freed to repent, we confess that we have *taunted*, *mocked*, and *discriminated*. God forgive us.

Freed from bondage so that we may hope for a free-style future, we declare and defend a just cause. We stifle the stench and acts of loveless, vengeful, mocking, and barbaric tyranny, burying it in trenches of annihilation.

Finally and forever heartbroken and haunted—but free to *want it to be so*—we can *Never Again* forget to ask according to Psalm 140:1–3:

> God whose council stands forever,
> help us to love our neighbors as ourselves.
> Rescue us, O Lord, from evil men; protect us from men of violence,
> who devise evil plans in their hearts and stir up war every day.
> They make their tongues as sharp as a serpent's;
> the poison of vipers is on their lips. —*Amen*

Covenant and Dedications

Today, we covenant to dedicate subjects that are influenced by the legacies of our parents' generation, even as we live out those legacies today.

> Today We the Passengers covenant:
> To dedicate Occupations, Transportation, Technology, Communication,
> Science, and Traditions in America and all Nations to
> God's Glory and Honor.

Night Watch

199. Patrick Henry, March 1775, to the Virginia House of Burgesses. Quoted in Federer, *America's God and Country*, 288.

Scripture Course and Focus Points

Personal, family, church, state, and national legacies and assumed responsibilities were shared today as a *Full Sail* "denouement" (according to dictionary. com, "the final resolution for a plot") before giving thanks to God for sharing his course for our lives and world during our last Cruise Day. I pray you will discern more legacies for filling sails in these Scriptures and as God grants you peace and counsel.

Scripture: Nehemiah 9; Psalms 24, 89, 129:8, 130; Proverbs 3:21–24; 28; Isaiah 29; 49; 60; Mark 13:36; 1 Corinthians 2:6–16; 2 Corinthians 4:4–6; Philippians 1:9–11; 1 Thessalonians 5; James 5:20.

Add more to these Focus Points: Honor, bless, curse, inheritance, times and dates, prophecy, watch, terror, tyrannical ruler, wealth, prayer, door, taunt, mocked, glory.

Song
God Bless America

To fill sails and prepare for our last cruise day, sing or say aloud Irving Berlin's wonderful prayer, first performed by Kate Smith on Armistice Day, 1938. I remember listening to the radio performance with my parents. If you don't remember the words, please just hum along, or find the words in a music book or on the Web. Lyrics are not included here for copyright reasons.

We rest assured in Christ's Blessings as he ends this day.

End of Cruise Day Twelve

Cruise Day Thirteen Program
First and Last Things

〰〰〰〰〰〰〰〰〰

Scripture Course

First and Last Wake-Up Calls!

First and Last Introductions
Cruise Host's Generation

First and Last Briefing: You Are Graciously Invited
to a Thanksgiving and Remembrance Feast

First and Last Library Visit

First and Last Cruise Bonuses
Poems and "A Cold War Immigrant Story"

First and Last Free Time Options

Thanksgiving and Remembrance Feast

First and Last Covenant and Dedications

First and Last Night Watch

Disembarkation Procedure

〰〰〰〰〰〰〰〰〰

Scripture Course
I will give thanks to the Lord because of his righteousness
and will sing praise to the name of the Lord Most High.
Psalm 7:17

Scripture: Exodus 6:6–8; 1 Chronicles 16:8–9; Isaiah 44:6; Luke 12:32–40, 13:28–30; John 13; Romans 11:33–36; 1 Corinthians 5:6–8, 11:17–34; Galatians 3:26–29; Ephesians 3:21; Revelation 1:7–8.

First and Last Wake-Up Calls!

[This] book represents an honest attempt to depict truthfully one of the most remarkable groups of persons in our Country's history. They lived in stern times, and yet in the face of what seemed to be unsurmountable obstacles, they devoted themselves to their ideals and were willing to give their property and lives for conscience sake. They placed their trust in God and "accomplished the impossible."

The Pilgrims are not here to answer the untruths spread concerning them. It is the duty of those who revere this country and its founders to protect their memories. (Francis R. Stoddard, *The Truth About the Pilgrims*)

General Secretary Gorbachev, if you seek peace, if you seek prosperity for the Soviet Union and Eastern Europe, if you seek liberalization: Come here to this gate! Mr. Gorbachev, open this gate! Mr. Gorbachev, tear down this wall! (President Ronald Reagan, "Tear Down This Wall" Speech, Berlin Wall, June 12, 1987)

On this day 390 years ago the great explorer Sir Francis Drake died aboard ship off the coast of Panama. In his lifetime the great frontiers were the oceans. And a historian later said, "He lived by the sea, died on it, and was buried in it." Today we can say of the "Challenger" crew: Their dedication was, like Drake's, complete.

The crew of the space shuttle "Challenger" honored us by the manner in which they lived their lives. We will never forget them, nor the last time we saw them—this morning, as they prepared for their journey, and waved goodbye, and "slipped the surly bonds of earth" to "touch the face of God." (President Ronald Reagan, "Challenger" Speech to the Nation, Oval Office, January 28, 1986)[200]

---

200. "Slipped the surly bonds to touch the face of God" is from a poem called "High Flight" by John Gillespie Magee, Jr. Peggy Noonan wrote Reagan's speech, which comforted a shocked America after the *Challenger* space accident when seven space explorers were lost. www.presidentreagan.info/speeches/challenger.cfm

First and Last Introductions: Cruise Host's Generation Thirteen Generations from the **Mayflower**

Beverly Pierce Stroebel   b. 25 October 1931 Blue Earth County, MN
                            m. 19 June 1954 Blue Earth County, MN
William Stroebel   b. 26 November 1930 Blue Earth County, MN

First and Last Briefing: You Are Graciously Invited to a Thanksgiving and Remembrance Feast

Welcome to the last day of our thirteen-day *Full Sail* spiritual cruise on board the *Mayflower!* The Wake-Up Calls of Francis R. Stoddard and President Reagan fill sails by advancing history and faith. Because you already know so much about me, and so that we may remember the Pilgrim's Thanksgiving while still on our *Mayflower* platform, today's course is set for giving thanks—beginning with mine for you.

Loyal Passengers, please receive my sincere thanks for coming on board to preserve, protect, purify, and dedicate aspects of Judeo-Christian, American, and international life and liberty to God's glory and honor. After we have declared our allegiances and trusted that the three-strand rope representing America's financial, civil, and spiritual moorings would be strengthened and lengthened during our cruise, thanksgiving is the most obvious final aspect of life and liberty to purify and dedicate today. My final Library Visit choice provides more background and fills our sails all the more.

First and Last Library Visit

Stoddard's book, *The Truth About the Pilgrims*, was a rare book found while I was researching.

> Thanksgiving is a day which will be forever associated with the Pilgrims because they introduced it to America. It really was adopted from the Dutch who in turn had adopted it from the early Christians who in turn had taken it from the Bible in which the early thanksgivings of the Jewish People are described. The Dutch during their Eighty Years War with Spain used it to show their thanks to the Creator for His aid in the repelling of the invaders. The hymn, "The Prayer of Thanksgiving," was of Dutch origin and was first sung in the sixteenth century.
>
> The first real day of Thanksgiving by the Pilgrims was when they were driven to take refuge on Clark's Island before the landing at Plymouth on Monday, December 21, 1620. The event is described by Bradford as follows: "for the next

day was a faire sunshining day, and they found themselves to be on an iland secure from the Indeans, wher they might drie their stufe, fixe their peeces, and rest themselves, and gave God thanks for his mercies in their manifould deliverances. And this being the last day of the weeke, they prepared ther to keepe the Sabath."

It was in 1623 that no rain fell between the third week in May and the middle of July. All of their plantings began to dry and wither because of the lack of water, and it seemed that all crops would be lost and famine would be their lot. The Indians appealed to their God for rain but in vain. Eventually the Pilgrims decided to call on their God by a day of humiliation and prayer. Bradford describes what took place as follows: . . .

"It came without either wind, or thunder, or any violence, and by degreese in that abundance, as that the earth was thorouwly wete and soked therwith. Which did so apparently revive and quicken the decayed corne and other fruits, as was wonderful to see, and the Indeans astonished to behold; and afterwards the Lord sent them such seasonable showers, with enterchange of faire warme weather, as, through his blessing, caused a fruitfull and liberall harvest, to ther no small comforte and rejoicing. For which mercie (in time conveniente) they also sett aparte a day of thanksgiveing." In 1637, an ordinance was passed "that it be in the power of the governor and assistants to command solemn days of humiliation, and also for thanksgiving, as occasion shall be offered." When the other New England colonies were formed, they eventually followed the example of Plymouth and fixed a certain day for Thanksgiving by formal proclamation.

Thanksgiving became a national day of observance when the Continental Congress on November 7, 1777, by formal proclamation, recommended that Thursday, December 18, 1777, be recognized as such . . .

On October 3, 1789, President George Washington, at the request of Congress, issued his first National Thanksgiving proclamation recommended and appointing Thursday, November 26, 1789, as the day.

[BPS note: Stoddard lists dates when other presidents through Madison issued proclamations, until 1815.] Thereafter the practice was discontinued for forty-seven years.

On his own initiative, President Abraham Lincoln issued a formal proclamation dated April 10, 1862, selecting Sunday, April 13, 1862, as a day of National Thanksgiving.[201]

First and Last Cruise Bonuses
Poems and "A Cold War Immigrant Story"

Today's Cruise Bonuses were written by two friends and are shared with you as my way of saying thanks for being *Full Sail* prayer partners, along with thanks to all who pray for me and my fellow twentieth-first-century *Mayflower* Passengers.

First, meet Jone Bosch, a poet and writer who has earned M.Div and Th.M. graduate school degrees and has taught adult Sunday School and Bible study classes for over twenty years. She writes science fiction and biblical studies, and she is seeking a publisher for *Song in the Night,* a collection of poems for meditation.

Jone had Luke 12:32–34 in mind as she penned "Treasures Found." "Life has" is in her unpublished poetry book. *Song in the Night.*

Treasures Found	Life has
Treasures	Life has followed
found	paths we never
along the	thought we'd see.
way	We felt the hand of
wealth	God showing us the
acquired	paths of life and
day by	as we
day	near the end, we
value	sense God's
given	presence with
pound for	joy, knowing
pound	what waits for
tell us	us when we'll spend
where our	eternity at
heart is	God's right hand,
found.	basking in the
	pleasure of his
	presence eternally.

---

201. Stoddard, *Truth About the Pilgrims,* 10–13.

Next, let me introduce you to Elzbieta Zielinska, who emigrated from Poland and is now an American citizen and a member of the Hearts for Israel group with Bill and me. She earned a Master's Degree in geography in Poland; a Master's in screenwriting in America. When I first heard her story, I wondered if I was hearing a movie in the making! See what you think.

Cold War Immigrant Story
by Elzbieta (Elizabeth) Zielinska

I entered the United States in December 1986 to begin a new way of life with my son. I was born in Poland during the communist system. My father was a journalist and a member of the Communist Party. Thus our family could cut through the Iron Curtain to travel in the western European countries where I realized that the world was divided into two different realms: one free, and the other not really that free.

Communism is a satanic system devised by dangerous minds to aim at and destroy God's given individuality to each of us. It leads countries under its regime to inevitable economic disaster, enslaving their own people by distorting and trampling on their basic human rights and unleashing the massive machine of destruction, murder, and fear. These societies became ill-fed and degraded, sunk in apathy, idleness, and alcoholism, fearful, distrustful, despising honest labor, envious, and hateful toward their rulers.

The reigning class in communist Poland, party members called the Nomenclature, pretended that they didn't exist; they invented a massive cover-up by propaganda claiming that the working class was in fact ruling the country. But it was this hated privileged elite that maintained oppressive terror, using murder and imprisonment to stay in power. Their muscle was local forces long established by the Soviets in their own image: Internal Troops, Border Troops, and of course, State Security.

My favorite activity during this oppressive martial-law era was underground Free Solidarity broadcasts. My husband and I and a friend recorded and transmitted the news from our room in the university dormitory where we lived while special military units tried to locate us.

I was in despair when my sister was arrested for smuggling a matrix for the underground newspaper and had to await her military trial in jail. She was released after a few long months in jail for lack of sufficient proof. But later both of us were arrested and interned in the same camp on the seashore of the Baltic Sea.

The time I spent in an internment camp was very significant and interesting to me. I met many famous intellectuals, dissidents, and Solidarity leaders, among them Tadeusz Mazowiecki, the first Prime Minister of free Poland. After 1989, they became people in power in Free Poland—senators and representatives using moral power that was able to wipe out the aftermath of the disastrous communist system from my country.

I taught in a small country grammar school after my release from prison: again, the communists persecuted me because it was a common knowledge that I was a "subversive element." The director of the school, a party member, fired me on illegal grounds and took away my apartment. I sued them, but the judicial system was subordinate to the party, so my efforts were in vain—or so I thought. I fought them in their own courts of law for a year. To my astonishment, I won! Even the representative of the school congratulated me.

When a friend encouraged me to leave Poland for exile in America, I remembered my teenage dreams to dwell in the USA. I began my journey to American citizenship in the American Embassy where I was ushered immediately before the consul who told me that in two weeks I'd get a visa for myself and my son. I waited ten months for a passport from the communists.

When I landed in California, right away I told my sponsors, a group of Poles, that I would study in a film school here. They thought I was crazy because I could barely speak English. However, in 1990, I was accepted into the University of Southern California graduate screenwriting program, which I finished with a Master's Diploma. Now I'm writing scripts and awaiting my big breakthrough. That will be my twenty-first-century American dream come true.

Thank you, Jone and Elzbieta. We now pray for you.

Prayer
Almighty Providential Master,
Because we believe that you place people in the right places at the right time,
we believe that you will bless and use Jone, Elizabeth,
and many other unknown, gifted believers in free-style life and liberty
for your glory and honor. Fulfill their dreams and use their gifts to
fill today's sails and bless America. —*Amen*

First and Last Free Time Options

If you are taking a break at this time on our last day, take out a map and find the Netherlands— where Jone's ancestors emigrated from—and Poland, the original homeland of Elzbieta Zielinska. Locate where your ancestors came from, then thank God for the gifts immigrants have brought to America. Pray for your ancestral nations.

If you are meeting as a group, discuss why your ancestors emigrated. Without discussing personal and political opinions, pray for America's legal and illegal immigration problems to be solved.

As you feast today, consider how to use items on the menu during future Thanksgiving feasts with family and friends.

Thanksgiving and Remembrance Feast

Feast Menu
Welcome
Thanksgiving Treasures
Thanks to the Netherlands and the Dutch People
Song: "We Gather Together"
Edward Winslow's Thanksgiving Letter
George Washington's 1789 Thanksgiving Proclamation
Thanksgiving Law
Mayflower Thanksgiving Prayer
Thanksgiving and Remembrance Communion

Welcome

Welcome to our last day's feast, where we will give thanks, sing, and review some American Thanksgiving treasures.

Thanksgiving Treasures

"Over the River and Through the Woods" was written by Lydia Maria Child (1802–1880) and published in the collection *Flowers for Children* in 1844. Look on the Web for more verses.
Poem
Over the River and Through the Woods

Over the river, and through the woods,
To Grandmother's house we go;
The horse knows the way to carry the sleigh
Through the white and drifted snow.

Over the river, and through the woods—
Oh, how the wind does blow!
It stings the toes and bites the nose
As over the ground we go.

Over the river, and through the woods,
To have a first-rate play.
Hear the bells ring, "Ting-a-ling-ding,"

Hurrah for Thanksgiving Day!

Over the river, and through the woods
Trot fast, my dapple-gray!
Spring over the ground like a hunting-hound,
For this is Thanksgiving Day.

Over the river, and through the woods—
And straight through the barnyard gate,
We seem to go extremely slow,
It is so hard to wait!

Over the river, and through the woods—
Now Grandmother's cap I spy!
Hurrah for the fun! Is the pudding done?
Hurrah for the pumpkin pie!

Poem

Come home to Thanksgiving!
Dear children, come home!
From the Northland and the South,
From West and East,
Where'er ye are resting, where'er ye roam,
Come back to this sacred and annual feast.
(Horace Greeley, editor and political leader, "To All New Englanders,"
1846)

Thanks to the Netherlands and the Dutch People

We the Passengers, on behalf of every American and the people in other nations who are blessed by America, pause now in our reading and prayers to say a long overdue thanks to the Netherlands and the Dutch people for sheltering the Pilgrims from 1608 to 1620.

We are "the children after" that William Bradford and other Pilgrims spoke about in this letter to the Dutch Governor in New Amsterdam:

To the honoured, etc.
The Governor and Council of New Plymouth, wishes, etc. We have received your letters, expressing your good-will and friendship towards us, but with over high titles, more than is our right, or it is fitting for us to receive. But for your

good-will and congratulations of our prosperity in these small beginnings of our poor colony, we are much obliged to you, and acknowledge them with many thanks, accepting them as a great honour to us and a sure proof of your love and good neighbourhood . . .

. . . many of us are under further obligations for the courteous treatment we received in your country, having lived there for many years in freedom, as many of our friends do to this day; for which we and our children after us are bound to be grateful to your nation, and shall never forget it, but shall heartily desire your good and prosperity as our own, forever.

By The Governor And Council Of New Plymouth,
New Plymouth, March 19, 1627[202]

Song

Perhaps the Separatist Pilgrims heard and even sang this Dutch folk song while living in Holland for twelve years before they sailed in 1620. We know for sure that early Dutch settlers brought the song to New Amsterdam. In the twenty-first century, "We Gather Together" is a favorite American Thanksgiving hymn—presented here to say thank you to the Lord, to the Jews, to the Hollanders, and to the Pilgrims for establishing a praise and thanksgiving "attitude" for America.

We Gather Together

We gather together to ask the Lord's blessing—
He chastens and hastens His will to make known;
The wicked oppressing now cease from distressing:
Sing praises to His name—He forgets not His own.

Beside us to guide us, our God with us joining.
Ordaining, maintaining His kingdom divine;
So from the beginning the fight we were winning:
Thou, Lord, wast at our side—all glory be Thine.

We all do extol Thee, Thou leader triumphant,
And pray that Thou still our defender wilt be;
Let Thy congregation escape tribulation:
Thy name be ever praised! O Lord, make us free! *Amen*[203]

---

202. Bradford and Paget, *Of Plymouth Plantation*, 184–5.
203. Translated by Theodore Baker.

Cruise Day Thirteen Program

Edward Winslow's Thanksgiving Letter

Edward Winslow was a seventeenth-century *Mayflower* passenger and a published and significant historical author. These examples are excerpts from his letter to England about the Pilgrim's Thanksgiving with the Natives, meant to promote interest in sailing to Plymouth and to whet appetites even today.

> We have found the Indians very faithful in their covenant of peace with us, very loving and ready to pleasure us. We often go to them, and they come to us . . . yea . . . to be under the protection, and subjects to our sovereign Lord King James. So that there is now great peace amongst the Indians themselves, which was not formerly, neither would have been but for us; and we walk as peaceably and safely in the wood as in the highways in England.[204]

> Our bay is full of lobsters all the summer and affordeth variety of other fish; in September we can take a hogshead of eels in a night, with small labor, and can dig them out of their beds all the winter. We have mussels . . . at our doors. Oysters we have none near, but we can have them brought by the Indians when we will; all the spring-time the earth sendeth forth naturally very good sallet herbs. Here are grapes, white and red, and very sweet and strong also. Strawberries, gooseberries, raspas, etc. Plums of tree sorts, with black and red, being almost as good as a damson; abundance of roses, white, red, and damask; single, but very sweet indeed . . . These things I thought good to let you understand, being the truth of things as near as I could experimentally take knowledge of, and that you might on our behalf give God thanks who hath dealt so favorably with us.

George Washington's 1789 Thanksgiving Proclamation

> Whereas it is the duty of all nations to acknowledge the providence of Almighty God, to obey His will, to be grateful for His benefits, and humbly to implore His protection and favor; and Whereas both Houses of Congress have, by their joint committee, requested me "to recommend to the people of the United States a day of public thanksgiving and

---

204. Quoted in Heath, *A Journal of the Pilgrims at Plymouth*, 82–83.

prayer, to be observed by acknowledging with grateful hearts the many and signal favors of Almighty God, especially by affording them an opportunity peaceably to establish a form of government for their safety and happiness:

Now, therefore, I do recommend and assign Thursday, the 26th day of November next, to be devoted by the people of these States to the service of that great and glorious Being who is the beneficent author of all the good that was, that is, or that will be; that we may then all unite in rendering unto Him our sincere and humble thanks for His kind care and protection of the people of this country previous to their becoming a nation; for the signal and manifold mercies and the favorable interpositions of His providence in the course and conclusion of the late war; for the great degree of tranquility, union, and plenty which we have since enjoyed; for the peaceable and rational manner in which we have been enabled to establish constitutions of government for our safety and happiness, and particularly the national one now lately instituted for the civil and religious liberty with which we are blessed, and the means we have of acquiring and diffusing useful knowledge; and, in general, for all the great and various favors which He has been pleased to confer upon us.

And also that we may then unite in most humbly offering our prayers and supplications to the great Lord and Ruler of Nations and beseech Him to pardon our national and other transgressions; to enable us all, whether in public or private stations, to perform our several and relative duties properly and punctually; to render our National Government a blessing to all the people by constantly being a Government of wise, just, and constitutional laws, discreetly and faithfully executed and obeyed; to protect and guide all sovereigns and nations (especially such as have show kindness to us), and to bless them with good governments, peace, and concord; to promote the knowledge and practice of true religion and virtue, and the increase of science among them and us; and, generally to grant unto all mankind such a degree of temporal prosperity as He alone knows to be best.

Given under my hand, at the city of New York, the 3rd day of October, A.D. 1789.

Thanksgiving Law

On October 3, 1863, President Abraham Lincoln established Thanksgiving as a national holiday to be celebrated on the last Thursday of November—"a day of Thanksgiving and praise to our beneficent Father who dwelleth in the heavens."

From the beginning, the thanksgiving was to God. The national Thanksgiving combined the religious observance with harvest time and national and civil aspects of American life and liberty. On December 26, 1941, Congress established the official date in Public Law #379.

Mayflower Thanksgiving Prayer

Today we join with the *Mayflower* Society to pray.

Our Father,
We thank you for Thy care during the time we have been apart.
Be with us as we celebrate another Thanksgiving Season.
May the beat of the drums that summoned the Pilgrims to church
and communion with Thee, still beat in our ears to continue the fight
for freedom, which our forefathers fought and died for.
We fight another battle now, preservation of everything that stands for the
American Dream. May we be strengthened to press forward, and be given
understanding and courage to meet the challenge. Bless our President,
our country, and our soldiers who are far from home,
and give them the assurance that you are with them always,
and that good will prevail in the end.

We are thankful Father, for all your bountiful blessings for soul, mind,
and body. We thank you especially for the food provided for our use today,
acknowledging that all good things come from Your Loving Hands.
We pray in the name of Him who is the "Bread of Life."—*Amen*[205]

Thanksgiving and Remembrance Communion

The communion served on our last Cruise Day is in the original context of Christ's last Passover *Seder*, or the Last Supper.

If you are cruising as a group through time, please participate in the original context by serving unleavened *matzah* bread. First, we prepare with a Scripture course.

---

205. Ruth M. Oberhelman, quoted in Teal and Folger, *Pilgrims at Prayer*, 34.

Christ, our Passover lamb, has been sacrificed. Therefore let us keep the Festival not with the old yeast, the yeast of malice and wickedness, but with bread without yeast, the bread of sincerity and truth. (1 Corinthians 5:7–8)

THE AFIKOMEN

LEADER: "For the transgression of my people he was stricken" (Isaiah 53:8). It is time for us to share the *afikomen*, the final *matzah* eaten at Passover. Messiah broke *matzah* and gave thanks to the Lord.

ALL: *Barukh atah adonai eloheynu melekh ha'olam hamotzi lekhem min ha'aretz.* Blessed are You, O Lord our God, Ruler of the universe, who brings forth bread from the earth.

LEADER: Then the Messiah added, "This is my body given for you; do this in remembrance of me" (Luke 22:19). As we eat the *matzah* and the taste lingers in our mouths, we meditate on the broken body of the Lamb of God who takes away the sin of the world.

THE CUP OF REDEMPTION

LEADER: The cup of redemption symbolizes the blood of the Passover lamb. It was the cup "after supper," when Messiah identified himself.

ALL: "I will redeem you with an outstretched arm" (Exodus 6:6).

LEADER: The prophet Isaiah reminds us, "Surely the arm of the Lord is not too short to save" (Isaiah 59:1). "It is our own righteousness that falls short. Though the Lord searched, He could find no one to intercede . . . so his own arm worked salvation for him, and his own righteousness sustained him" (Isaiah 59:16). Yeshua the Messiah lifted the cup, saying, "This cup is the new covenant in my blood, which is poured out for you" (Luke 22:20). Just as the blood of the lamb brought salvation in Egypt, so Messiah's atoning death can bring salvation to all who believe.

ALL: *Barukh atah adonai eloheynu melkh ha'olam borey pri hagafen.* Blessed are you, O Lord our God, Ruler of the universe, who creates the fruit of the vine. Let us all gratefully drink.

THE CUP OF PRAISE

LEADER: Let us lift the fourth cup and give thanks to God, our great redeemer, and bless the Name of the Lord.

ALL: *Barukh atah adonai eloheynu melekh ha'olam boey pri hagafen.* Blessed are You, O Lord our God, Ruler of the universe, who creates the fruit of the vine.

224

LEADER: Our Passover *Seder* is now complete, just as our redemption is forever complete. Let us conclude with the traditional prayer that we may celebrate Passover next year in Jerusalem.

Prayer

> May the Prophet Elijah come soon in our time with the Messiah,
> son of David. —*Amen*

First and Last Covenant and Dedications

On this last Cruise Day we have feasted on God's glorious provisions and enjoyed the fruits of freedom as reflected in the words and music of our past. We have listened to a modern-day immigrant story which poignantly portrayed how deeply people all over the world *hunger* for the feast of freedom we enjoy in this exceptional nation—for which we have just given heartfelt thanksgiving. We have communed and now covenant and dedicate as one body to glorify God our great redeemer.

> We the Passengers covenant:
> To dedicate Amazing Grace, Truth, Thanksgiving,
> and Free-Style Life and Liberty in Full Sail
> from the First to the Last
> *to God's Glory and Honor for Ever and Ever.*

First and Last Night Watch

This pilgrimage was a first for everyone on board, including me, your Cruise Host. I hope that in the days, weeks, months, and years to come, we will return again and again and invite family and friends to cruise on board the *Mayflower*.

> Oh, the depth of the riches of the wisdom and knowledge of God!
> How unsearchable his judgments, and his paths beyond tracing out!
> Who has known the mind of the Lord?
> Or has ever given to God, that God should repay him?
> For from him and through him and to him are all things.
> To him be the glory forever and ever! Amen.
> (Romans 11:33–36; Ephesians 3:21)

Disembarkation Procedure

On this cruise, We the Twenty-First-Century Passengers have sailed through time and many aspects of free-style life and liberty. Next, we will go out into the world for Christ—by praying for nations and supporting missionaries, ministries, and outreaches.

The prayers are not just for disembarking from *Full Sail*. Please remember where the book is stored in your house to return to for prayer if you hear of or read about any of these nations—or issues we've prayed for— in the news.

Rest assured, Christ will be our helmsman on any pilgrimage through time, history, and Judeo-Christian faith.

**End of Cruise Day Thirteen
and the Full Sail Cruise**

Disembarkation
On the Deck at the Dock

Commissioning Course

Commissioning Song

Disembarkation Briefing

Prayers for Continents and Nations

Covenant and Dedication
Missionaries and Ministries and Fulfillment
of the Great Commission

Song of Choice

Full Sail Cruise Benediction

Commissioning Course
The Great Commission

Then Jesus came to them and said: "All authority in heaven and on earth has been given to me. Therefore go and make disciples of all nations, baptizing them in the name of the Father and of the Son and of the Holy Spirit, and teaching them to obey everything I have commanded you. And surely I am with you always, to the very end of the age." (Matthew 28:18–20)

Commissioning Song
We've A Story to Tell to the Nations

We've a story to tell to the nations That shall turn their hearts to the right,
A story of truth and mercy, A story of peace and light,
A story of peace and light. *Refrain.*

We've a song to be sung to the nations That shall lift their hearts to the Lord,
A song that shall conquer evil And shatter the spear and sword,
And shatter the spear and sword. *Refrain.*

We've a message to give to the nations—That the Lord who reigneth above
Hath sent us His Son to save us And show us that God is love,
And show us that God is love. *Refrain.*

We've a Savior to show to the nations Who the path of sorrow hath trod,
That all of the world's great peoples Might come to the truth of God,
Might come to the truth of God. *Refrain.*

Refrain
For the darkness shall turn to dawning, And the dawning to noonday bright,
And Christ's great kingdom shall come on earth, The kingdom of love and
light.[206]

Disembarkation Briefing

Disembarking from a ship usually means that a voyage has ended. Our
pilgrimage, by contrast, is forever. We do not know when or how, but we know
our time on earth will end, and we'll pilgrimage to our eternal home—our life
after earthbound life.

We boarded this ship with baggage—now-confessed sins—that God has
hurled into the sea as we sailed through time. Good riddance! After reviewing,
purifying, and dedicating many facets of free-style life and liberty—with our
life's adventure designated for the glory and honor of God—we are prepared to
disembark with vigor and vision for the future.

Before we do, please pause to dedicate the following reputation to God,
because he is the course-setter and commissioner in our lives. Former American
pilgrims have set disembarkation examples for many years.

According to the Mayflower Institute, 80–85% of gospel and missionary
resources sent to the world in the name of Christ over the past two hundred
years have come from America.

> A nation's rank among the peoples depends upon the
> contribution which it makes to God's purpose for mankind
> and upon its homage to His universal rule. (G. A. Cook)[207]

---

206. Words and music by H. Ernest Nichol (1896).
207. Cook, *Ezekiel*, 282.

228

Before disembarking through prayer for the nations, please take time to think about nations not mentioned by name in Scripture, including America—although I suggest, for your consideration, that all nations are mentioned. Look through God's eyes—and a space traveler's—to see the Bible's "islands" as continents surrounded by water, such as those mentioned in Isaiah 11:11; 18; 24:15; 40:15; 41:1–5; 42:4, 10–15; 49:1, 22; 51:5, 18; 60:9, 19; Ezekiel 26:18; and Revelation 21. Take careful thought about idolizing any continent or nation, because Peter warns that islands and homelands will disappear.

> The day of the Lord will come like a thief. The heavens will disappear with a roar; the elements will be destroyed by fire, and the earth and everything in it will be laid bare. Since everything will be destroyed in this way, what kind of people ought you to be? You ought to live holy and godly lives as you look forward to the day of God and speed its coming. (2 Peter 3:10–12)

The *day* is approaching, every day closer than yesterday. Many peoples and nations are not prepared for Judgment Day and the New Jerusalem, and even we who are warned and prepared need equipping by missionaries and immigrants who know why and how to pray.

Many were invited on board to lead prayers as we disembark alphabetically according to continents and nations. The Cruise Library contains contact information for supporting these missionaries and their ministries. Many missionaries exist on support that provides less than their needs. A warning: if we have more than we need, in prayer we may hear a call to give generously to those who have learned that no better or higher blessing exists than to be called by God!

Prayers for Continents and Nations
Africa

Prayers for Nigeria
By Steve and Jan Volker
"Jesus Film" Campus Crusade for Christ

Nigeria is the most populous country in Africa, located on the west central coast. Many mission groups and Nigerian denominations have seen great growth in the South over the last several years. The Jesus Film Ministry by Campus Crusade has played a significant part in leading large numbers of new believers to grow in discipleship and to provide leadership now for the spreading of the gospel in the central and northern parts of the nation. There are now over 140 translations of the Jesus Film along with the Book of Luke or the whole New Testament for 140 distinct language groups.

The Nigerian Jesus Film staff have also used the Hausa Jesus Film and New Testament (Hausa is the official trade language). Now there is a desperate need for thirty to forty new translations and more Jesus Film teams to reach out where false religions and occult practices and mistreatment of women abound in the north.

Please pray with us:

Our Father who made all the nations and tongues:
We trust you to meet the great needs for more Bible training centers,
more film team workers, and more support for the many unreached language
groups in Nigeria. We pray that your solid truth and growing character
within your people will overcome and defeat the lying and corruption
that has plagued this nation.
We also pray your will for all nations in Africa and on other
continents as in Isaiah 60:1–2: "Arise, shine for your Light has come and
the glory of the Lord rises upon you. See, darkness covers the earth
and thick darkness is over the peoples, but the Lord rises upon
the nations, and His glory appears over you." —*Amen*

Christ's Hope International and a Prayer for AIDS Ministry in Africa
by Dave Kase, National Director of Christ's Hope USA
www.christshopeusa.org

The numbers of HIV-infected people range from 5–30% in most African countries. They die painful deaths, alone, without dignity and without hope. A staggering number of orphans and vulnerable children are left behind without homes, adult protection or the loving arms of caring parents.

Christ's Hope International partners with supporters throughout the world to bring care, nurturing love, dignity and the hope that can only come through the saving grace of Jesus Christ.

Our three core ministries are:

1. Choose to Wait: Breaking the cycle of AIDS through sexual purity.
2. Care and Compassion: Ministering to those infected by HIV/AIDS.
3. Orphan and Vulnerable Children Care: Nurturing and caring for children affected by HIV and AIDS.

Dear Lord,
You know Africa has been hit hard with the scourge of AIDS. You alone
attend every death and see every tear that is shed by the millions of orphans
who have been left behind. We thank you for calling your people to reach out

in your name to the hurting and to care for these widows and orphans. We
have seen your Hope rise up in the middle of great suffering,
and we have learned the lesson that you are enough. Thank you for your
faithfulness to "comfort all who mourn, and to provide for those who grieve
. . . to bestow on them a crown of beauty instead of ashes, the oil of gladness
instead of mourning, and a garment of praise instead of a spirit of despair."
I have witnessed you doing this with my own eyes in Africa.
Thank you for the tremendous work you are doing there to
draw all people to yourself. We pray for a continued outpouring
of your Holy Spirit to convict, and to teach and comfort our
brothers and sisters in Africa. In Jesus' Name. —*Amen*

Antarctica

Pray for the "seven nations—Argentina, Australia, the United Kingdom,
Chile, France, New Zealand, and Norway—that claim territory in Antarctica.
Other nations, including the United States and Russia, do not acknowledge
these claims and make no claims of their own, but reserve rights to claim territory in the future. Since 1961 the continent has been administered under
the Antarctic Treaty, an international agreement to preserve the continent for
peaceful scientific study."[208]

Asia

Prayer for China
by Douglas and Wendy Miller

Dear Heavenly Father,
We are grateful for your sovereign working in our lives today and
throughout history. O Lord, consider and grant these requests toward
the nation and peoples of China in the coming years:
Pour out the Holy Spirit upon the land to bring healing to the many
Chinese peoples and cultures. O Lord, draw near to those who are hopeless
and brokenhearted. Open the eyes of the Chinese leaders and intellectuals
and raise up a godly cadre of true believers, effective teachers, and leaders
from the ashes of communism and atheism to lead the people of China to
practice kindness, mercy, and truth as taught by your Word.
Break through every wall constructed by man under the influence
of the powers of darkness to shine the True Light of Salvation
through Jesus Christ upon China.

---

208. "Antarctica," Microsoft Encarta Online Encyclopedia 2009. http://encarta.msn.com

We ask that Chinese Christians will have greater access to
Bibles and receive the correct teaching of your Word.
In the powerful Name of Jesus Christ, by faith alone,
we ask for these things by your hand. —*Amen*

Australia and Oceania

Prayer for Australia
by Rev. Liberty Savard, Liberty Savard Ministries, Inc.

I was blessed to have several Australian students come to America and attend two of my Keys of the Kingdom Schools in Sacramento, California, in 2005. Aussie Christians love the Lord with a unique passion and tears of compassion just below the surface of their humor.

This country's history has been long, rich, and sometimes turbulent. But Australia seems to be poised today for a sweep of God's Spirit over the nation. The 2001 Census stated that Australian beliefs break down like this: Catholic 26.4%, Anglican 20.5%, other Christian 20.5%, Buddhist 1.9%, Muslim 1.5%, other 1.2%, unspecified 12.7%, none 15.3% . Because the Australian believers long for a total surrender to Christ in their nation, join me to pray for Australia:

Lord,
We bind every person in Australia to your will and purposes for their lives.
We ask you to bless them, encourage them, and pour out
your mercy and grace upon them. Reveal your Son, Jesus,
to them in divine and miraculous ways. Bind their minds to the mind of
Christ and loose wrong patterns of generational bondage thinking
from them. Loose the effects and influences of wrong agreements
from them. Bind their emotions to the healing comfort of the
Holy Spirit and loose unforgiving thoughts and the reactions
and distractions of their souls' desires to pursue the ways of the world.
We ask you to arise and shine in this precious country, Lord.
Make Australia an example to the world. Raise up strong Christian
leaders in Australia and especially in the Aboriginal tribes.
Let them all see Jesus in each other and draw their
strength from that unity.
Bless the Australians, Father, and cause them to light the way for
other countries. Cause them to show the world how you are
perceived in the Body of Christ from "down under." —*Amen*

Prayers for Indonesia
by Philip and Diane Messah
(Born in Jakarta, Indonesia; emigrated to the U.S. in 1976)

The Republic of Indonesia is a country of cultural diversity and natural wealth. Most areas are predominantly Muslim, a few areas are predominantly Christian, and the island of Bali is predominantly Hindu. Although there are many strict Muslims in the country, for the average Indonesian, religion is built on top of a deeper spirituality involving ethnic tradition, animism, cultural taboos, and ancient legend. Indonesia is home to over one hundred unreached people groups.

Almighty God:
We pray about Indonesian national issues:
★ Endemic corruption affecting every level of society including the Church (Proverbs 22:1, 4).
★ Fanaticism breeding ethnic and religious hatred (Proverbs 2:5–8, 21:21).
★ The president and his government as they seek to tackle these issues including poverty and multiple natural disasters such as tsunamis, earthquakes, and volcanic eruptions (Proverbs 3:3–6,14:34, 16:12, 31:8–9).

We pray for the Indonesian Christians:
★ For victims of violence, church burnings, and persecution, particularly those in the Maluku Islands and Central Sulawesi (Revelation 2:2–3, Revelation 26–29, and Romans 12).
★ For a greater unity among the Body of Christ, the growth of a national prayer movement, and a commitment to outreach in Indonesia and beyond (Colossians 2:2–3, Colossians 3:1–4:6; Acts 2:38-47; and Romans 1:16).
★ For Muslim-background believers who need great wisdom to know how to express their faith in Christ and great strength to persevere (2 Thessalonians 2:13–3:5 and 2 Timothy 4:1–8).
To you be all honor, glory, and praise now and forever. In His Name. —*Amen*

Prayer for Israel, India, Nepal, and Thailand
Jews for Jesus Massah Program
by Sterling Reed

Jews for Jesus is providing young Jewish believers with an amazing opportunity to get involved in ministry overseas. Through a program called *Massah* ("The Journey"), college-age Jewish believers can experience ministry and discipleship and learn about Jewish identity.

God, open the eyes and hearts of the travelers and people living
in India, Nepal, and Thailand. In these nations where so many people
are looking for something, looking for truth, looking for identity,
looking for answers, I know you are the only one who can satisfy what
they're searching for. Please be merciful to open and prepare
their hearts for the message we bring. I know that by ourselves
we are capable of so little, but with you we can do anything.
I know that we may feel inadequate facing the task set before us,
but you have prepared us for such a time as this and have equipped us
with all we need. I know that in the end all we can do is to be obedient,
and that the rest depends on you. I've seen you at work, and
I'm so hungry to see more. Lord, you are good and faithful,
and I ask you for more. We won't be satisfied
until we see you glorified. —*Amen*

Prayer for Iraq
by Anonymous Servants for Christ

Father, we pray:
★ that you will make the eastern church rise in boldness such as it once had.
★ that you will protect and use Iraqi Christians who confess Jesus Christ.
★ that your justice will prevail here so that corruption and
favoritism might die.
★ that the church will stand as an example instead of an embarrassment to
God's righteousness.
★ that people will have faith in what is true, instead of having faith in money.
★ that people will bow to the true God, instead of to Mammon.
★ that you will start a chain reaction of love in this country.
★ that your power will cross every political, ethnic, and religious barrier and
unite people in love.
★ that the country will come to know your peace through
men and women of peace. —*Amen*

Israel

And Still They Come
by Raymond "Bob" Fischer
Author, American and Israeli Dual Citizen

The modern-day State of Israel was established on May 14, 1948. The emigration of the Jews to Israel began in earnest in 1950 with the Law of Return, which granted every Jew the automatic right to immigrate to Israel and become a citizen. My wife, Donna, and I were clearly called by the Lord in early 1992 to "make aliyah" (emigrate to Israel).

Sadly, as many as half of the Jewish remnant in Israel are below the poverty level, with unemployment among them continuing at about 15%. Many cannot afford medical or dental care which, contrary to common understanding, is not provided by the government. Mortgage foreclosures, eviction for non-payment of rent, utility termination, inadequate clothing and food—these are a way of life for many brothers and sisters.

And still they come! And still they come! And still they come!

Because our fellow Jews in the Diaspora continue to hear the Biblical call and come to Israel despite the difficulties that may await them, we established the "Olim Fund of the Land of Israel," an official Israeli tax-free charity, in 2004.

Detailed information about the Fund and how you can join us in this effort is at our Web site, www.olimpublications.com. Please pray with me.

Heavenly Father:
In the name of Yeshua, your Son, we praise and thank you on
behalf of your people, Israel, for your never-failing love and provision.
We ask you to quicken the hearts of our fellow believers in Yeshua
around the world to help new immigrants with their continuing plight.
We pray that the Olim Fund might continue to grow and
prosper to help meet growing survival-level needs.
Father, as you know, Israel is surrounded by enemies sworn to
wipe our country from the map and to kill us all, each and every
Jew who would dare to reside here in the Land of our inheritance.
Persecution is growing in many nations. We ask you to protect us.
Hear prayers for our enemies and for our Arab-Christian cousins,
and remain faithful as in past generations.
Finally, we ask you to lift curses and abundantly bless every
brother and sister in Yeshua who selflessly reaches out to us in prayer,
encouragement, and material support. We ask these things in the
Holy name of Yeshua. —*Amen*

Ministry and Prayer for Arabs and Jews in Israel
by Carol and Wayne King

We ministered among the Arab community in Israel for thirty-nine years, training local Arab Christians to lead the ministry of Child Evangelism Fellowship in Israel. We have left a team of teachers there, led by Fadi Hanna. Their ministry includes Teacher Training, Good News Clubs, summer 5-Day

Clubs, camps, puppet ministry, school chapels, special classes for kindergartens, Christmas and Easter clubs, and translation of CEF literature. Most of our Arab teachers also speak Hebrew fluently and have been privileged to also minister within the Messianic Jewish community. God has abundantly blessed all these ministries, and praise to him, many boys and girls have come to know Jesus personally. Many of the adult leaders in the Christian community today are the result of CEF ministry in Israel.

Heavenly Father:
We praise you for all you have done to make your
Name known in your Land. We pray that many more children, moms
and dads, both Arab and Jew, will come to know Jesus personally
and become part of your family. We pray that many more people,
from all over the world, will be burdened for this strategic
ministry and get involved with prayer and financial support.
We pray that the proclamation of God's Word will not be hindered
during this harvest season because of man's sinful inclinations
and the devil's work to prevent the Good News from being spread.
"Pray ye the Lord of the harvest to send forth
[protect and provide for] laborers into His harvest."
In Jesus' Name, —*Amen*

Ray of Hope in Israel: Presenting the Gospel to the Jew And the Nations

Ray of Hope Ministries includes Shabbat services, a humanitarian aid center which supplies food and other items to new immigrants as they assimilate into the country, and a ministry at the camps where Chinese construction workers live while working in Israel.

Father, we ask for discernment, boldness, and your protection for
those who love the unsaved Jews, Arabs, and Gentiles so much
that they are willing to pay the price for their faith.
We ask for your intervention for several families throughout Israel who
are in jeopardy of deportation and for your grace for those Christians and
Jewish believers who have been already systematically removed from the land.
We especially ask for the Russian-speakers and others who have been sent
back to countries where they no longer have citizenship.
We pray for truth, righteousness, and justice to prevail in the
court cases that are presently before the Supreme Court.
We cry to you on behalf of the many Christian Gentile women
in Israel who do not have citizenship although they are married
to Jewish Israeli citizens.

We also petition for the Ethiopian Jewish believers who have not yet been allowed to enter Israel. Lord, raise up compassionate men and women who will lobby for this group of people who are perishing for the name of Yeshua. In Yeshua's name we pray. —*Amen*

Prayer for Japan and Japanese People Around the World
by Kevin and Peggy Grip

Our ministry is many faceted.

Reaching women with the gospel: Pray for Peggy's English Bible study for moms who come, mostly as friends of other participants, with little or no background in the Bible and learn about Jesus for the first time.

Reaching men with the gospel: Pray for men who come to afternoon barbecues with their family and friends.

Reaching young people with the gospel: Some young people in Japan stop going to school, or even contemplate suicide, because of the social stresses and struggles at school. Pray for our eighth-grade daughter and her friends, who started a fun-filled evangelistic gathering for their Japanese friends. Now others are trusting in Jesus as their Savior.

Reaching the world: Pray for Kevin. As missions coordinator for Campus Crusade's ministry in Japan, he has the challenge and privilege of helping send short- and long-term missionaries from Japan.

While we are encouraged by the things God is doing, the spiritual ground is hard, and Japanese Christians and missionaries struggle with discouragement. Please pray that believers will stand in the midst of spiritual battle and that unbelievers' hearts will be prepared to hear and receive the gospel. Please pray for a breakthrough with "the first husbands" in families to set in motion a movement for trusting in Christ.

Prayer for Jordan
by Anonymous Agape Servants
(Names Withheld for Privacy and Protection)

The Jordan Kingdom is an Arab country bordering the State of Israel. It is 93% Muslim and 3% Christian. We have lived in Jordan as agape Christians since the late 1990s. We worship with a Messianic Jewish congregation. We are known and accepted as Christians. Arab friends accept our offer to pray when they are ill and under trauma. Even King Abdullah II and Queen Rania, during the one time we met them, seemed pleased when told we pray for them every day. Please pray with us:

Abba Father:

You have given us your agape love for your Arab people, both Christian and Muslim alike. In spite of what we see, we know that Yeshua died for each one of your creation and that you have not wanted anyone to be lost for eternity. Knowing your desire, we agree with you and become intercessors for this people who have been deceived by the enemy.

The Kingdom of Jordan is an earthly kingdom that has a king in leadership. You tell us to pray for those in authority over us, so we lift King Abdullah II and Queen Rania up to you and ask for your will to be done in their lives. We ask you to import godly wisdom and biblical understanding to them, that they will lead their people in paths of righteousness.

The Arabs are sons of Abraham, and you have blessed them because Abraham asked you to do this for Ishmael. So we take the authority in Jesus' name and ask you to release them from the lies of the enemy and bind them to your will, Abba Father. Also release them from the bondage to telling lies and fighting, even amongst themselves.

Specifically, we pray for the children, especially those in orphanages and those needing wheelchairs and better nourishment and education. —*Amen*

A Prayer for Taiwan
by Chia Hong-bun, translated by David Alexander

> For Taiwan's islands, we ardently pray.
> Come, Holy Spirit, to enlighten our way.
> For Taiwan's people, we humbly implore,
> fill us with Jesus' love to our very core.
> O Almighty Father, your kingdom come here,
> that sickness and poverty we may nevermore fear.
> Our Father in Heaven, may your will be done.
> May justice and righteousness shine as bright as the sun.

The Rev. David Alexander is a minister of the Reformed Church in America. He grew up in Canoga Park, California, and received his ministerial training at New Brunswick Theological Seminary in New Jersey. Finishing college in 1976, he went to Taiwan on a missionary intern program and stayed for two years. Returning to the U.S. for theological education, he eventually married Charlene Bos from McBain, Michigan. They returned to Taiwan in 1982 and have lived there ever since in various ministry capacities, including campus evangelism, parish work, publications, university teaching, and theological education.

Prayer for Russia
by Sara Robinson, student at California Baptist University
(Mission trip to St. Petersburg, Russia, through Sunergos International in May 2008)

Dear Lord,
I ask that you be in the hearts of the orphans of Russia. Bring someone into each of their lives to show them your love and your light. Please help these children and teenagers know that there is a better way to live than turning to alcohol, crime, and prostitution. Thank you for placing people in Russia to minister to the people of this country. I pray that you would strengthen the missionaries that you have placed there so they can continue your work.
I pray that the people would see past traditions and really understand what a relationship with you is like. I thank you for the work that you are doing and will continue to do.
I pray that we would be able to unite as Christians around the world and glorify and lift your name up in all nations. In your Holy Name, —*Amen*

Europe

Why And How To Pray For Poland
by Elizabeth Zeilinska

In a sense, World War II didn't end in 1945 for Poland, but rather ended when the Soviet Union relinquished control over her in 1989. Mainly thanks to the Polish Pope, John Paul II, the Solidarity movement, and America's leadership, the communistic regime collapsed in Eastern Europe.

Dear God:
You know that Poles went through many sufferings,
including betrayal by friendly allies after WWII.
Heal the land and wounds of the people, and bestow your blessing there.
We ask that Poland will be open to your plan for Europe.
Protect Poland's boundaries, wedged between two countries,
Germany and Russia, historically expansive and hostile toward her.
We ask for cleansing of the land from shedding Jewish blood during the
Nazis' reign. We ask that Poland and other European nations will
repent of idolatry and sins against the Jews, God's chosen people.
We ask that renewal in the Holy Spirit, which has powerfully started in the
Catholic Church, will blossom and increase in Poland, and we pray for breaking of a religious spirit, that people will go directly to God in prayer.
We ask for governments to be established by God and anointed by him in his
power, wisdom, and grace. —*Amen*

Seeing the Light in the Netherlands
by Emma Hansen

Emma Hansen is a Hawaii/California native who was deeply impacted by Jesus Christ in her university years. God grew her heart for other nations over several years working in university ministry, during which she met Steve and Julie Kramer. They shared their vision for reaching the 16.3 million people in the Netherlands and a generation who have turned away from Christ. So she packed up her bags and set sail for the old country, desiring to bring hope to a lost generation.

Now Emma writes,

The Netherlands is home to many things, but also home to the famous painter Rembrandt, known as the Painter of Light. One of the famous sayings in Dutch around Leiden when they were celebrating Rembrandt's four hundredth birthday is, "In Leiden, Rembrandt saw the light."

Father God:
We pray that your "light would shine in the darkness"
and that truth would be illuminated here in the Netherlands.
We pray that the universities would again be a place of enlightenment,
drawing students to the love of Christ and compassion to reach the world.
We pray that the Dutch churches would come alive and be freed
from the oppression of "religious duty" and guilt.
God, raise up a generation who bypass the skepticism of their
forefathers and jump passionately into the faith that comes from you.
We ask you to give confidence and courage to our Christian family who are
seeing and following the light for the first time.
Just as Rembrandt "saw the light" in an artistic sense,
we pray that the Dutch and all of the Netherlands would see and
come to the "Light" of Jesus Christ. —*Amen*

A Prayer for Scotland
by Karah Baker
(*Full Sail* cover artist, who served with Youth With a Mission in Scotland. Karah graduated from the San Francisco Art Institute in 2009.)

Dear Father:
Please renew the Scots' passionate fire for the gospel,
and renew your sending call to the people in Scotland.
Renew and restore the churches, drawing people of all ages into
your kingdom. May the warrior-spirit in the Celtic heart be stirred
for the glory and praise of God, the Creator of all. Jesus,

may your love heal all wounds and cleanse all the darkness away.
Thank you for the many gifts and callings with which you've blessed the
Scots, and we bless your will in the nation. —*Amen*

North America

Prayer for Host Native Nations in the USA
by Ed LaRose

As a Pitt River and Pomo Nations man—and a man of God—I speak
God's vision for our world—Revelation 5:9: "And they sang a new song, saying, thou art worthy to take the book, and to open the seals thereof: for thou
wast slain, and hast redeemed us to God by thy blood and out of every kindred
and tongue, and people and nation" (KJV).

Lord:
Your vision is for every nation. We will believe and pray for nothing
less than this being done in Yeshua's Name. —*Amen*

Comfort Israel and Prayer for Mexico

Comfort, yes comfort My people says your God, speak comfort to Jerusalem. (Isaiah 40:1)

Comfort Israel is a division of International Disciple Training, Inc. (I.D.T.).
The heart of this ministry is to comfort, encourage, and express unconditional
love and solidarity to the Jewish people worldwide and to the nation of Israel.

I.D.T. is a twenty-two-year-old Christian interdenominational ministry
that enjoys legal status in the United States (California), Mexico, Canada, and
Liberia, West Africa. Our work in Baja, Mexico, spans from building free hous-
ing for the poor to running a child daycare center and an orphanage, working
with local churches, and providing feeding and clothing programs and most
importantly, discipleship.

Let us join Brandy Cook in this prayer for Mexico:

Blessed are You, Lord our God, King of the Universe,
Master of our lives who is faithful to complete all good things you have
begun! Lord, we turn our hearts and our eyes toward you; we seek you,
O God, for your favor upon the nation of Mexico,
a nation that abstained from the UN vote in 1948 for Israel to
receive internationally recognized statehood.
We thank you, dear Father, for the awakening in the church in Mexico,

for the Mexican people, for the Mixteco people, for the Triqui people, for all
the tribes represented in this nation to whom you have revealed your truth.
We ask, as Holy Spirit fire descends upon the precious nation of Mexico, that
the people will send missionaries into the world to proclaim your salvation.
We ask that Mexico would radiate the Glory of the Living God, that the light
of Jesus Christ would be the outstanding characteristic of this nation!
Hear our praises, Heavenly Father, for your grace and mercy.
May you be high and lifted up and glorified in the earth.
Amen in the mighty name of Jesus Christ, *B'Shem Y'shua HaMashiach*.

Prayer for Canada
by Rachel Robinson, student at California Baptist University
(Mission trip to The Connection, Vancouver, May 2008)

Dear Heavenly Father,
Thank you for all you have done and all you are going to do in Canada.
Thank you that your people have been burdened to share your gift of sal-
vation, and continue to burden us to spread the gospel. Let the hearts of
Canadians be softened to who you are and their need for you in their lives.
Let the workers in Canada draw their strength and wisdom from you. Let the
people of Canada be set on fire for you so that their nation may be a light to
the world. As your work is done in Canada, be glorified.
In Jesus' Name, —*Amen*

Arts Ministries and a Prayer for the Church and Peoples of Canada
by Rachel Starr Thomson

I am an author, editor, and small publisher, and I co-direct the Canadian
professional dance company Soli Deo Gloria Ballet. We are passionate about
presenting old truths in new ways that will touch hearts and lives through the
power of God's Holy Spirit. You can find my writings online at www.rachelstar-
rthomson.com or visit Soli Deo Gloria Ballet at www.solideoballet.com.

Our Father, which art in heaven,
From the cities, mountains, and fields of Canada, we praise and worship
your holy name. You have been faithful to provide for us, surrounding us with
incredible beauty, abundance, and peace.
We pray that you would strengthen and purify your church, imparting
passion and conviction to your people in these times when it is so much easier
to be moderate and apathetic. We pray that your glory, your holiness, and
your love would mark your people, making us truly "the true north strong
and free." We pray that you would end the scourge of abortion in our land,
turning the hearts of fathers and mothers to their children.

Disembarkation

And we pray, dear Lord, in the name of Jesus your unspeakable gift,
that you would bring the nations of this nation to yourself—the First Nations
peoples, immigrant communities, and French and English-speaking groups
that dwell here together. For thine is the kingdom, the power,
and the glory, forever and ever. —*Amen*

South America

Prayer for Brazil and the Work of Hope Unlimited
(Prayer by Antonio Oliveria)

In Brazil, there are an estimated 7 million street children. They suffer every imaginable form of abuse, neglect, violence, and exploitation. The average survival for street kids is only three to four years. These children desperately need a new beginning.

We minister to the physical, educational, and spiritual needs of Brazil's street children who live in mortal risk. Using a comprehensive, Christ-centered model, these children experience personal transformation while being equipped to live successful, productive lives as adult members of society.

Father,
We pray that you'll keep touching people with the gospel and raise up
prophets to purify the church. We pray that the enormous Church of
Brazil will get more involved with the things that your son was involved
with, preaching the gospel to the poor, healing the sick, discipling people,
and caring for the needy, instead of focusing most of our efforts
and resources in liturgical aspects of religion.
We ask for the revival of Brazil not to stop, but to mature in saintliness
and sacrifice. We pray that you will give intelligence and wisdom to Brazilian
Christians so we can affect our nation and the world. Most of all, we pray for
uniting love in the church. That Christians might forget the small things that
separate us and gather around God's love showed on the Cross. —*Amen*

Ministries in Multiple Nations

My Ministry To Three Nations: Columbia, Sudan, Angola
by Fran Gralow

Twenty-six years of my life were spent as a missionary/linguist in Colombia, South America. A coworker and I lived among the Koreguaje people for several years, learned their language, made an alphabet for it, taught people to read it, and translated the New Testament and an abridgment of the Old Testament into that language.

Through the Word of God in their language, people have been delivered from alcohol and evil spirits, received courage to stand up to the drug trade, and found meaning for their lives.

Next, I spent five and a half years in East Africa training Sudanese Bible translators and literacy workers, most of this time laboring with poor health. Of these Sudanese, some young Christian men who were not listened to when they tried to preach the gospel to older members of their society found that the Scriptures they translated were considered authoritative and worth listening to.

Now, after many years as refugees in neighboring countries, these newly trained men are returning with many of their countrymen to the land of their birth and continuing their ministries in their home areas.

By the time you read my story, I hope to be in Angola with a different organization to initiate a Bible translation program there. Through all these years working in South America and Africa, I could not have done anything if it weren't for the prayers and financial support of people at home. The people I have worked with and will work with in these various countries need our prayers.

Lord, we pray for the Koreguaje people of Colombia, that you will protect them and continue to work in hearts to bring them to yourself. Help those who have turned to you to continue to be faithful to you and to share their faith with others. Make it possible for the remaining copies of the Koreguaje Scriptures to get into the hands of those who will read them and follow them. We pray Sudanese Christians will apply Scriptures to their lives. We pray national Christian workers in Sudan will make good progress in translating more Scripture and success in literacy efforts in the many languages of Sudan. Protect them from hostile influences and the temptations of materialism. We pray especially for the persecuted people of Darfur, for protection from danger and the strength to carry on. We pray for the country of Angola as it recovers from decades of war, for physical and emotional healing and the ability to forgive one another. Raise up willing workers to labor in the translation of the Bible into the languages that still need it and provide ways to sustain them and their families as they work. Prepare the hearts of the peoples of Angola to receive the Word of God in their own tongues. —*Amen*

Sisters in Service: Extending God's Love to Unreached Women and Children by Michele M. Rickett

The news for women and children in lands least reached with the gospel is bleak. Women and children are least-fed, least-educated, abused, abandoned, abducted, and enslaved. They comprise 80% of all refugees, 70% of the poor, and two-thirds of illiterates. Each year, 500,000 girls die of shock and infection from female circumcision, and 4 million are trafficked. Though they are the least valued in our troubled world, God invites us to speak up for them and reach out to help them in practical ways. By working with local Christian women who know the language and the culture, we provide resources to bear the light of God's love, woman by woman, project by project.

Last year, nearly 40,000 women and children heard and experienced the gospel from a woman of their own culture strengthened by Sisters In Service. We work in the least reached places: Afghanistan, Indonesia, China, Iraq, Egypt, Mali, Ethiopia, Senegal, India, and the Sudan.

Dear Heavenly Father:
We know that you are very near to the brokenhearted. Be very near to the women and children who suffer so much and do not know your everlasting love in Jesus Christ. Strengthen our hearts and hands, so that your nearness can be experienced by those of us who say we follow you.
Father, allow women who live in virtual cultural prisons to meet women who look and sound like them who can communicate your love.
Grant our sisters courage and protection where they reach out under persecution and poverty. Supply their needs.
Each region presents different forms of oppression:
Indian girls are told they are less valuable than a cow, underfed and undereducated.
African girls endure mutilation and are sold off to marry older men.
Rural Chinese women have the world's highest rate of suicide.
Arab women are kept as slaves.
Widows and orphans have no way to feed themselves.
Sexual exploitation resulting in disease is rampant.
And you see all the ravages of a sin-sick world on each vulnerable one.
Show mercy to them through your people.
Awaken the hearts of those who have been given so much.
Teach us to leverage our freedom, education, time, and giftedness for those who suffer to serve the least of these.
May your renown be spread over the whole earth
through the least likely vessels: humble women of faith and faithfulness.
For that worthy Name, Jesus! —*Amen*

Prison and Released Prisoner Ministry

Disciples of Christ: Outreach to Inmates

D.O.C. began in Placer County Jail, Auburn, California, in October 2005 and grew to just under one thousand members in thirteen months!

Inmate Damon Bates had a vision: to bring the truth of freedom in Christ to men and women who saw themselves and their lives as hopeless, useless, and unloved. And for the future, to develop a physical location with resources for men and women being released into society: a safe place, a learning place, a place to grow in the Word of God and become servants as well as serve their surrounding communities.

After Damon told his cell mate his vision, D.O.C. was born through God's Word and excitement, hope, and love for their fellow inmates. They began holding Bible study in the day room and praying for inmates who were hurting or scared. Inmates began asking questions, asking for prayer, and joining the Bible study time.

"New Men/Women" are required to sign a commitment form stating that the signer is willing to surrender to the Lord and follow the "two great commandments":

1. To love the Lord your God with all your mind, might and strength.
2. To love your brother as yourself.

Each "New Man/Woman" is required to have an established member as a Sponsor to encourage spiritual growth and be held accountable for reading the Word, praying, participating in Bible studies, and serving brothers and sisters—Christians or not.

Members carry the message of Jesus Christ's freedom to prisons and sponsor other inmates. Released D.O.C. members, like Damon, meet together weekly for Bible study and attend Celebrate Recovery group meetings.

Father, we pray for nonbelievers behind the walls to find Jesus Christ.
We pray for safety for all behind the walls and courage for those
who speak the Word on the yards and those who call prayers at night.
We especially pray for Muslims who oppose the Word.
We ask for financial and volunteer help. —*Amen*

Covenant and Dedications

These and additional missionaries, ministries, and humanitarian organizations to pray for and support are listed in the Cruise Library and on Disembarkation pages at www.mayflowerfullsaillogbook.com. Individually or if meeting as a group, please add other nations, missionaries, ministries, and organizations to your prayer list to fulfill the words of Scripture:

He has sent me to bind up the brokenhearted, to proclaim freedom for the captives and release from darkness for the prisoners, to proclaim the year of the Lord's favor and the day of vengeance of our God. (Isaiah 61:1–2)

This gospel of the kingdom will be preached in the whole world as a testimony to all nations, and then the end will come. (Matthew 24:14)

Prepared to Disembark, We the Twenty-First-Century *Full Sail* Pilgrims covenant:

To dedicate Missionaries, Ministries, and Organizations
Fulfilling the Great Commission
in all Nations on all Continents to God's Glory and Honor.

Song of Choice

Choose a favorite song or hymn from the Cruise or your own songbook. Whether we sing or recite the benediction alone or with a group, God hears our voices as We the Passengers end this cruise.

Full Sail *Cruise Benediction*

Hallelujah!
Salvation and glory and power belong to our God;
for true and just are his judgments.
Blessed are those who are invited to the wedding supper of the Lamb!
Hold to the testimony of Jesus.
Worship God!
For the testimony of Jesus is the spirit of prophecy.
(Excerpts from Revelation 19)

Cruise Library Catalog

The Library contains books and resources quoted on our cruise, along with a listing of promoted ministries and others that provided motivation for writing *Full Sail*. Three appendices will help you explore history and the Christian roots of America further.

The Full Sail *Selected Bibliography (Recommended Reading)*

Categories for Checkout

> General
> *Mayflower*, Plymouth Colony, New England, and Puritan Books
> Books for Children and Youth
> Genealogy Books and Resources
> Dictionaries, Commentaries, Encyclopedias
> Marriage Resources
> Messianic and Other Jewish Resources
> Memoirs and Letters

General

Andrews, Charles M. *The Colonial Period of American History*. Vol.1, *The Settlements*. New Haven, CT: Yale University Press, 1964.

———. *The Colonial Background of the American Revolution: Four Essays in American Colonial History*. New Haven, CN: Yale University Press, 1958.

Bailyn, Bernard. *Faces of Revolution, Personalities and Themes in the Struggle for American Independence*. New York: Vintage Books, 1990.

Baron, Robert C., ed. *Soul of America: Documenting Our Past*. Vol. 2, 1858-1993. Golden, CO: North American Press, 1994.

Bennett, Ivan L., ed., *The Hymnal Army and Navy*, Washington, D.C.:U.S. Government Printing Office, 1942.

Bennett, William J. *America The Last Best Hope*. Vol. 1, *From the Age of Discovery To a World at War*. Nashville: Nelson Current Books, 2006.

Boorstin, Daniel J. *The Americans: The Colonial Experience*. New York: Random House, 1958.

Brookhiser, Richard. *What Would the Founders Do?: Our Questions, Their Answers.* New York: Basic Books, 2006.

Butel, A. J. *Overshadowed.* E-book, available at www.ajbutel.com. Published By: Deep Image, 2009.

Butterfield, Herbert. *Christianity and History.* New York: HarperCollins, 2009.

Butterfield, L. H., ed. *The Book of Abigail and John: Selected Letters of the Adams Family* 1762-1884. Cambridge, MA: Harvard University Press.

Calkins, Carroll C., ed. *The Story of America.* Pleasantville, NY: Reader's Digest Association, 1975.

Collins, Ace. *Songs Sung Red, White, and Blue: The Stories Behind America's Best-Loved Patriotic Songs.* New York: HarperCollins, HarperResource, 2003.

Colson, Charles W. *Life Sentence.* Waco, TX: Chosen Books, 1979.

Cook, G.A. *Ezekiel.* International Critical Commentary. New York: Charles Scribner's Sons, 1937.

Farrow, Anne, Joel Land, and Jenifer Frank. *Complicity: How the North Promoted, Prolonged, and Profited from Slavery.* New York: Ballantine Books, 2006.

Flint, Cort. R., ed., *The Quotable Billy Graham.* South Carolina: Droke House, 1966.

Gaustad, Edwin S. *Roger Williams: Prophet of Liberty.* New York: Oxford University Press, 2001.

Gingrich, Newt. *Rediscovering God in America: Reflections on the Role of Faith in Our Nation's History and Future.* Franklin, TN: Integrity Publishers, 2006.

Grant, George. *The Courage and Character of Theodore Roosevelt: A Hero Among Leaders.* Nashville: Cumberland House, 2005.

Greene, Lorenzo Johnston. *The Negro in Colonial New England 1620-1776.* New York: Columbia University Press, 1942.

Grun, Bernard. *The Timetables of History: A Horizontal Linkage of People and Events.* Based on Werner Stein's *Kulturfahrplan.* New York: Simon & Schuster, 1979.

Heath, Dwight B., ed. *A Journal of the Pilgrims at Plymouth: Mourt's Relation.* New York: Corinth Books, 1963.

Hosmer, James K. *Samuel Adams.* Boston and New York: Houghton Mifflin Company, The Riverside Press Cambridge, 1913.

Hughes, Thomas. *Indian Chiefs of Southern Minnesota: Containing Sketches of the Prominent Chieftains of the Dakota and Winnebago Tribes from 1825 to 1865.* Minneapolis: 2nd ed. Ross & Haines, 1969. Originally available at the Blue Earth County Historical Society, Mankato, MN 56001.

Hutson, James H. *The Founders on Religion: A Book of Quotations.* Princeton, NJ: Princeton University Press, 2005.

Kaiser, John Edmund. *Winning on Purpose: How to Organize Congregations to Succeed in Their Mission.* Nashville: Abingdon Press, 2006.

LaRose, Ed. *Our Trail of Tears: The Journey of Reconciliation.* Scotland, PA: Healing the Land Publishing, 2006. P.O. Box 73, Scotland, PA 17254. www.healingtheland.com

Larsen, David L. *Jews, Gentiles and The Church: A New Perspective on History and Prophecy.* Grand Rapids: Discovery House Publishers, 1995.

Mann, Charles C. *1491: New Revelations of the Americas Before Columbus.* New York: Alfred A. Knopf, 2006.

Marshall, Catherine, ed. *The Prayers of Peter Marshall.* New York: McGraw Hill Book Company, 1954.

Marshall, Peter J. Jr. and David B. Manuel Jr. *The Light and the Glory.* Old Tappan, NJ: Fleming H. Revell, 1977.

——. *From Sea to Shining Sea.* Old Tappan, NJ: Fleming H. Revell, 1986.

McCullough, David. *John Adams.* New York: Simon & Schuster, 2001.

Millard, Catherine. *The Rewriting of America's History.* Camp Hill, PA: Horizon Books, 1991.

Maloney, Elbert S. *Chapman Piloting, Seamanship & Small Boat Handling.* New York: Hearst Marine Books, 1958.

Molotsky, Irvin. *The Flag, The Poet & The Song: The Story of the Star-Spangled Banner*. New York: Dutton, 2001.

Morgan, Robert J. *Then Sings My Soul: 250 of the World's Greatest Hymn Stories*. Nashville: Thomas Nelson, 2003.

Nabokov, Peter, ed. *Native American Testimony: A Chronicle of Indian-White Relations from Prophecy to the Present, 1492-1992*. New York: The Penguin Group, 1991.

Noonan, Peggy. *On Speaking Well*. New York: Regan Books/HarperPerennial, 1999.

———. *When Character Was King: A Story of Ronald Reagan*. New York: Viking, 2001.

Novak, Michael. *On Two Wings: Humble Faith and Common Sense at the American Founding*. San Francisco: Encounter Books, 2002. www.encounterbooks. com

Pearce, Jane. *The Pearces: Persons of Quality*. Hobbs, NM: Southwest Printing Co., 1982.

Pierce, Clara Weldon McClurkin, James Pierce, Graham L. Pierce. *The Pierces and Their Posterity*. Nashville: Parthenon Press, 1981.

Pierce, Frederick Clifton. *Pierce Genealogy: Being the Record of the Posterity of Capt. Michael, John and Capt. William Pierce Who Came to this Country from England*. 1889. Bowie, MA: Heritage Books, Inc., Reprint 2002.

Schweikart, Larry, and Michael Allen. *A Patriot's History of the United States from Columbus's Great Discovery to the War on Terror*. New York: Sentinel, 2004.

Shelley, Bruce L. *Church History in Plain Language*. 2nd ed. Nashville: Word Publishing, 1995.

Shepherd, Jack. *The Adams Chronicles: Four Generations of Greatness*. Cambridge: Harvard Univ. Press, c1975

Shirer, William L. *The Rise and Fall of the Third Reich*. New York: Simon & Schuster, 1960.

Sittser, Gerald L. *The Will of God as a Way of Life*. Grand Rapids: Zondervan, 2000.

———. *A Grace Disguised: How the Soul Grows Through Loss.* Grand Rapids: Zondervan, 1996.

Stark, Rodney. *The Victory of Reason: How Christianity Led to Freedom, Capitalism, and Western Success.* New York: Random House, 2005.
Stratton, Eugene Aubrey. *Plymouth Colony: Its History & People 1620-1691.* Salt Lake City: Ancestry Publishing, 1986.

Strobel, Lee. *The Case For A Creater: A Journalist Investigates Scientific Evidence that Points Toward God.* Grand Rapids: Zondervan, 2004.

Tada, Joni Eareckson. *Heaven Your Real Home.* Grand Rapids: Zondervan, 1995.

Toby Mac and Michael Tait. *Under God.* Bloomington, MN: Bethany House, 2004.

de Tocqueville, Alexis. *Democracy in America: Specially Edited and Abridged for the Modern Reader.* Edited by Richard D. Heffner. New York: New American Library, Penguin Putnam, 1984.

Washington, Booker T. *The Story of My Life and Work: An Autobiography.* Naperville, IL: J. L. Nichols & Co., 1901.

Weatherford, Jack McIver. *Native Roots: How the Indians Enriched America.* New York: Crown Publishers, 1991.

Weiss, Benjamin. *God in American History.* Grand Rapids: Zondervan, 1966.

Wood, Betty. *Origins of American Slavery: Freedom and Bondage in the English Colonies.* New York: HarperCollins, 1997.

Wood, Peter H. *Strange New Land: Africans in Colonial America.* New York: Oxford University Press, 2003.

Wroth, Lawrence C. *The Colonial Printer.* Charlottesville: Dominion Books, 1964.

Mayflower, Plymouth Colony, New England, & Puritan Books

Anthony, Bertha Williams. *Roger Williams of Providence, R.I.* Vol. 2. England: Oxford University Press, 1966.

Ballam, Anthea and Julia Ballam. *Mayflower: The Voyage that Changed the World.* New York: O Books, 2003.

Beale, David. *The Mayflower Pilgrims: Roots of Puritan, Presbyterian, Congregationalist, and Baptist Heritage.* Greenville, SC: Emerald House Group, 2002.0, 2002. This book contains the complete second Pierce/Peirce Patent of 1621.

Bradford, William. *Of Plymouth Plantation 1620-1647.* Edited by Samuel Eliot Morison. New York: Alfred A. Knopf / Random House, 2002.

Bradford, William. *Of Plymouth Plantation: Bradford's History of the Plymouth Settlement 1608–1650.* Original Manuscript Rendered into Modern English by Harold Paget, 1909. San Antonio, TX: Vision Forum, 2007.

Deetz, James and Patricia Scott. *The Times of Their Lives: Life, Love, and Death in Plymouth.* New York.: V. H. Freeman and Company, 2000.

Dunn, Richard S., and Yeandle, Laetitia, eds. *The Journal of John Winthrop 1630-1649.* Belknap Press of Harvard University Press, 1996.

Harrison House. *Pray for Our Nation: Scriptural Prayers To Revive Our Country.* Tulsa, OK: Harrison House, 1999.

Jehle, Dr. Paul. *Plymouth in the Words of Her Founders: A Visitor's Guide to America's Hometown.* San Antonio: Vision Forum Ministries, 2002.

Johnson, Caleb H. *The Mayflower and Her Passengers.* Bloomington, IN: Xlibris, 2006. www.mayflowerhistory.com

LaPlante, Eve. *American Jezebel: The Uncommon Life of Anne Hutchinson, The Woman Who Defied the Puritans.* New York: HarperCollins, 2004.

Libby, Charles T. *Mary Chilton's Title to Celebrity.* Rhode Island: Society of Mayflower Descendants, 1978.

Morgan, Edmund S. *The Puritan Dilemma: The Story of John Winthrop.* Edited by Oscar Handlin. Boston: Little, Brown & Company, 1958.

Plooij, D. *The Pilgrim Fathers from a Dutch Point of View.* New York: AMS Press, 1969.

Philbrick, Nathaniel. *Mayflower: A Story of Courage, Community, and War.* New York: Viking, 2006.

Teal, Alice C., and Harry P. Folger 3rd. *Pilgrims at Prayer*. Plymouth, MA: General Society of Mayflower Descendants, 2005.

Roser, Susan E. *Mayflower Marriages: From the Files of George Ernest Bowman at the Massachusetts Society of Mayflower Descendants*. Baltimore: Genealogical Publishing, 1990.

Sherman, Robert Moody, Robert S. Wakefield, Lydia Dow Finlay. *Mayflower Families Through Five Generations*. Vol. 15: *James Chilton–Richard More*. Plymouth, MA: General Society of Mayflower Descendants, 1997.

Skousen, W. Cleon. *The 5000 Year Leap: A Miracle That Changed the World*. Malta, ID: National Center for Constitutional Studies, 1981. www.nccs.net

Stoddard, Francis. *The Truth About the Pilgrims*. Baltimore: Genealogical Publishing, 1976.

Stoll, Ira. *Samuel Adams: A Life*. New York: Free Press, 2008.

Stratton, Eugene Aubrey. *Plymouth Colony: Its History & People 1620-1691*, Salt Lake City: Ancestry Publishing, 1986.

Thacher, James. *History of the Town of Plymouth, from its First Settlement in 1620 to the Present Time*. 3rd ed. Yarmouthport: Parnassus Press, 1972.

Turnbull, Ralph G. *Jonathan Edwards The Preacher*. Grand Rapids: Baker Book House, 1958.

Willison, George F. *Saints and Strangers, Being the Lives of the Pilgrim Fathers & Their Families, and Their Friends & Foes; & an Account of Their Posthumous Wanderings in Limbo, Their Final Resurrection & Rise to Glory, & the Strange Pilgrimages of Plymouth Rock*. New York: Reynal & Hitchcock, 1945.

Winslow, Edward. *Good Newes from New England*. Bedford, MA: Applewood Books, 1996. First Published in 1624.

Books for Children and Youth

Anderson, Joan. *The First Thanksgiving Feast*. Photographed at Plimoth Plantation by George Ancona; enriches readers' perception of one of the most popular moments in American history. New York: Clarion Books, c1984.

Bennett, William J. *Our Country's Founders: A Book of Advice for Young People Adapted from Our Sacred Honor*. New York: Simon & Schuster Books for Young Readers,1998.

Resources

Cheney, Lynne. *America: A Patriotic Primer*. Illustrated by Robin Preiss Glasser. New York: Simon & Schuster Children's Publishing, 2002.

———. *A is for Abigail: An Almanac of Amazing American Women*. Illustrated by Robin Preiss Glasser. New York: Simon & Schuster Books for Young Readers, 2003.

———. *Our 50 States: A Family Adventure Across America*. Illustrated by Robin Preiss Glasser. New York: Simon & Schuster Books for Young Readers, 2006.

Fast, Howard. *Haym Salomon: Son of Liberty*. New York: Julian Messner, 1941.

Fleming, Thomas J. *One Small Candle: The Pilgrims' First Year in America*. New York: W.W. Norton & Company, 1963.

Greene, Rhonda Gowler. *The Very First Thanksgiving Day*. Paintings by Susan Gaber. New York: Atheneum Books for Young Readers, 2002.

Hall, Verna M. *The Christian History of the American Revolution: Consider and Ponder*. Chesapeake, VA: Foundation for American Christian Education, 1976. www.face.net
Lawton, Wendy. *Almost Home*. Chicago: Moody Press, 2003.

Marshall, Peter, David Manuel, and Sheldon Maxwell. *Mercy Clifton: Pilgrim Girl*. The Crimson Cross Series. Nashville: B&H Publishing Group, 2007. www.CrimsonCrossBooks.com

———. *Nate Donovan: Revolutionary Spy*. The Crimson Cross Series. Nashville: B&H Publishing Group, 2007. www.CrimsonCrossBooks.com

Paterson, Katherine. *Bridge to Terabithia*. New York: HarperTrophy, 2007.

Schmidt, Gary D. *William Bradford: Plymouth's Faithful Pilgrim*. Grand Rapids: Eerdmans Books for Young Readers, 1999.

Schultz, Charles and Lee Mendelson. *The Mayflower Voyagers*. VHS. Produced by Lee Mendelson and Bill Melendez Productions in association with Charles M. Schultz Creative Associates and United Media. Directed by Evert Brown, 1988. United Feature Syndicate, Inc.

Waters, Kate. *Sarah Morton's Day: A Day in the Life of a Pilgrim Girl*. Photographs taken by Russ Kendall at Plimoth Plantation, a living history museum in Plymouth, MA, and based on real people of the time. New York: Scholastic Inc.

Genealogy Books and Resources

BOOKS

Melnyk, Marcia D. Yannizze. *Family History 101: A Beginner's Guide to Finding Your Ancestors.* Cincinnati, OH: Family Tree Books, 2005.

Powell, Kimberly. *The Everything Guide to Online Genealogy.* Avon, MA: Adams Media, an F+W Publications Company, 2008.

Schweitzer, George K., Phd, ScD. *Massachusetts Genealogical Research* by *Genealogist's Handbook for New England Research.* Knoxville, TN: George K. Schweitzer, 1999.

Westin, Jeane Eddy. *Finding Your Roots: How to Trace Your Ancestors at Home and Abroad.* New York: Jeremy P. Tarcher/Putnam, 1998.

OTHER RESOURCES

New England Historic Genealogical Society
A National Center for Family and Local History
101 Newbury Street, Boston, MA, 02116-3007
(617) 536-5740 | www.NewEnglandAncestors.org

National Society of the Sons and Daughters of the Pilgrims
www.nssdp.com

Plimoth Plantation
A living history museum of Plymouth, Massachusetts.
P.O. Box 1620, Plymouth, MA, 02362
www.plimothplantation.org.

Dictionaries, Commentaries, Almanac, Encyclopedias

Federer, William J. *America's God and Country: Encyclopedia Of Quotations.* St. Louis, MO: FAME Publishing, Inc., 2000.

Nave's Topical Bible. Orville J. Nave. Classic Reference Series. Revised and compiled by Edward Viening. Grand Rapids: Zondervan, Regency Reference Library, 1969.

Nelson's New Christian Dictionary. George Thomas Kurian, ed. Nashville: Thomas Nelson, 2001.

Ryken, Leland, James C. Wilhoit, and Tremper Longman, eds. *Dictionary of Biblical Imagery: An Encyclopedic Exploration of the Images, Symbols, Motifs, Metaphors, Figures of Speech and Literary Patterns of the Bible.* Downers Grove, IL: InterVarsity Press, 1998. *The World Book Encyclopedia.* Chicago, IL.: Field

Enterprises Educational Corporation, 1966 Edition. http://www.britannica.com.

Time Almanac, 2004. Pearson Education, Inc., Needham, Mass.

Ask.com

MSN Encarta, 2009.

Yahoo.com

Marriage Resources

Chosen People Ministries. *Joined Together*. DVD. Presents an intimate portrait of four interfaith couples. Directed by Nikki Hevesy. Chosen People Ministries, 2004.

Gross, David C. and Esther R. *Under the Wedding Canopy: Love & Marriage in Judaism*. New York: Hipporene Books, 1996.

Lash, Jamie. *The Ancient Jewish Wedding . . . and the Return of Messiah for His Bride*. Ft. Lauderdale, FL: Jewish Jewels, 1997.

Lowery, Dr. Fred. *Covenant Marriage: Staying Together for Life*. West Monroe, LA: Howard Publishing, 2002.

Thomas, Gary L. *Sacred Marriage: What if God Designed Marriage to Make Us Holy More Than to Make Us Happy?* Grand Rapids: Zondervan, 2000.

Mason, Mike. *The Mystery of Marriage: As Iron Sharpens Iron*. Portland, OR.: Multnomah Press, 1985.

Monsarrat, Ann. *And the Bride Wore . . . : The Story of the White Wedding*. New York: Dodd, Mead, 1974. Provides interesting information about Pilgrim and Puritan weddings and famous British and American weddings.

Messianic Jewish books, ministries, Gentile authors about Isreal, and other resources

Bernis, Jonathan. Messianic Jewish author and ministry founder. Excellent Web site Messianic belief: www.Jewishvoice.org

Brickner, David. *Future Hope: A Jewish Christian Look at the End of the World*. San Francisco: Purple Pomegranate Productions, 1999.

Dolan, David. *Israel in Crisis: What Lies Ahead?* Grand Rapids: Flaming H. Revell, 2001.

Fuchs, Daniel. *Israel's Holy Days in Type and Prophecy.* Neptune, NJ: Loizeaux Brothers, 1985.

Finto, Don. *Your People Shall Be My People: How Israel, the Jews and the Christian Church Will Come Together in the Last Days.* Ventura, CA: Regal Books, 2001.

Fischer, Raymond Robert. Books: *Provision, Messianic Seal, Children of God, Full Circle, The Door Where It Began*; DVD teaching series: *The Jewish Origins of Christianity* © Raymond Fischer ©Olim Publications. www.OlimPublications.com.
———. *The Ways of the Way.* Lake Mary, FL: Creation House, a Strang Company, 2009.

Flynn, Leslie B. *What the Church Owes the Jew.* Carlsbad, CA: Magnus Press, 1998.

Glaser, Mitch and Zhava Glaser. *The Fall Feasts of Israel.* Chicago: Moody Bible Institute, 1987.

Goetz, Marty. Messianic Jewish worship leader, singer, songwriter. www.martygoetz.com

Goll, James W. *Praying for Israel's Destiny: Effective Intercession for God's Purposes in the Middle East.* Grand Rapids: Chosen Books, 2005.

Grose, Peter. Israel in the Mind of America. New York: Knopf, 1984.

Howard, Kevin and Marvin Rosenthal. *The Feasts of the Lord: God's Prophetic Calendar from Calvary to the Kingdom.* Nashville: Thomas Nelson, 1997.

Jews for Jesus. *The Messianic Movement: A Field Guide for Evangelical Christians.* Edited by Rich Robinson and Naomi Rose Rothstein. San Francisco, CA: Purple Pomegranate Productions, 2005.

Joyner, Rick. *The Passover.* Pineville, NC: MorningStar Publications, Inc., 1989.

Juster, Dan and Keith Intrater. *Israel, the Church and the Last Days.* Shippensburg, PA: Destiny Image Publishers, 2003.

Kasdan, Barney. *God's Appointed Times: A Practical Guide for Understanding and Celebrating the Biblical Holidays.* Baltimore: Lederer Books, 1993.

Frymer-Kensky, Tikva, David Novak, Peter Ochs, David Fox Sandmel, and Michael A. Signer, eds. *Christianity in Jewish Terms.* Boulder, CO: Westview Press, 2000.

Kinzer, Mark S. *Post-Missionary Messianic Judaism: Redefining Christian Engagement with the Jewish People.* Grand Rapids: Brazos Press, 2005.

McCartney, Bill and Aaron Fruh. *Two Minute Warning: Why It's Time to Honor Jewish People Before the Clock Runs Out,* VMI Publishers, 2009.

Mills, Gerrie Hyman. *Oy Vey! Such a Deal: Jazzed by Faith & Chocolate Pudding,* Lake Mary, FL: Creation House, a Strang Company, 2007.

Nadler, Miriam. *Sense & Sensibility* and other books. Charlotte, NC: Word of Messiah Ministries.

Nadler, Sam. *Growing in Messiah* and other books. Charlotte, NC: Word of Messiah Ministries.

Resnik, Russell L. *The Root and the Branches: Jewish Identity in Messiah.* Albuquerque, NM: Adat Yeshua (Messianic Jewish Congregation), 1997.

Rosen, Ceil and Moishe Rosen. *Christ in the Passover: Why is this Night Different?* Chicago: Moody Bible Institute, 1978.

Teplinsky, Sandra. *Israel's Anointing: Your Inheritance and End-Time Destiny Through Israel.* Grand Rapids: Chosen Books, 2008.

——. *Why Care about Israel? How the Jewish Nation Is Key to Unleashing God's Blessings in the 21st Century.* Grand Rapids: Chosen Books, 2004–5.

Wilbur, Paul. Messianic Jewish praise and worship musician. www.wilburministries.com

Telchin, Stan. *Abandoned: What is God's Will for the Jewish People and the Church?* Chosen Books, 1997.

Memoirs and Letters

Bush, George H.W. *All the Best: My Life in Letters and Other Writings.* New York: Scribner, 1999.

Jeter, William F. *Boyhood Along the Brook Called Horn: "A Nouveau Huck Finn."* Seattle: Hara Publishing, 2003.

Osborne, Jack. *Makers of Mischief: A Boomer's Adventures in Childhood.* San Jose, CA: DreamAway Books, 2007. www.makersofmischief.com

Van Regenmorter, Richard. *Because He Loves Me, There is Life Beyond Trauma.* Sioux Center, IA: P&R Publishers, 2000. Memoir about the Providence of God and the physical and emotional pain that combat veterans endure. Order from P&R Publishers, 1440 1st Ave. SE, Sioux Center, Iowa, 51250. richand-phyllis@gmail.com.

Listing of Ministries and Other Organizations

Outreaches, Missions, and Missionaries

Prison Fellowship
44180 Riverside Parkway, Lansdowne, VA 20196
1-877-478-0100 or 1-703-478-0100
For donations only: P.O. Box 1550, Merrifield, VA 22116-1550
Information and donations online: www.pfm.org

D.O.C.: Disciples of Christ Outreach to Inmates
P. O. Box 4554. Citrus Heights, CA 9561-4554
(916) 726-4242

Child Evangelism Fellowship, Inc.
North American address for financial gifts/support:

P.O. Box 348, Warrenton, MO 63383
Designate for CEF of Israel #06122

Israeli address:
P.O. Box 292
Nazareth, Israel

Chosen People Ministries International Headquarters
241 East 51st Street
New York, NY 10022-6502
www.chosenpeople.com

Campus Crusade for Christ
Tokyo, Japan: Kevin and Peggy Grip
Staff #0368454
Jesus Film Outreach, Nigeria: Steven and Janet Volker
Staff #0054749
Send support for Grips and/or Volkers to
Campus Crusade for Christ, PO Box 628222, Orlando, FL 32862-8222

Fran Gralow
For more information about Fran's work in Angola, email Fran.Gralow@sim.org.
To contribute to this ministry, see www.missiongo.org.

Hope Unlimited - Brazil
www.hopeunlimited.org

International Discipleship Training (I.D.T.)
Rance and Brandy Cook
www.idtmissions.org
Comfort Israel: www.idtmissions.org/comfortisrael

Jews for Jesus International Headquarters
60 Haight Street
San Francisco, CA 94102-5895
www.jewsforjesus.org • jfj@jewsforjesus.org

Liberty Savard Ministries
Liberty Savard
Information about ministry beliefs, purpose, writing classes, books, and LSS
schedule are available at www.libertysavard.com.

Light of Zion
Sandra and Kerry Teplinsky
www.lightofzion.org

"Light of Zion" is a ministry mediating Messiah Yeshua (Jesus, the Jewish
Bridegroom-Savior), He who is the Light of Zion, to God's people through Bible teaching, prophetic intercession/worship, and ministry to the poor among
Israeli believers. The ministry also provides financial aid to needy Israeli believers, assisting the poor in accordance with the biblical priority to remember our
brothers and sisters in faith (Galatians 6:10). Light of Zion is a nonprofit corporation, and U.S. contributions are tax-deductible under I.R.C. 501(c)(3).

Ray of Hope - Israel
To contribute to the expenses of Ray of Hope, please make checks payable to:
Ray of Hope Israel
P.O. Box 893
Winnemucca, NV 89446

Sisters in Service
2975 Northwoods Parkway, Suite 100
Norcross, GA 30071
(770) 783-1665
www.sistersinservice.org

Soli Deo Gloria Ballet
Rachel Starr Thomson or Carolyn Currey
solideoballet@gmail.com
3807 Bertie St., Stevensville, ON L0S 1S0
Canada
To see pictures, video, and performance and support information, visit
www.solideoballet.com

Synseis Alliance International (SAI)
SAI facilitates synergistic mentoring alliances between individuals, institutions and organizations that are passionate about securing and mobilizing academic infrastructure in Christian higher education throughout the world.

Mentoring and coaching newly appointed national leaders for seminaries, Bible colleges and ministry training institutes in the developing world is the first priority of this ministry with strategic services as follows:
Governance Training
Strategic Planning
Faculty and Staff Development
Curriculum Review
Accreditation Preparation
Policy and Procedure Development
Financial Advisement
Technology and Library Support

Inquiries concerning the purpose, projects and operations of SAI to Dr. Ron Freeman at rfreeman@synseis.org or (916) 243-8852.

Send tax-deductible gifts to Synseis Alliance International, 5017 Dory Way, Fair Oaks, CA 95628

Rachel Starr Thomson
Author of Heart to Heart: Meeting With God in the Lord's Prayer, Letters to a Samuel Generation, the Seventh World Trilogy, and other books.
Visit Rachel online at www.rachelstarrthomson.com or e-mail thomson.rachel @gmail.com.

World Wide Christian Radio
Broadcasting the gospel into the Middle East
Eugene Ridings
1337 Middleton Road, Taneyville, MO 65759
(417)299-8205.

Law and Justice Ministries

American Center for Law and Justice
Chief Counsel: Jay Alan Sekulow
P.O. Box 90555
Washington, D.C. 20090-0555

American Center for Law and Justice is a d/b/a for Christian Advocates Serving Evangelism, Inc., a Section 501(c)(3) not-for-profit religious corporation that is involved in education, promulgation, conciliation, and where necessary, litigation, to the end that religious freedoms are protected under the law. The organization has participated in numerous cases before the Supreme Court, Federal Court of Appeals, Federal District Courts, and various state courts regarding freedom of religion and freedom of speech.

Pacific Justice Institute
www.pacificjustice.org

Pacific Justice Institute is a non-profit 501(c)(3) legal defense organization specializing in the defense of religious freedom, parental rights, and other civil liberties. Pacific Justice Institute works diligently, without charge, to provide their clients with all the legal support they need.

Pacific Justice Institute's strategy is to coordinate and oversee large numbers of concurrent court actions through a network of over one thousand affiliate attorneys nationwide. According to former United States Attorney General Edwin Meese, "The Institute fills a critical need on the West Coast for those whose civil liberties are threatened."

International Justice Mission
www.ijm.org

A U.S.-based Christian non-profit human rights organization that operates in countries all over the world to rescue victims of individual human rights abuse, working to combat human trafficking, forced labor slavery, illegal detention, unprosecuted rape, police brutality, and illegal land seizure.

Humanitarian Aid, Volunteer Organizations, and Health Ministries

Christian Volunteering.org
ChristianVolunteering.org matches volunteers with Christian volunteer service

opportunities. According to the Corporation for National and Community Service, the value of the donated time of faith-based volunteers in 2005 was $51.8 billion dollars.

Joni and Friends
www.joniandfriends.org
Joni and Friends reach out to people with disabilities and their families across the U.S. and around the world.

Olim Fund of Israel
Tax-exempt donations may be sent payable to Word of Life Association:
155 Corinth Court, Roswell, Georgia 30075
Contact Dr. Fischer at olim@012.net.il or at Olim, P.O. Box 2111, Tiberius, Israel
For book, fund, and personal information, visit www.olimpublications.com.
Powerhouse Ministries
www.powerhouse-ministries.org

Rebuilding Together
www.rebuildingtogether.org

Appendix One: Two Dictionary Chart

Two Dictionaries. Two Definitions. Which Dictionary is on Your Shelf?
Two Dictionary Chart by Foundation for American Christian Education
(www.face.net.) Used with permission.

1828 Noah Webster's American Dictionary of the English Language	*1981 Webster's New Collegiate Dictionary*
"MARRIAGE" The act of uniting a man and woman for life . . . Marriage was instituted by God himself ... "Marriage is honorable in all" Heb. 13.	**"MARRIAGE"** ... man and woman are joined in a special kind of social and legal dependence for the purpose of founding and maintaining a family ... an intimate or close union.
"EDUCATION" Education comprehends ... instruction and discipline intended to enlighten the understanding, correct the temper, and form the manners and habits of youth, and fit them for usefulness in their future stations. To give them a religious education is indispensable.	**"EDUCATION"** The action or process of [developing mentally or morally].
"MERCY" That benevolence, mildness or tenderness which disposes a person ... to treat an offender better than he deserves. "The Lord is long-suffering and of great mercy." Num.14.	**"MERCY"** Compassion or forbearance shown esp. to an offender or to one subject to one's power ... an act of divine favor or compassion ... a fortunate circumstance.
"TRUTH" Conformity to fact or reality ... We rely on the truth of scriptural prophecies. "Sanctify them through thy truth ..." John 17	**"TRUTH"** Sincerity in action, character, and utterance ... the body of real thing ... a judgment ... that is true or accepted as true.

Appendix Two: State Preambles, with Acts and Bills of Rights

Alabama 1901, Preamble: We the people of the State of Alabama, invoking the favor and guidance of Almighty God, do ordain and establish the following Constitution.

Alaska 1956, Preamble: We, the people of Alaska, grateful to God and to those who founded our nation and pioneered this great land...

Arizona 1911, Preamble: We, the people of the State of Arizona, grateful to Almighty God for our liberties, do ordain this Constitution...

Arkansas 1874, Preamble: We, the people of the State of Arkansas, grateful to Almighty God for the privilege of choosing our own form of government...

California 1879, Preamble: We, the People of the State of California, grateful to Almighty God for our freedom...
Colorado 1876, Preamble: We, the people of Colorado, with profound reverence for the Supreme Ruler of Universe...

Connecticut 1818, Preamble: The People of Connecticut, acknowledging with gratitude the good Providence of God in permitting them to enjoy...

Delaware 1897, Preamble: Through Divine Goodness all men have, by nature, the rights of worshipping and serving their Creator according to the dictates of their consciences...

Florida 1885, Preamble: We, the people of the State of Florida, grateful to Almighty God for our constitutional liberty ... establish this Constitution...
Georgia 1777, Preamble: We, the people of Georgia, relying upon protection and guidance of Almighty God, do ordain and establish this Constitution...

Hawaii 1959, Preamble: We, the people of Hawaii, Grateful for Divine Guidance ... establish this Constitution...

Idaho 1889, Preamble: We, the people of the State of Idaho, grateful to Almighty God for our freedom, to secure its blessings...

Illinois 1850, Preamble: We, the people of the State of Illinois, grateful to Almighty God for the civil, political and religious liberty which He hath so long permitted us to enjoy and looking to Him for a blessing on our endeavors...

Indiana 1851, Preamble: We, the People of the State of Indiana, grateful to Almighty God for the free exercise of the right to choose our form of government...

Iowa 1857, Preamble: We, the People of the State of Iowa, grateful to the Supreme Being for the blessings hitherto enjoyed, and feeling our dependence on Him for a continuation of these blessings ... establish this Constitution.

Kansas 1859, Preamble: We, the people of Kansas, grateful to Almighty God for our civil and religious privileges ... establish this Constitution.

Kentucky 1891, Preamble: We, the people of the Commonwealth of Kentucky grateful to Almighty God for the civil, political and religious liberties...

Louisiana 1921, Preamble: We, the people of the State of Louisiana, grateful to Almighty God for the civil, political and religious liberties we enjoy...

Maine 1820, Preamble: We the People of Maine. acknowledging with grateful hearts the goodness of the Sovereign Ruler of the Universe in affording us an opportunity ... and imploring His aid and direction...

Maryland 1776, Preamble: We, the people of the state of Maryland, grateful to Almighty God for our civil and religious liberty...

Massachusetts 1780, Preamble: We ... the people of Massachusetts, acknowledging with grateful hearts, the goodness of the Great Legislator of the Universe ... in the course of His Providence, an opportunity and devoutly imploring His direction...

Michigan 1908, Preamble: We, the people of the State of Michigan, grateful to Almighty God for the blessings of freedom ... establish this Constitution
Minnesota, 1857, Preamble: We, the people of the State of Minnesota, grateful to God for our civil and religious liberty, and desiring to perpetuate its blessings...

Mississippi 1890, Preamble: We, the people of Mississippi in convention assembled, grateful to Almighty God, and invoking His blessing on our work...

Missouri 1845, Preamble: We, the people of Missouri, with profound reverence for the Supreme Ruler of the Universe, and grateful for His goodness ... establish this Constitution...

Montana 1889, Preamble: We, the people of Montana, grateful to Almighty God for the blessings of liberty, establish this Constitution.

Nebraska 1875, Preamble: We, the people, grateful to Almighty God for our freedom ... establish this Constitution.

Nevada 1864, Preamble: We the people of the State of Nevada, grateful to Almighty God for our freedom, establish this Constitution...

New Hampshire 1792, Part I. Art. I. Sec. V: Every individual has a natural and unalienable right to worship God according to the dictates of his own conscience.

New Jersey 1844, Preamble: We, the people of the State of New Jersey, grateful to Almighty God for civil and religious liberty which He hath so long permitted us to enjoy, and looking to Him for a blessing on our endeavors...

New Mexico 1911, Preamble: We, the People of New Mexico, grateful to Almighty God for the blessings of liberty...

New York 1846, Preamble: We, the people of the State of New York, grateful to Almighty God for our freedom, in order to secure its blessings...

North Carolina 1868, Preamble: We the people of the State of North Carolina, grateful to Almighty God, the Sovereign Ruler of Nations, for our civil, political, and religious liberties, and acknowledging our dependence upon Him for the continuance of those...

North Dakota 1889, Preamble: We, the people of North Dakota, grateful to Almighty God for the blessings of civil and religious liberty, do ordain ...

Ohio 1852, Preamble: We the people of the state of Ohio, grateful to Almighty God for our freedom, to secure its blessings and to promote our common...
Oklahoma 1907, Preamble: Invoking the guidance of Almighty God, in order to secure and perpetuate the blessings of liberty ...

Oregon 1857, Bill of Rights, Article. Section 2: All men shall be secure in the Natural right, to worship Almighty God according to the dictates of their consciences ...

Pennsylvania 1776, Preamble: We, the people of Pennsylvania, grateful to Almighty God for the blessings of civil and religious liberty, and humbly invoking His guidance ...

Rhode Island 1842, Preamble: We the People of the State of Rhode Island, grateful to Almighty God for the civil and religious liberty which He hath so long permitted us to enjoy, and looking to Him for a blessing ...

South Carolina, 1778, Preamble: We, the people of the State of South Carolina. grateful to God for our liberties, do ordain and establish this Constitution …

South Dakota 1889, Preamble: We, the people of South Dakota, grateful to Almighty God for our civil and religious liberties …

Tennessee 1796, Art. XI.III: That all men have a natural and indefeasible right to worship Almighty God according to the dictates of their conscience …

Texas 1845, Preamble: We the People of the Republic of Texas, acknowledging, with gratitude, the grace and beneficence of God …

Utah 1896, Preamble: Grateful to Almighty God for life and liberty, we establish this Constitution …

Vermont 1777, Preamble: Whereas all government ought to … enable the individuals who compose it to enjoy their natural rights, and other blessings which the Author of Existence has bestowed on man …

Virginia 1776, Bill of Rights, XVI: Religion, or the Duty which we owe our Creator … can be directed only by Reason and that it is the mutual duty of all to practice Christian Forbearance, Love and Charity towards each other …

Washington 1889, Preamble: We the People of the State of Washington, grateful to the Supreme Ruler of the Universe for our liberties, do ordain this Constitution …

West Virginia 1872, Preamble: Since through Divine Providence we enjoy the blessings of civil, political and religious liberty, we, the people of West Virginia, reaffirm our faith in and constant reliance upon God …
Wisconsin 1848, Preamble: We, the people of Wisconsin, grateful to Almighty God for our freedom, domestic tranquility …

Wyoming 1890, Preamble: We, the people of the State of Wyoming, grateful to God for our civil, political, and religious liberties … establish this Constitution.

Appendix Three: Address of Secretary Charles Evans Hughes at the Laying of the Cornerstone of the National Baptist Memorial to Religious Liberty, at Sixteenth and Columbia Road, Saturday, April 22, 1922

from *The Religious Herald*, April 27, 1922

This memorial is at once a tribute and a pledge. It is a tribute, in this capital where the services and ideals of those who founded and preserved the Union are fittingly memorialized, to one of their great forerunners, to the pioneer who first in America erected the standard of religious liberty. It is also a tribute to that earnest group of believers who, amid scorn and persecution, were steadfast to their distinctive tenet which was to become the vital principle of our free institutions. It is a pledge that this principle shall be held inviolate.

The conception of religious liberty is so familiar to us that we find it difficult to realize that it is not a natural one; that it is one of the late fruits of political experience; and that when first declared it was deemed of all doctrines the most pernicious and dangerous. It is distinctively an American doctrine, for here the principle first found effective expression in governmental institutions. "Of all the differences between the Old World and the New," says Boyce, "this is perhaps the most salient. Half the wars of Europe, half the internal troubles that have vexed European States, from the Monophysite controversies of the Roman Empire of the fifth century down to the Kuiturkampf in the German Empire of the nineteenth have arisen from theological differences or from the rival claims of Church and State."

It was inevitable that monarchs, believing themselves to occupy the throne as of divine right, should exert their sway over the consciences of their subjects. It was natural, deeming itself to represent the divine rule upon earth, that the church should seek either direct control or pervasive influence over political institutions. Nor was religious liberty the aim of the leaders of the Reformation. It was recognized to be the province of the head of the State to ordain the religion to be observed within the State, at least to the extent of stamping out heretical doctrine. It was a position easily understood and plausibly defended. What would become of the State without religion? Would not subversive religious views and pernicious doctrines threaten the very existence of the State? And who should suppress them if not the ruler of the State? How could pure religion be maintained if the State did not define it and support it by its authority? Never was political precept deemed to be more solidly based in unanswerable logic. Thus was found the ready justification for civil disability, proscription and persecution. "The chief duty of the magistrate," it was formally declared, "is to defend religion and take care that the Word of God is purely preached." He was to remove and destroy "all false service of God."

Against this almost universal opinion, against the voice of authoritative dogma and of philosophical exposition in its support on the part of the learned, with rare exceptions, against what was conceived to be the essential defense of both civil and religion institutions—what chance remained for freedom of conscience and of equality before the law? There were indeed a few scattered prophets of the new era. And there was one group, contemned and persecuted—to whom the light was given when the brightest intellects of Europe were clouded. To the Anabaptists, the most scorned of sects, belongs the imperishable honor of declaring and persistently urging the fundamental doctrine that rulers of States should not intervene in affairs of conscience and that civil disability should not be predicated upon religious belief. Said they, "The magistrate is not to meddle with religion or matters of conscience, nor compel men to this or that form of religion, because Christ is the King and lawgiver of the church and conscience."

This demand for religious liberty was not an incidental declaration or an effort to obtain a mere immunity for religious practice. Others might flee from persecution only in turn to persecute those who disagreed with them. Others might pledge toleration or maintain a passive resistance to authority. The Anabaptists were not asking to be tolerated; they were fighting for a cardinal principle of their faith. Persecution intensified their struggle, but it was not sufficient for them to escape persecution. Their demand for the absolute freedom of religion from civil control was an essential part of their conception of religious truth and was pressed with the ardor of the deepest religious feeling. They went to the root of the matter—the relation of the individual soul to its Maker. The kingdom of God was not of this world and was not within the keeping of any prince.

This contribution is the glory of the Baptist heritage, more distinctive than any other characteristic of belief or practice. To this militant leadership, all sects and faiths are debtors. Let this memorial proclaim the indebtedness in the capital of the republic where the once despised dogma has become the foundation of the civic structure.

The soil of Europe was not congenial for the growth of the radical doctrine of religious liberty. Tradition, the supposed requirements of organized society, political authority, ecclesiasticism of whatever name, the learning of the schools, were all against it. Even toleration, as the word implies, fell far short of its advocacy. There was only the persistent effort of weak things which were to put to shame things which were strong. The seeds of liberty were blown across the Atlantic and found fruitage here.

But it was a long process. The New World, despite its freer atmosphere, was affected by the traditions of the Old. Freedom to worship God was one thing. Freedom for someone else to worship God was quite another. Of course, persecution was only for error. Was it not desirable to stamp out error? Was not punishment clearly needed if one continued after warning to sin "against his own conscience?" In the colonies there were various religious establishments reflecting variety of origin and creed and all the inveterate prejudices and hatreds to which age-long religious strife had given rise. Even the truth cannot prosper without leadership, and liberty waited for the appearance of the prophet of the new thought. Able, well-trained, aflame with zeal, came Roger Williams.

An exile banished by the theocratic religionists because of his treasonable demand for freedom of conscience, he was, as his enemy put it, "enlarged" out of Massachusetts. And in Rhode Island he founded the commonwealth where for the first time religious liberty was a foundation principle. To him, who established the liberty of the soul in the New World; who, not with indifference to religious truth, but with profound religious conviction, demanded the emancipation of the spirit of man from the fetters of civil rule; who pointed the coming nation to the true pathway of a free people, to Roger Williams— preacher, prophet and statesman—we erect this memorial of the lasting obligation of men and women of all creeds and races.

These were his principles: "The civil sword may make a nation of hypocrites and anti-Christians, but not one Christian. Forcing of conscience is a soul-rape. Persecution for conscience hath been the lancet which hath let the blood of the nations. Man hath no power to make laws to bind conscience. The civil commonwealth and the spiritual commonwealth, the church, not inconsistent, though independent, the one of the other. The civil magistrate owes two things to false worshippers: (1) permission, (2) protection."

And in 1663 his fundamental tenet was embodied in the following memorable and discriminating language of the charter for the Colony of Rhode Island.

"No persons within the said colony, at any time hereafter, shall be in any wise molested, punished, disquieted, or called in question, for any differences in opinion, in matters of religion, who do not actually disturb the civil peace of our said colony; but that all and every person and persons may, from time to time, and at all times hereafter, freely and fully have and enjoy his own and their own judgments and consciences, in matters of religious concernments, throughout the tract of land hereafter mentioned, they behaving themselves peaceable and quietly and not using this liberty to licentiousness and profaneness nor to the civil injury or outward disturbance of others."

This was the ancestor of the provisions of our Federal Constitution adopted one hundred and twenty-four years later: "Congress shall make no law respecting an establishment of religion or prohibiting the free exercise thereof," and of the familiar provisions of similar import of the respective State Constitutions.

These Constitutional declarations are not forms of words conveying an abstract idea. They have definite and well-understood practical implications. Men of all religious beliefs stand equal before the law. They are not to be punished by reason of their creeds or forms of worship so long as they respect the public peace and the equal rights of others. No one is exposed to civil disability either as a witness in our courts or with respect to qualification for any public office by reasons of his religious faith. Nor are the people to be taxed and public moneys to be used for the support of any sort of religion.

This principle of our institutions also carries with it an inhibition, respected by all good citizens, that no one should seek through political action to promote the activities of religious organizations or should intrude differences of religious faith or practice into our political controversies. The extent to which we manifest that self-restraint marks our degree of attachment to the liberty we proclaim. The right to religious liberty has become a truism, and we are so familiar with this conception that we are likely to forget at what cost freedom of conscience has been won and also the danger to which we are constantly exposed of a recrudescence of bigotry. The hardest lesson mankind has had to learn is that the religious truth which is held to be most precious cannot prosper by attempts forcibly to impose it upon others. Strong conviction, especially religious convictions, are apt to develop tyrannical purpose and no faith is so pure that it is ever in danger of being made the instrument of the mistaken zeal of those who would deny to others the right to think as they choose.

It is a sound instinct that couples civil and religious liberty in one phrase, in our description of free institutions, however distinct theoretically they may be. The effort to dominate the conscience of men by the use of civil power has always been destructive of civil liberty itself. If there are any who would pervert our institutions to make them servants of religious dogma, they should be regarded as enemies of both religion and the State, as the success of their endeavors would undermine both.

The principle of Roger Williams is not only one of absolute justice with respect of equality before the law, but it is the essential principle of religious culture. When we look beyond form and ritual to the spiritual life of which they are the expression, it must be realized that its vital breath is the liberty of the soul in following its highest aspirations. It is only in the atmosphere of religious freedom that we may hope either for protection against error and delusion or for the maintenance of that spiritual power upon which all progress depends.

Charles Evans Hughes Sr. (April 11, 1862–August 27, 1948) was a lawyer and Republican politician from the State of New York. He served as Governor of New York (1907–1910), United States Secretary of State (1921–1925), Associate Justice of the Supreme Court of the United States (1910–1916) and Chief Justice of the United States (1930–1941). He was the Republican candidate in the 1916 U.S. presidential election, losing to Woodrow Wilson.

This speech was transcribed from its original source, *The Religious Herald*, on microfilm, 2008, by Aaron Weaver, J. M. Baylor University Dawson Institute of Church-State Studies, Doctoral Student, Religion, Politics & Society.

Sail On!

The Pilgrim's faith, the Pilgrim's courage grant us,
Still shines the truth that for the Pilgrims shone.
We are his seed; nor life nor death shall daunt us.
The port is Freedom! Pilgrim heart, sail on!

—Dean LeBaron Russell Briggs[209]

---

209. End of poem delivered at the 1920 Plymouth Celebration. Stoddard, 104.